HARMONY KINGDOM

The Original Box Figurine®

The Harmony Kingdom Reference Guide

by Leanna Barron

Copyright © 2002 by Harmony Ball Company
All rights reserved

No part of this publication may be reproduced in whole or in part in any form without written permission of the Harmony Ball Company. For information regarding permission, write to Harmony Ball Company, ATTN: Permissions Dept., 232 Neilston Street, Columbus, OH 43215.

Editorial Assistance by Corinna Perry, Lisa Yashon and Kim Cinko
Production and Design by EWC Design, Ltd., and Harmony Ball Company

ISBN 0-9676908-1-1

Third edition, July 2002
Printed by Robin Enterprises, Columbus, Ohio

Table of Contents

Welcome
The Creators
- Introduction to Harmony Kingdom 6
- The Cotswolds 7
- Martin and Corinna Perry 8
- Noel Wiggins and Lisa Yashon 9
- Peter Calvesbert 11
- David Lawrence 12
- Monique Baldwin 13
- Adam Binder 14
- Julie Bharucha 14
- Sherman Drackett 15
- Mel Heald 15

Ingenuity and Change
- The Garden Shed Days: 1989 16
- A Cottage Industry Forms: 1993 18
- When Jewellery and Boxes Come Together: 1994 19
- Griffin Mill: 1994 20
- Introducing Harmony Kingdom: 1995 20
- Variations on the Animal Theme: 1995 21
- The Royal Watch Collector's Club: 1995 22
- Harmony Kingdom on the Internet: 1995 22
- Harmony International Ltd.: 1996 23
- The Re-incarnation of Lord Byron: 1996 23
- Harmony Kingdom Travels to the Far East: 1997 24
- Independent Collector Clubs: 1997 25
- Events and Conventions: 1997 25
- Focus on Charity: 1998 25
- Goodbye Griffin, Hello Wimberley: 1998 26
- The House of Peers: 1999 26
- Picturesque: 1999 27
- Signing Events: 1999 28
- The Millennium Party: 2000 28
- 2001:Planet HK 29
- Rule Britannia: 2002 29
- Lord of the Aisles: 2002 29

Introduction to the Box Figurines
- How Harmony Kingdom Box Figurines Are Made 30
- Why Variations Occur 32
- Photography 33
- Production Numbers 33
- Origination 33
- Dates 34
- Measurements 34
- Hallmarks 34
- Issue Price 37

Secrets Revealed (Box Details) 38
Appendix/Index 256

Welcome

It has been nearly three years since the publication of the Millennium Edition of *The Harmony Kingdom Reference Guide*. My, how time flies! I had hoped that company headquarters would release an updated version earlier, but they felt that the Harmony Kingdom website pre-empted the need for a new edition. The website (www.HarmonyKingdom.com) is a fabulous treasure trove for us on-line collectors. It is regularly updated and provides comprehensive information about our collections and HK events, news and shops. It really is a must-go destination for any Kingdom aficionado.

With this said, all of us aren't quite ready to partake of the "electronic information age". And, there's something so intimate about a 5" by 8" book that you can easily carry about town or curl up with. Even the super lightweight titanium laptops don't provide this luxury. Headquarters acquiesced, and I proudly present to you Edition III of *The Harmony Kingdom Reference Guide* with over 100 additional pages.

Over the last three years, there has been much positive change within our favorite collectible company. The Box Figurines themselves have undergone further refinement and are even more enchanting than before. Each piece released prior to July 2002 is presented in the guide, with color photos, secrets, and all of the vital information that we care about. Production has moved back to England's Wimberley Mills, so we can once again say that Harmony Kingdom is a true English collectible in every sense. We have seen new and very talented artists join the HK family of carvers, and Peter Calvesbert's absolutely unique vision of the world and unsurpassable carving abilities have become even more elegant and sophisticated.

Speaking of Peter, I'm sure that many of you had the opportunity to meet this quiet, quirky, and kind-hearted man while he visited eighteen retailers throughout the U.S. on the Summer 2002 House of Lords Tour, or at the Rosemont International Gift & Collectible Exposition the last weekend of June. I had the wonderful opportunity of escorting him and Harmony Ball Company (HBC) President Noel Wiggins to four of the East Coast events. The time I spent with these two gentlemen again reminded me why I love the Kingdom as I do.

Another highlight of the past few years has been my involvement with the Independent Collector Clubs and the HK House of Peers (HOP), which serves as liaison between the clubs and the company. HOP and the Indy Clubs have raised well over $100,000 for various charities, including HBC's chosen charity - The National Alliance for the Mentally Ill (NAMI).

I would like to thank Kim Cinko of HBC for updating the current guide. Her talents are seen in its layout, secrets, and piece details. Anna Greashaber, HBC's Marketing Director, has provided me continual support on this project and HOP work over the last few years. And lastly, I'd like to thank all of you collectors who have been so encouraging. Recently, I've noticed a kinder and gentler spirit sweep through the Kingdom - an unusual harmony not typically found amongst such a diverse group. As always, I welcome your input and comments. Please contact me via e-mail at leannab@optonline.net or write Leanna Barron, PO Box 1116, Yonkers, NY 10703.

- *Leanna Barron*

Harmony Kingdom

The Creators
Introduction to Harmony Kingdom

As I stated in the first edition, Harmony Kingdom is not your typical company, nor are the pieces it creates ordinary. While its inspiration and joy come from nature, those responsible for its creation have distinct backgrounds, each lending a unique contribution to the kingdom. In this edition, I will take you deeper into the history and backgrounds of these people and places.

The history of Harmony Kingdom is full of chance encounters and unusual parallels. Two couples on two continents, Martin and Corinna Perry in the U.K. and Noel Wiggins and Lisa Yashon in the U.S., began their humble businesses in flea markets around the same time. Today the principals are still very involved with the day-to-day activities of the company. Each has said that their greatest satisfaction comes from the communities that have formed as a result of Harmony Kingdom. Many friendships, even trans-Atlantic, have been created as collectors worldwide meet one another via the Internet and at collector events in both the U.S. and U.K. Harmony Kingdom is truly a tale of two countries.

What first piqued my interest in Harmony Kingdom was that it was British-based. You probably can tell that I am a bit of an Anglophile, with the British spelling and terms that are found throughout the reference guide. However, as I learn more about Harmony Kingdom, I realise that it is as much a U.S. creation as a U.K. creation. All of Harmony Kingdom's carvers live in England, and Martin's studio is located in the village of Brimscombe. However, many of the ideas originate in the U.S. In fact, the idea of elaborate interior carvings sprang from Noel's very vivid imagination, as did the emphasis on hidden secrets. Noel is also responsible for drawing the pieces that comprise the Harmony Garden collection. A fourth generation painter and a graduate of the arts, he adds an artistic dimension to Harmony Kingdom that is both inborn and schooled. Harmony Kingdom is unique in that it is very accessible and welcomes suggestions of all kinds. Many concepts and design elements for the box figurines have actually come from collectors and retailers on both sides of the Atlantic.

The places from which Harmony Kingdom originates are as much a part of the collection as its creators. Each box figurine is infused with the beauty of the Cotswolds. It is here where the carvers live, where Wimberley Mills and Martin Perry Studios are located and where distribution outside of the Americas takes place. The company headquarters are in Columbus, Ohio, where marketing and distribution to the Americas is centred. A humble and friendly Midwestern city, Columbus is where the disparate parts are integrated into a harmonious whole.

The Cotswolds

Harmony Kingdom's U.K. headquarters, Wimberley Mills, is privileged to be located in one of the most beautiful rural areas in England, the South Cotswolds. Designated as an Area of Outstanding Natural Beauty, the Cotswolds is famous for its honey-coloured stone cottages, grand manor houses and impressive churches.

The name 'Cotswolds' refers to rolling hills and broad river valleys. These wooded hills and valleys are especially suitable for grazing, particularly for the native Cotswold sheep, which in medieval times were responsible for the growth of the wool trade. For centuries Cotswold wool was used in more than half of England's cloth and was exported to the continent, bringing great wealth to the wool merchants who donated large sums to the local churches and built themselves magnificent houses.

The river valleys form the setting for the towns and villages, which nestle snugly amongst the hills. The market town of Stroud is the central point where the five valleys meet. Cirencester, the capital of the Cotswolds, was known during Roman times as Corinium Dubonnorum and was the second largest city in Roman Britain.

Throughout the Cotswolds historic sites are in abundance, as are wildlife activities. The canal that runs alongside Wimberley Mills was once the only means of transport, except for the donkey paths that wind their way down the steep hills. Today the canal acts as an animal reserve. To the south of Wimberley Mills is Bath, the Georgian spa town, rich in Roman history. To the north is Stratford-upon-Avon, Shakespeare's birthplace, close to Warwick Castle, one of the largest medieval castles in the country. To the east is the university town of Oxford, city of dreaming spires.

This setting has had great influence on the creators of Harmony Kingdom. The box figurines share the same reverence towards nature, feeling of antiquity and subtle colouration as the place in which they are created.

RIVER FROME, CHALFORD, ENGLAND
PHOTOGRAPH COURTESY OF
BRUNO PACINI

Martin and Corinna Perry

Martin is the founder and owner of Antiquark Ltd., the company responsible for manufacturing English-made Harmony Kingdom pieces. He is also the artistic director of Martin Perry Studios, a consortium of English carvers who sculpt the figurines. He and his wife Corinna live in the Cotswolds region of England near Wimberley Mills, which houses Antiquark Ltd., Martin Perry Studios and Harmony International Ltd.

Martin Perry left school at the age of 14 and began his professional career in London as a gofer for his uncle, a film producer. At the age of 22, feeling disenchanted with the film industry, Martin moved to Snowdonia, a mountain region of North Wales. Here he adopted a puppy, the runt of a litter, which seemed to have a natural calling for sheep herding. Since Martin didn't have any idea what he wanted to do with his life, he followed the dog's lead. Martin found a romantic-looking mountain and offered his services as shepherd to the local farmer. Because Martin had no experience he offered to work for free, a proposition the farmer couldn't refuse.

For the next five years Martin and his dog tended sheep in the Welsh mountains, living a decidedly rustic life. Martin had human contact only once a week but kept occupied by walking an average of 20 miles a day. After meeting his future wife Corinna, he knew they could not continue to live such a secluded life, and they moved to the lowlands near Chalford, England, where Martin continued shepherding for a large farm. Martin did not like the rigidity and demands of business farming, yet he stayed with it for four years until he injured his back shearing sheep, which ended his shepherding career forever.

While she was growing up, Corinna listened to her mother speak French, German, Italian and Spanish around the house. Corinna, too, became quite a linguist and eventually a teacher of language. Her father was an illustrator of children's books, an animal lover, and an early conservationist, and her brother is a sculptor. At university Corinna studied art history and travelled extensively, spending a year in India. On a visit to her father in Wales, Corinna met Martin. During Martin's shepherding years near Chalford, Corinna taught "English as a second language" to corporate and military personnel. After their daughter and son were born, Corinna began working with the children of the village.

It was Corinna who introduced Martin to the owner of History Craft, a company that manufactured replicas for art museums around the world. No longer shepherding, Martin got a job in History Craft's packing department, sending out everything from large marble statues to tiny Roman coins. Sometimes items were needed that were not yet made so Martin would make the replicas himself. Martin says, "I can still remember the satisfaction from making that first thing. I

Harmony Kingdom

was so pleased with it. I've still got it - it was a rabbit, a replica of Japanese netsuke [the traditional, intricately carved ivory miniatures from Japan used primarily as fasteners for kimonos]."

For the next decade, Martin created replicas of museum artworks, including 18th and 19th century netsukes. He developed a special process that gave marble resin an antique, ivory look (later to be further refined and used in Harmony Kingdom box figurines). As he discovered and honed his artistic skills, he began to grow tired of copying other works. Eventually he left History Craft and began sculpting "a Westerner's idea of a netsuke."

In 1989 Martin decided to form his own business, Antiquark Ltd., and developed the current finishing process. He cast his new pieces from netsuke and oriental ivory moulds, as well as crafting scrimshaw reproductions. At this time his enterprise was a modest one, selling his pieces mostly to friends and at London flea markets.

Noel Wiggins and Lisa Yashon

Also in 1989, two college mates from the U.S. formed their fledgling business, Harmony Ball Company.

Noel and Lisa met in 1982 as freshmen at Brown University in Providence, Rhode Island. They both studied filmmaking and film theory, though Noel's emphasis was on the visual and Lisa's was on writing. They collaborated on many projects, including "Harmony Magazine," a satirical "politically incorrect" underground magazine which led to Noel's dismissal from the university for one year and a write-up in the *New York Times*.

After graduation Lisa and Noel temporarily went their separate ways. Lisa wrote for a newspaper in New England, while Noel worked as a motorcycle messenger in New York City. By 1988 Noel and Lisa decided it was time to take a break from their routines and embark on a new adventure. That October, Noel headed to Columbus, Ohio, in his rusty Toyota Chinook camper to pick up his old friend. The two continued southward into the heart of Mexico with $1500, a couple changes of clothing and the desire for adventure. They arrived in Patzcuaro, Mexico on November 1 during the holiday "El Dia De Los Muertos" (The Day of the Dead) and fell in love with the playful, satirical "calaveras" made by Mexican artisans from clay, wood, paper mache and sugar to commemorate the dead.

Spurred on by the kindness of the people and the intriguing folk art, Noel and Lisa travelled from region to region in Mexico. After a month, they had filled the camper with unique treasures from tiny villages throughout central and southern Mexico, and returned stateside to sell some of their finds in flea markets in and around New Orleans, Memphis, and Atlanta. At this time, Noel and Lisa decided to form a company, The Here After, which was to be a 24-hour coffee shop, movie house and purveyor of odd little trinkets from around the world. They also decided to repeat the trip the following year.

A year later, Noel and Lisa travelled to Taxco, the sterling silver capital of Mexico. Here they found a small handful of marble-sized chiming balls. On their trip home through the flea market circuit the balls were extremely popular, much more than the painted, fragile clay figurines had been the year before. They decided to have the craftspeople that made the chiming spheres enhance them with overlay designs of nature themes and attach bails so that they could be worn as pendants. Baby rattles, key chains, bracelets and earrings soon followed, and The Here After was officially incorporated in June 1991, dba The Harmony Ball Company. Business was so brisk that the coffee shop and movie house were left by the wayside. Instead the company's mission was to find unusual and creative trinkets and crafts from around the world to be sold in the U.S.

Noel moved from Brooklyn to Columbus in March 1991, and The Harmony Ball Company (HBC) office was set up. By 1992 HBC was a multi-million-dollar business that employed 400 Mexican artisans. The next HBC sensation, which came in 1993, was the Love Letter. These sterling silver cubes with letters and symbols were such a phenomenon that they were copied within a few months. Next came Birthstone Kids, but the same fate befell them. Jewellery was nearly impossible to copyright, so new items were constantly needed. Running a fast-growing business, innovating new products and producing and marketing them quickly before they could be copied proved extremely challenging. At its height HBC offered over 3,000 jewellery items with pieces made throughout the U.S., Mexico, Thailand, Italy, and Germany. When Noel and Lisa met Martin in 1994, they were not yet 30 years old but felt almost like seasoned pros.

Today, the stateside headquarters of Harmony Kingdom is located in a turn-of-the-century warehouse listed on the National Historic Register in downtown Columbus, Ohio.

HBC OFFICES, COLUMBUS, OHIO
PHOTOGRAPH COURTESY OF
BRAD FEINKNOPH

Peter Calvesbert

As master carver, Peter is the man responsible for the humorous Treasure Jest® series. His works have captured the attention of collectors worldwide, although interestingly he has had no formal arts training.

Born in 1960 in Hereford, England, he first picked up a piece of modeling clay at the age of three but didn't pursue sculpting for nearly thirty years. He worked odd jobs during his youth, and when he fell short of money he painted china, a craft he had acquired when he worked as a ceramic artist at Boehms of Malvern.

In 1990 Peter experienced a stroke of good fortune. By that time Martin had realised he needed to hire a master carver for Antiquark and was interviewing for the position. Michael Tandy, Peter's friend, was one of the candidates and asked Peter to accompany him on the interview. As his friend was leaving the interview with the promise to carve some samples, Peter whispered to Martin that he thought he could carve a couple too. Michael returned with "The Ram" and what was later known as "Who'd A Thought." Peter brought a series of six ducks, four of which later became part of the Harmony Kingdom "Large Treasure Jest" series.

By 1992 Peter was earning a modest income from his carvings for Antiquark and from painting china. However, he felt it was time to embark on a "real" career, so he enrolled in a university journalism course. It is here where he met his wife Andrea, who was also studying journalism. By 1994 they were planning their wedding, which took place in September 1995. Many box figurines from this time are encrypted with wedding references. Both Peter and Andrea love wildlife, so their honeymoon was spent on a South African safari, which also figures prominently in some of his pieces.

Peter and Andrea live a bucolic life in the English countryside. Peter counts the birth of their son, Samuel, in February 2001 as one of the most moving moments of his life. Many secrets on Peter's recent box figurines refer to Sam. They share their home with "Spike" the cockatiel, Peter's beloved dog Murphy, and a small ginger coloured cat named "LG" for Little Ginger, whose "pet" name is "Algy". Andrea is a great sport in letting Peter reveal in his art private details of their lives together.

Thank goodness Peter gave up his journalistic aspirations. He works full-time as Harmony Kingdom's most prolific and well-recognised master carver. We can still enjoy his writings in the column "Planet Calvesbert" in Harmony Kingdom's newsletter "The Queen's Courier."

TREASURE JESTS

David Lawrence

Collectors of Harmony Kingdom were introduced to David Lawrence's work with "Chatelaine," the first holiday angel released in 1995, followed by the 1996 release of the Harmony Circus™. Harmony Circus box figurines reflected his very English and very eccentric sense of humour. It would be hard to say which of his circus characters proved the most extraordinary. Was it the multirubberlimbed Il Bendi, the intrepid Henry the Human Cannonball or the silver-throated sword-swallower Vlad the Impaler?

David's next range, Angelique™, was on a completely different tack. The childlike angels that comprise Angelique were a reflection of the circumstances in which the artist found himself: his daughter Rose and her various friends from around the village filled his house with laughter and song and served as inspiration and models. He has contributed larger format animal box figurines for the Zookeepers Series and his most recent creations are wonderful, whimsical cats, complete with hidden messages both inside and out.

David has always enjoyed the challenge of working in different fields and different media, the result of a "restless imagination" he says. Initially he was a painter in photo-realistic style and a medical illustrator. A good technical grounding enabled him to graduate to the hothouse of the advertising industry of West End London in the eighties.

The desire to work at something more lasting and meaningful led David to Harmony Kingdom and to the small village in Wessex where he lives with his wife and two daughters in a home that dates back to 1690. He loves the solitude of village life and takes great pride in its history. In addition to family and work, he has two other passions. He can be seen throughout the countryside performing with the Taunton Deane Morris Men, a troupe which practices the ancient English dance form known as Morris Dancing. His second passion is for his neighbourhood pub, which is as much a way of life in his village as the daily milk delivery.

Monique Baldwin

One of the more unique aspects of Martin Perry Studios is that it is comprised of both accomplished artists as well as younger, aspiring ones. Monique falls into the second category and is truly a product of Martin's guidance.

Monique was born in Dominica but has lived in Stroud most of her life. She studied art and design at Stroud College for two years before attending Carmarthen College in Wales where she pursued an HND in surface design, jewellery design, ceramics and stained glass. After graduation, with college loans to repay, she found work in the finishing department at Antiquark. After a year and nearly debt free, she decided "it was time to start looking for a job where my four years of art school could be utilised." Fortuitously, Martin was looking for someone to help in the new research and development department and learned that Monique had a strong arts background.

For six months she experimented with colour and mixing stain, and she worked in every department so she could get a thorough understanding of the production process. She then began to re-design masters, which involved sanding areas that had chipped in the machine or adding to parts that were too thin, before production began. From this exercise, Martin realised that Monique was quite adept at carving, so he had her sculpt many of the interior scenes in Harmony Garden Chapter II, as well as the "Rose Bud" which was the first piece she carved entirely. She went on to carve the open edition pieces for Chapters III and IV of the Harmony Garden collection. Monique also regularly contributes exclusives for buying groups and special events.

I asked Monique if she had a garden of her own. She had just moved into a new home and had begun to create a living Harmony Garden, planting those flowers that she sculpts. Her first trip to the U.S. and first public Harmony Kingdom appearance was in June 1999 at the International Collectibles Exposition in Rosemont, Illinois. The number of people that enjoy her work overwhelmed her. Little did she know how delighted we are by the fruits (and flowers) of her labour.

Adam Binder

Adam Binder joined Martin Perry's circle of talented artists in 1999. "I had always greatly admired the Harmony Kingdom line," Adam says, "and I was thrilled when Martin invited me to become an HK artist." Adam is a native of Cirencester, Gloucestershire, and attended Art College at Cheltenham. After travelling throughout Europe and South Africa, he returned to England to become a potter. While making a living from producing ceramics, Adam learned the fundamentals of the giftware business.

The delightful Roly Polys, chubby little animals full of personality, were Adam's first additions to the whimsical realm of Harmony Kingdom. He has also carved event pieces, the Two By Two and Interchangeables series, Royal Watch box figurines and the 2001 Holiday Edition angel "Beau Geste."

ROLY POLYS

Julie Bharucha

Originally a potter, Julie Bharucha was used to working with porcelain, later turning to clay. After an amusing discussion with Martin Perry, Julie went on to sculpt a series of voluptuous women in opulent settings. This series, Clair de Lune, captures the feel of Paris in the Jazz Age of the 1920's and served as the inspiration for Harmony Kingdom's Year 2000 Convention.

Clair de Lune

Harmony Kingdom

Sherman Drackett

Born in Jamaica, Sherman is a former member of the British Army and traveller extraordinaire. He ranks a six-week safari in Africa as his most exciting experience. Sherman describes himself as "creative, curious, and open-minded." Proud to be a Harmony Kingdom carver, his first Box Figurine was the exclusive piece for the Atlanta 2000 International Collectible Exposition's Memories Dinner. "The oval shape, colors and textures of the fruit basket made for appealing work," he says.

Sherman has made numerous contributions to Harmony Kingdom's collection, including limited editions and members-only exclusives for the Royal Watch, Harmony Kingdom's official collectors' club. His attention to detail is exhibited in his creation of the Longaberger® basket figurines. All of his creations are imbued with a sweetness and sense of wonder.

In a recent visit with Sherman, we discussed his interest in trout fishing. He would love an opportunity to go trout fishing in the U.S.!

Mel Heald

Mel Heald is a recent addition to Martin Perry Studios. Born in South Yorkshire, Mel taught classic guitar while teaching himself the art of fine cabinet making. He became increasingly interested in the sculptural aspects of furniture, eventually moving on to other materials. For some years he designed and sculpted items in silver, gold and pewter.

Mel is a self-proclaimed "River Gypsy" and currently lives on a barge on a canal in Bath. Collectors at the 7th Birthday Bash at Wimberley Mills enjoyed the opportunity to meet this mild-mannered artist.

Ingenuity and Change

The Garden Shed Days: 1989

The garden shed outside of Weaver's Cottage, Martin & Corinna's former home, is where the quirky little boxes were born. Weaver's Cottage is nestled on one of the steeply sloping hillsides of Chalford, a village that dates back to 1842. The garden shed has a spectacular view of the surrounding Cotswold countryside. It is here where Martin first began to craft the box figurines. The year was 1989, and Martin's sole objective was to make a modest income to support his young family.

Martin's "assembly line" consisted of a table top that held a set number of pre-cast pieces that translated into a set amount of pound sterling once sold. The manufacturing process was too ambitious at the time so a company in Somerset did the moulding and casting, after which Martin tinted and hand-painted each piece. Martin's creations were sold in flea markets and nearby shops. His older brother assisted in the sales of these early pieces – the netsuke reproductions, animal piles and what are now referred to as Large Treasure Jests.

With the netsuke reproductions, a mould was made from the original ivory carving. Since these pieces were hundreds of years old, they were not copyrighted. Soon Martin began to make original models, often from the designs of some of his friends. From this practice came what were called "piles," carved stacks of animals piled atop one another.

The following listing contains some of the netsuke and piles previously produced by Antiquark. The codes shown are the alphanumeric system that Martin began in 1989 and which he still uses to this day to track his moulds.

Netsuke Reproductions:

Code	Description
M2	Pigs
M3	Pillar of Men
M5	Monkeys
M6	Cat on Catfish
M7	Rat in Pumpkin
M8	Frog on Lily Pad
M9	Ducks
M10	Chick in Egg
M11	Face Pot
M12	Frogs on Tortoise
M13	Rooster
M14	Rats on Cornsack

Animal Piles:

Description
Frog
Pig
Tortoise
Armadillo
Rat
Puppy
Hedgehog
Monkey
Seal
Cat
Bear

During this time there were also six duck box figurines that are now referred to as Large Treasure Jests. Sculpted by Peter, four were later included in the Harmony Kingdom collection.

In October 1990 Studio Ann Carlton (SAC) approached Martin and wanted to finish and market his pieces, so he sold them white bodied castings. SAC's finishing process was similar to Martin's, but not identical so the pieces looked different – glossier and less like ivory. What became of the two remaining ducks that weren't included in the Harmony Kingdom collection? "Widgeon Duck" and "Marble Duck" were shipped from October 1990 through October 1991. Approximately three hundred of each were cast, with two thirds of these finished and sold by Studio Ann Carlton. Another large box from this time was the large rooster. Only 821 of these were produced. When Martin cancelled the contract with SAC in September 1995, SAC was still only finishing and selling large boxes.

During these early days, quite a few of Peter's carvings were never produced as Martin was still learning what could and could not be done in the manufacturing process. One such experiment was Peter's "Punk Rock Hedgehog." Getting the castings out of the moulds was extremely difficult, and polishing the spines was impossible. However, a few very rare pieces are in existence, albeit somewhat flawed.

In 1992 Martin began to focus on what are now referred to as "Small Treasure Jests" as he could fit more of the smaller pieces on his worktable. The first small box figurine carved by Peter was "Forty Winks," a downsized version of "Sunnyside Up," finished in March 1992. It was soon followed by "Princely Thoughts" in April 1992, a miniature version of "Awaiting A Kiss." Soon thereafter, Peter began studying journalism, so Martin started to produce Michael Tandy's "The Ram" and "Who'd A Thought."

After Peter's one-year course was completed, Martin lured him back with the offer of a full-time job. By September 1993, Peter created five new small box designs, including "All Tied Up," "Hammin' It Up," "At Arm's Length," "Shell Game" and "Reminiscence." With these designs, Peter introduced his signature mouse.

At this time, two other companies besides SAC began to distribute Martin's pieces. The stained and painted small boxes were sold to DoZen Ltd. for sale throughout Europe and to Mascott Direct for sale in the U.S. Both distributors were modest in size: DoZen was a six-man jewellery company, and Mascott was owned and operated by one man, who has since joined with Gallo Pewter and formed "Surprise It's A Box." The listing on the next page is from an early Mascott Direct brochure and includes Martin's replicas and Traddles, Martin's first box. For Traddles, Martin used a tortoise shell to cast the piece and Corinna created the head using the family pet Traddles as model. There are no itemised sales records for Traddles, but the quantity of pieces produced is less than fifteen.

Mascott Code	Description
R1	Bird in Egg
R2	Face Pot
R3	Frog Under Leaf
R4	Two Ducks
R5	Rat on Pumpkin
R6	Cat on Catfish
R7	Frogs on Tortoise
R8	Cockerel
R9	Pig Pile
R10	Armadillo
R11	Monkey Pile
R12	Puppy Pile
R13	Seal Pile
R14	Frog Pile
R15	Afterglow
R16	Rat Pot
R17	Men & Dogs
R18	Suckling Pig
R19	Tortoise Box (Traddles)

A Cottage Industry Forms: 1993

By 1993, finishing and painting the boxes were too much for one person to handle, so Corinna joined Martin. She began by painting the pieces on her kitchen table. Soon, other women from the village were enlisted to help. Corinna formed her guild of painters and tinters, comprised mostly of women with young children who enjoyed working out of their homes in the Cotswold tradition of cottage industry manufacturing.

Kay Roseblade

One of these women was Kay Roseblade. Later Kay became the first Antiquark employee and is now its General Manager. Another woman, Carole Clayton, was pregnant when she began painting with Corinna. She now paints only part-time, but because of her skill and experience she is given the most challenging work.

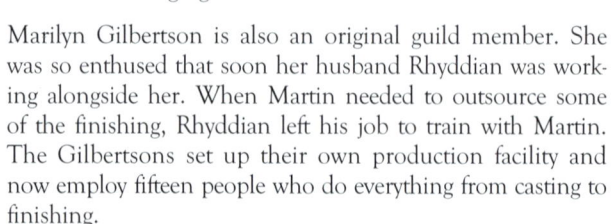

Carole Clayton

Marilyn Gilbertson is also an original guild member. She was so enthused that soon her husband Rhyddian was working alongside her. When Martin needed to outsource some of the finishing, Rhyddian left his job to train with Martin. The Gilbertsons set up their own production facility and now employ fifteen people who do everything from casting to finishing.

Marilyn Gilbertson

When Jewellery and Boxes Come Together: 1994

In early 1994, Noel and Lisa decided to introduce their own line of Limoges porcelain boxes, and they travelled to Limoges, France, to explore opportunities. There they quickly surmised that the exclusivity they were looking for would not be possible due to manufacturing procedures and distribution channels. At the time HBC was looking for exclusive designs that could be copyrighted. Since Noel and Lisa were already in Europe, they decided to attend a gift fair in Germany. They walked the show and stumbled upon DoZen Ltd.'s jewellery display where a small selection of animal boxes from England were on exhibit.

Noel and Lisa returned to the U.S. to pursue the source of the British boxes. Noel spoke with Martin for the first time in late February 1994 and said he "would like to buy thousands of his little boxes." Martin simply replied, "We do not make thousands." Martin was offered advance payment and a deal was struck. The original order made by Harmony Ball Company to Antiquark was:

Qty	Code	Animal	Name
400	M17	Toad	Princely Thoughts
350	M20	Owl	Who'd A Thought
500	M26	Elephant	Reminiscence
450	M32	Hare	All Ears
350	M104	Chimps	Inside Joke
400	M106	Penguins	Unexpected Arrival
300	M107	Cat	Purrfect Friends

In typical Antiquark fashion, they shipped what was available. The first shipment arrived in the U.S. in March 1994, and included:

Qty	Code	Animal	Name
95	TJAL	Alligator	Swamp Song
50	TJPO	Pony	Day Dreamer
90	TJTI	Tiger	Of The Same Stripe
95	TJWH	Whale	Jonah's Hideaway
95	TJTU	Turtle	Shell Game
94	TJFR	Toad	Princely Thoughts
95	TJFI	Fish	School's Out
94	TJCR	Crow	Trunk Show
93	TJEL	Elephant	Reminiscence
96	TJPI	Pig	Hammin' It Up

More shipments soon followed, including the original order along with eight of the large boxes. If not for Noel's forceful entreaty, Harmony Kingdom as we know it today would never have existed.

HBC initially sold the small boxes with a 16mm chiming pendant on sterling chain and the large boxes with a 25mm chiming bead, later replaced with a 25mm chiming sphere. The boxes were called "Treasure Jests" because they served as treasure chests for jewellery, and also bore humorous designs. Within three months retailers asked for the boxes without the interior jewels and it was clear that the "Treasure Jest" was much more than a glorified jewellery box.

In August 1994, Martin, Corinna and their two children made their first trip to the U.S. to meet with Noel and Lisa, who were exhibiting at the New York International Gift Fair. The four bonded immediately. "From day one, Noel and Lisa saw what could be done with these little boxes," Martin says. However, he was reluctant to make major changes in his life. "I had a simple existence in my garden shed and was making a living." Noel's enthusiasm for the boxes finally convinced Martin to work exclusively with HBC and he did not renew his contracts with Mascott Direct and DoZen Ltd. effective December 31, 1994. HBC was given official worldwide distributorship outside of the U.K. commencing January 1995. At this time, Mascott Direct came out with their me-too line "Surprise It's A Box" and promoted it heavily throughout the U.K.

In September 1994, shortly after returning from the New York Gift Fair, Martin hired Pam and Robin Miles to distribute the boxes in the U.K. The Miles' company, Arktype, had little product as the U.S. market was absorbing nearly all of Martin's production. In addition, Arktype was undercapitalised and costly to Antiquark, which was forced to put forward substantial start-up loans. The ark logo on the labels was introduced at this time. The relationship between Arktype and Antiquark dissolved in 1996, and the ark logo on the labels removed.

Griffin Mill: 1994

Toward the end of 1994, it became evident that the garden shed and outsourcing weren't enough to handle the growing demand for the box figurines. Martin moved Antiquark to Griffin Mill, where one third of a floor was acquired. Within months, an entire floor was rented and soon an entire building. The designs were becoming more ambitious, so Martin felt that casting should be moved in-house in order to oversee the process more closely. Antiquark spread to two more buildings for mould making and casting.

Introducing Harmony Kingdom: 1995

Just ten months after Antiquark's initial order arrived to HBC, another chance meeting took place that would irrevocably imprint Harmony Kingdom. While Noel Wiggins was attending the Chicago Gift Show in January 1995, he met Paul Osnain, an expert in the collectibles industry. Noel explained to Paul the difficulty HBC had with copyrighting its jewellery products and retaining customer loyalty due to competition from copycat companies. He then showed Paul HBC's new product line, the Treasure Jests. Noel explained how popular the little boxes were and how people were even beginning to collect them. Paul seized the opportunity and gave Noel invaluable advice on how a proper collectible company operates: a brand name is essential, the pieces should have colourful names and be divided into distinct subsets, some pieces should be limited edition while others should be retired, and a collector's club should be formed.

When Noel returned from Chicago he explained the blueprint to Lisa, who at first was sceptical as she felt that a collectible shouldn't be "planned" but should naturally evolve over many years. Noel convinced her that Treasure Jests were already being collected and setting things up right from the start would benefit potential collectors. So the two immediately put their heads together to come up with the name "Harmony Kingdom." They then named the sixty box figurines currently in the line, retired four of the boxes ("Let's Do Lunch," "Who'd a Thought," "Untouchable," and "Back Scratch"), divided the current selection into categories, introduced the first limited edition piece ("Unbearables"), created the first Harmony Kingdom catalogue, and retained a booth at the International Collectibles Exposition in Long Beach, California, to be held in April, 1995. Paul Osnain even flew to Columbus to assist them at no charge. Harmony Kingdom is forever indebted to Paul for his invaluable and selfless advice.

The first four retired box figurines were selected due to the controversial subject matter ("Let's Do Lunch") or the simplicity of design and lack of humour (the other three selections). Including these four, there were forty-three pieces in the "Small Treasure Jest Series," twelve pieces in the "Large Treasure Jest Series," four pieces in the "Hi-Jinx Series," and the limited edition "Unbearables."

At the Long Beach International Collectibles Exposition in April, collectors were won over by the humour, ingenuity, and detailing of the box figurines, and were further enamoured by their English origins. The fervour has continued ever since. Martin marvels at the growth of Harmony Kingdom: "It seems extraordinary to me that I can be a one-man business in my shed one day, and the next day a creator of fine collectibles sold throughout the world."

Variations on the Animal Theme: 1995

While at the 1995 Long Beach show, Martin, Noel, and Lisa discussed new themes to add to Harmony Kingdom. Treasure Jests had nearly limitless possibilities, but Martin didn't want to overtax Peter. In addition, Martin had recently met a promising new artist, David Lawrence, who was at work creating Harmony Kingdom's first holiday angel, 1995's "Chatelaine." One theme discussed at Long Beach that came to fruition was the Harmony Circus which was launched eight months later.

"I met Martin through one of those strokes of good fortune which seems to characterise the success and growth of Harmony Kingdom. Perhaps it is a strange conjunction of astrological phenomena – but at almost every turn people have come together with just the right skills at the right time. Martin was looking to expand on the wonderful success of Peter's work, and I was looking for a more meaningful form of creation. Advertising and illustration can be stimulating, but is a very aggressive and pressured world and I was constantly aware that today's all-important ad would be tomorrow's waste paper. I was looking to create something that people actually wanted and treasured and which would give them pleasure for years to come. So meeting Martin was the fulfillment of a dream," David mused.

When David was asked to carve Harmony Circus, "A period of hibernation, gestation and rumination took place. Then one morning I leapt out of bed – something had just clicked and within five minutes I had scribbled down the idea for Il Bendi, Winston, Henry, and half a dozen others. All that remained now was for me to make them. So I set to work. Martin allowed me great freedom. The one restraint he put on me was 'never sacrifice quality' which is a great luxury."

Royal Watch Collector's Club: 1995

By the end of 1995, the Royal Watch Collector's Club was formed and was officially debuted in Secaucus, NJ, at the International Collectibles Exposition in April 1996. As an incentive to join the club at the show, HK offered collectors a special version of the Garden Prince pendant. At the Rosemont Show in June of that year, another variation of the same pendant was available to people who joined the club. This pattern has continued with current members and new members who join the club at the expositions receiving the special event pendant while at the show. Harmony Garden rose pendants were the 1997 event pieces. David Lawrence's angel pendants were the event pieces for 1998, and Monique Baldwin created an adorable Lord Byron pendant for 1999. Bumbles the Bee appeared as a show pendant in 2000 and the sultry space cat Minx in 2001, with Murphy appearing in 2002. The Royal Watch continues to enjoy rapid growth. Membership benefits include club exclusive gifts, a free subscription to the club newsletter "The Queen's Courier," opportunity to purchase annual redemption pieces, and other exclusive benefits. For further information on The Royal Watch Collector's Club, residents of the Americas may e-mail RoyalWatch@HarmonyBall.com or call 614-469-0600; residents outside the Americas may e-mail RoyalWatch@HarmonyKingdom.co.uk or call +44 (0) 1453 885722.

Harmony Kingdom on the Internet: 1995

Computers have always been an integral part of Harmony Ball Company. HBC was fully computerised prior to its incorporation, thanks to Noel's interest and aptitude. Convinced that the Internet would be an extremely powerful means of communication, Noel hired a young Internet guru named Grasshopper in June 1995 who posted a primitive web site by late 1995. Grasshopper's successor, Christopher Sosa, was instrumental in creating the official Harmony Kingdom web site in September 1996. Towards the end of 1996 a chat room was created, the first of its kind in the collectibles industry. In addition, top retailers were listed on the web site, enabling collectors to locate hard-to-find pieces. Retailers and collectors had access to an unprecedented amount of information through the Harmony Kingdom web site, which generated enormous interest in the collection.

The International Collectibles Exposition in Long Beach in April 1997 brought another first to the collectibles industry. HBC's Internet Division (HBC-ID) broadcast via the Internet a live feed from the show, updating the Harmony Kingdom site every few hours. This enabled collectors and retailers who weren't able to attend to share in the festivities.

Harmony Kingdom's web site, http://www.HarmonyKingdom.com, is updated weekly and is a must-go destination for any avid collector. It has been visited over half a million times. Here you can read the latest news from Harmony Kingdom, view the entire collection, learn about upcoming events, and find dealer listings throughout the world.

Harmony International Ltd.: 1996

In the autumn of 1996, Harmony International Ltd. was formed to distribute the box figurines worldwide outside of the Americas. This company, jointly owned by Martin, Corinna, Noel, and Lisa, is headed by Nicholas Dangar and is headquartered in Wimberley Mills. Nick has put together a very able staff and through his tireless efforts has succeeded in spreading his enthusiasm for Harmony Kingdom throughout the United Kingdom and the Continent, into Hong Kong and Japan and to other far reaches of the globe. It seems that Harmony Kingdom's popularity is without territorial boundaries.

Nick's family is listed in the Doomsday Book and is part of the English aristocracy. At the age of eighteen, he left the "upper crust" Stowe School to attend the "university of life" as he calls it. He set out to Australia and worked as a floor sweeper for a wine merchant. Within eight months, he was manager of operations. After returning to England, he continued in the wine trade for seven years. While the benefits were good (wine at lunch every day), he was looking for something more challenging. He co-founded The Hazelbury House Collection Ltd., a company that manufactures replicas of 17th-19th century antiquities. In November 1996, after selling his shares in the company, he joined Harmony Kingdom.

It is unusual for an English aristocrat to be such a hard worker. What's even more extraordinary is that Nick is such good fun! He is full of life and has many loves – sports cars, his beautiful home "Lilac Cottage," cooking and women! Always greeting people with a giant smile, Nick is the backbone to operations outside of the Americas.

The Re-incarnation of Lord Byron: 1996

The inaugural issue of "The Queen's Courier" in spring 1996 featured an article entitled "Secrets of the Kingdom." By this time it was clear that collectors greatly enjoyed the "secrets" carved into and found within the figurines. Noel encouraged Martin to emphasise the importance of secrets to the master carvers. This has become a source of delight for both collectors and the artists themselves who very much enjoy encrypting their pieces.

The flowers were to be a variation on the secrets theme. Instead of having hidden secrets, they were to have elaborate interior scenes. The original flower prototypes had butterflies inside, but it was decided that a distinct character that meandered throughout each should be introduced. Noel did the original sketches for the first ten open edition Harmony Garden box figurines and created the outline for the saga, and Lisa came up with the name Lord Byron as a play on "Ladybug" or "Ladybird" (the English equivalent). The story of Lord Byron was to involve romance and adventure, so naming the character after the famous romantic poet seemed appropriate. Martin loved the idea of intricate interiors and immediately set out to tackle this very complex project.

The first ten open edition box figurines in Lord Byron's Harmony Garden™ were introduced in January 1997. In addition, six limited edition single roses were released throughout the year, "The Sunflower" was a club exclusive redemption piece for 1997, and the 1997 limited edition "Rose Basket" featured Lord Byron golfing on the moon. However, after a few months, Martin realised that the pieces were too complex to cast and paint. Since this collection was amongst Martin's favourites, a solution had to be found.

Harmony Kingdom Travels to the Far East: 1997

England and China have been trading partners as early as 1715, when the British East India Company set up headquarters in Canton. Martin knew the Chinese were expert painters, skilled in the art of calligraphy as early as 1300 BC. Moving production of Harmony Garden to China was explored at great length and the decision to do so was finally made in May of 1997. The first shipment of Harmony Garden Chapter I arrived from China in November 1997.

Mid 1997 another chance occurrence took place that helped to shape the future of Harmony Kingdom. Lee Cheng, president and artistic director of Concordia Corporation, was visiting the 225 Gift Building in New York City where Harmony Ball Company had a showroom. He happened upon the showroom and met with Noel, who was very impressed with him and introduced him to Martin. Lee Cheng is a classical violinist and his wife is a well-known watercolorist. Together they shared the artistic acumen needed to create Harmony Kingdom box figurines. With Lee in charge of production, Martin was able to unleash full creativity, knowing that his ambitious designs need not be compromised.

During the International Collectibles Exposition in Rosemont in June 1999, I had the pleasure of spending several hours with Lee Cheng. I found him to be a gentle, caring man who is proud to help the people in China make better lives for themselves. Inland China is extremely poor with little opportunity. Most people till a small piece of land with no prospects for the future. Many young people leave their homes to work in coastal areas where wages are as much as four times higher. Here they work for four or five years and save their earnings, after which they can return home, get married, build a house and live more comfortably. In Lee's factory all of the craftspeople are at least 18 years of age; most are in their early twenties and have a high school education. Each person is given room and board near the factory, so most of what is earned may be saved. Lee set up an exclusive HK production facility in year 2000. While Harmony Kingdom production moved back to England in 2002, Lee is kept busy creating Harmony Ball Company's unique and varied gift lines, as well as most Disney exclusives.

Independent Collector Clubs: 1997

By 1997 Harmony Kingdom's popularity was booming, yet one area was conspicuously absent – independent clubs formed by collectors themselves. The first independent club was founded midyear 1997. Within months others began to spring up throughout the U.S. and U.K., and as of June 2002 there were twenty-seven authorised independent clubs. Local clubs offer members a wide variety of benefits, including camaraderie with others and a source of information. Additionally, members of independent clubs are offered special figurines like "The Mouse That Roared."

Events & Conventions: 1997

Since June of 1997, Harmony Kingdom has sponsored wonderful collector events that coincide with the International Collectibles Expositions. One hundred and fifty people enjoyed the first such event named "The Three Hour Tour." It was held aboard the Eleanor R cruise ship which set sail on Lake Michigan for an enchanted Saturday evening that culminated in a spectacular fireworks display with the Chicago skyline as backdrop. In June of 1998 another Lake Michigan cruise – "The Ugly Duck" – hosted five hundred and fifty people. Nearly eight hundred attended "Harmony Kingdom's Grand Investiture" at Medieval Times in Schaumburg, Illinois, in June of 1999. The spring of 2001 saw Paradise Found and Peter Calvesbert was the guest of honor at Breakfast With An Artist in 2002.

In addition to one-night events, Harmony Kingdom hosted week long conventions for collectors. "Primordial Crooze" was the first convention – a floating five-day fiesta aboard a Royal Caribbean cruise ship – in April 1999. The ship sailed from Los Angeles to Baja, Mexico, with nearly six hundred Harmony Kingdom passengers aboard. The Year 2000 convention – "Clair de Lune" - was held at The Abbey Resort in Lake Geneva, Wisconsin, the last week of June 2000.

Focus on Charity: 1998

While Harmony Kingdom has made charitable contributions since its inception, a program was launched in 1998 that involved the box figurines themselves. The Zookeepers Collection was introduced as an ongoing series devoted to the care of needy animals through the world. David Lawrence carved the first four pieces, three of which were limited editions, with proceeds going to the Brookfield Zoo. The fourth, 1999's club redemption piece, benefited Pelican Island National Wildlife Refuge in Titusville, Florida. The program was so successful that two

Zookeepers were done in 2000: "Cow Town" benefitted the manatees of the Columbus Zoo and Aquarium and "Retired Racers" benefitted a greyhound rescue organisation. The Zookeepers continued in 2001 with "Gentle Giant" to benefit the National Zoo and 2002 with the Royal Watch redemption "Haji's Hero" to benefit Dickerson Park Zoo. With each Zookeeper, collectors are given the opportunity to adopt an animal for a small fee. They receive information from the adopting organisation, adoption papers and a Wee Beastie miniature figurine that depicts the animal that they have adopted.

Another on-going charitable campaign organised by The House of Peers involves raffling or auctioning rare prototypes donated by Harmony Kingdom. HOP and the independent clubs have raised over $100,000 for charity through 2001. For more information on upcoming charity auctions and raffles, please write to HK House of Peers, ATTN: HOP Charity Coordinator, P.O. Box 1116, Yonkers, NY 10703 or send e-mail to charity@houseofpeers.com.

Goodbye Griffin, Hello Wimberley: 1998

What with all of the energies surrounding Harmony Kingdom – new collections, clubs, the Internet, worldwide sales, events, conventions and charitable campaigns – it was inevitable that Antiquark would someday outgrow Griffin Mill. In February 1998 Antiquark relocated to Wimberley Mills in nearby Brimscombe. With nearly 20 times the space, Antiquark could now expand production in an effort to meet the ever-growing demand for Harmony Kingdom.

The House of Peers: 1999

Due to the growing number of independent Harmony Kingdom collector clubs and events, The House of Peers was formed in May 1999 as an administrative body to facilitate communication between clubs and the company and to coordinate collector events and charitable activities. Four officers were appointed by Harmony Kingdom and subsequently elected by their peers: Iris Harbert (president/facilitator), Nancy Hix (treasurer/charity coordinator), Leanna Barron (secretary/events coordinator), and Joe McLaughlin (webmaster/Internet coordinator). Each was a Harmony Kingdom collector and volunteered time to The House of Peers. Since then, the slate of officers has changed but the enthusiasm of the House of Peers remains strong. In addition, each independent club appoints two delegates to The House of Peers. For further information on Harmony Kingdom Independent Clubs, please write to Harmony Ball Company, Attn: Clubs, 232 Neilston Street, Columbus, Ohio 43215.

Picturesque: 1999

PICTURESQUE

"Epic Tales In Tile"

During the Rosemont International Collectibles Exposition in 1997, the idea of wall plaques first occurred to Martin. He had been talking to collectors throughout the day, and several said that they were having trouble fitting more collectibles into their curio cabinets. Ever the opportunist, Martin thought about all that empty wall space.

"Two things excited me about the idea," says Martin. "The first was that we could carve a tile in relief, which would by itself be an attractive addition to any collector's arsenal. Yet even better, this single tile could then be part of a larger scheme. We could carve other tiles that would expand the original image into a larger and larger picture. In other words, people could own one, two, five or twenty tiles, whatever suited them. The other equally exciting aspect to this idea was that the subject matter would be limitless."

Ann Richmond carved the first series in the Picturesque™ Collection, "Noah's Park," and Peter lent his hand to the centerpiece tile, "The Lost Ark." The series took a full year to finish. "It is a ravishing visual image full of humour and the typically enigmatic Harmony Kingdom detail," says Martin. Inspired by the result, Ann created a second series, "Byron's Secret Garden." Both series premiered in March 1999 at the International Coverings Show in Orlando Florida. "Noah's Park" was first introduced to collectors the following week at the first stop on the "Picturesque Tour" and "Byron's Secret Garden" at the Long Beach Collectibles Exposition in April. In September 1999, pre-production tile figurines of "Wimberley Tales," the third series in the Picturesque Collection, were premiered at the final two Picturesque events in the U.S. Carved by Mark Ricketts, this spectacular pastiche of a medieval deep relief carving portrays the fictional town of Wimberley, named after Wimberley Mills.

In addition to a variety of Picturesque accessories to showcase one to twenty tiles, stand-alone tile figurines have been carved. Peter's "Storm Brewing" and Ann's "Ruffians' Feast" and "Purrfect Tidings" have been enthusiastically received. With Picturesque, Harmony Kingdom has created its second collectible category – tile figurines.

Harmony Kingdom

Signing Events: 1999

Since 1995 collectors who visit collectible expositions have had the opportunity to have their Harmony Kingdom pieces signed by Martin, Noel, and attending master carvers. To meet more collectors and to launch the Picturesque collection, Martin and Noel travelled to the six top retailers in each region of the U.S. and one in the U.K. on the Picturesque Tour from March through November 1999. Noel began the "Cat's Meow" tour in October 1999, which continued through 2000. With the success of these signing events and the fun had by all, Peter visited 18 retailers for the House of Lords Tour in the summer of 2002.

The Millennium Party: 2000

During the year 2000, Harmony Kingdom hosted its first "Memories Dinner" at the Atlanta International Collectibles Exposition, introduced new collectible lines and the Fab Five Party Boys Series, as well celebrated the Royal Watch's fifth anniversary. For the first time, a Harmony Kingdom convention was held in England. The 5th Birthday Bash was a great opportunity to meet the artists and obtain an exclusive event piece.

Another highlight of 2000 was the Clair de Lune Convention, held after the Rosemont ICE. Collectors gathered at the Abbey Resort in Lake Geneva, Wisconsin, for an entire week of R & R and HK.

Creativity continued to flow out of Wimberley Mills, with the Clair de Lune limited editions, Mini Treasure Jests, NetsUKe and Roly Polys all introduced in 2000. Harmony Kingdom also began its series of box figurines designed exclusively for The Longaberger® Company, a hand-made collectible basket company based in Central Ohio, near HBC's Columbus headquarters.

2001: Planet HK

The Royal Watch boldly went where no collectors' club had gone before with "2001: Planet HK." A sexy sidekick was needed for the space journey, and so the character of Minx joined the "Space Boys" as part of the collectors' club kit for 2001. The stellar theme carried through to the Paradise Found collector event in Anaheim, California, where the event exclusive was "Planet Paradise," and the Space Ball, held as part of the RW 6th Birthday Bash.

Some changes took place as well. To bring the Royal Watch more in line with other collectible clubs, the membership year was changed. Those who joined in 2001 enjoyed a few extra months of membership, as the club year ended on March 31, 2002. The 2002 club year runs from April 1, 2002, through March 31, 2003.

Wimberley Mills opened its doors for visits for the first time in November 2001, giving collectors a chance to see the birthplace of Harmony Kingdom. Tours will continue throughout 2002 and beyond.

Rule Britannia: 2002

The theme for 2002 is "Rule Britannia," reflecting Harmony Kingdom's English roots. In addition to Royal Watch club gifts and redemptions made in Wimberley Mills, Lord Byron comes home as production of Chapter Six of Harmony Garden returns to England. And in keeping with British tradition, the annual in-store event is The HK Tea Party.

During the summer of 2002, Peter Calvesbert made a series of rare U.S. appearances on the House of Lords "Talk of the Town" tour. An English-made parrot box figurine was the exclusive event piece.

Lord of the Aisles: 2002

In 1999 one of the first activities of HOP was to help the independent clubs organise a parade of HK club banners through the aisles of the International Collectible Exposition. Our humble beginning saw thirteen club members proudly present their banners, led by bagpipes, HOP officers and the Royal Watch. Each ICE show parade has grown, and in 2002 almost every club participated, with 125 marchers at Rosemont. The significance of this popular club activity was recognised by the 2002 International Gift and Collectible event box figurine "Lord of the Aisles."

Introduction to the Box Figurines

How Harmony Kingdom Box Figurines Are Made

Sculpting And Master Mould Making

The artist uses a clay/plasticene mixture to carve the sculpture. One mould is made from the sculpture. The sculpture rarely stays intact after it is moulded. Twelve masters are then created from the original mould. Any edition changes are made to the twelve masters.

Production Mould Making

The twelve masters are used to make the production moulds. The production moulds are made of silicon rubber and can be used on average fifty times. More complex designs yield fewer pieces from each production mould.

Casting

A mixture of marble powder and resin is poured into the silicon moulds. The mixture passes through two vacuum chambers, once before pouring and again when the mixture is in the mould. This removes gas and air bubbles trapped in the mixture and pulls out any air pockets caught in the mould during pouring. The mixture is exposed to high temperatures and sets after two hours. Lids and bases are cast separately.

De-moulding

The white casting is removed from the mould and inspected for any defects. The mould is then cleaned, inspected, and returned to the casting department.

Dipping

The white casting is dipped into a specially formulated stain.

Polishing

After the stain dries, the casting is placed in a tumbler where it is gently polished.

Linishing

After polishing, the bottom and top are matched and inspected and the flashing is ground off.

Finishing

The Finishing Department cleans off the grinding dust, stains the undersides of the base and lid, and inspects the piece before applying the Harmony Kingdom stamp.

Painting

Having passed the quality checks at each of the previous stages, the piece is given to the Painting Department or distributed to outwork painters. All colours are mixed in-house.

Why Variations Occur

Colouration

For the most part, colouration changes are not considered variations, as these are not controllable. Because each box figurine is individually hand-painted, in many cases by villagers who live throughout the Cotswolds, the pieces take on the personalities of their painters. Even though the painters are given guidelines, their natural inclinations come through in their application of paint in the same way collectors have individual preferences. The pigments in the paint itself vary based on batch mixing, ambient temperatures and evaporation. On occasion, a planned colour change does occur to reduce the number of rejects or to lend the piece a more fanciful quality. One example of a planned colour change is "Bon Enfant," which underwent three distinct colour transformations.

Exterior Changes

Martin provides his artists with guidelines so that the master carvers are aware of the limitations of the production process. However, it is sometimes impossible to foresee production pitfalls until the piece has been moulded and hundreds of figurines already cast. If too many rejects occur, the mould must be changed. Antiquark endeavours to record production quantities for the different moulds so that these variations can be tracked. Other exterior changes are made if the design by the artist is flawed. An example of this is "Trumpeters' Ball" where an extraneous elephant trunk appeared and was later removed. Occasionally an external change is made to create a "story," as in the case of "Ed's Safari II."

Interior Changes

Originally, the box figurines had empty interiors. Some of the interiors of the early pieces have been enhanced. Other interiors are too obtuse, are difficult to produce, or are misunderstood, so the interiors have been modified. Occasionally interior changes are made just for the fun of it. The interior of "Algenon" in its original version, for example, portrayed artist Peter Calvesbert in a bubble bath with his rubber duck. This was replaced with a ball of yarn and knitting needles, as the new imagery was more universally understood. Antiquark endeavours to record production quantities for the different moulds so that these variations can be tracked.

Edition Changes

In January 1999 Harmony Kingdom changed its hallmarking system. With this, certain variations were introduced on some of the open and timed pieces carved from 1999 onward. The first 5,000 pieces of an edition are referred to as Version 1; subsequent pieces as Version Infinity (∞). Mould changes on the interior and/or exterior and colour variations exist on some of these pieces as they change from Version 1 to Version Infinity.

Transformations

Pieces are sometimes modified to create special event pieces. A jacket was added to "The Garden Prince" for the 1996 collectible exhibition event piece giveaways. "Tin Cat" was modified into "Tin Cat's Cruise," the event piece for the Ugly Duck cruise in 1998. "Primordial Soup" was altered to create "Primordial Sloop," the event piece for the first Harmony Kingdom convention, Primordial Crooze. "Catch A Lot" was transformed into "Camelot" for Harmony Kingdom's Grand Investiture in 1999.

Photography

Photographs are taken of early prototypes whose colours and design may not have been finalised at the time of photography. An example of this is "Joie De Vivre" which was photographed with her head down, but was changed shortly after production began to have her head up. The photographic process itself as well as scanning and printing of the publications may alter colouration.

Production Numbers

The number of pieces produced for limited and timed editions and retired pieces are provided in the Secrets Revealed section of this book. These numbers represent the total quantity of pieces produced in England and China, dating back to when Martin created pieces alone in his garden shed.

Origination

The initials PC for Peter Calvesbert, DL for David Lawrence, S for Sherman Drackett or M for Martin Perry are sometimes moulded into the box figurines. Peter Calvesbert and David Lawrence carve their own pieces. Modifications are made based on Martin's and Noel's suggestions, though PC and DL generally represent the two men's creations. Martin does not carve pieces that bear M. He closely supervises a team of select carvers that work under his tutelage to create the MP pieces. Often, multiple carvers work on an individual piece. In 1999 Monique Baldwin was given a unique signature hallmark, an eye. In 2000 Adam Binder began using a gecko for his signature hallmark. Mel Heald uses an H as the hallmark on his pieces.

Concepts for the figurines come from a variety of sources, including collectors. Noel Wiggins has sketched some of the designs, including parts of Harmony Garden, "Bon Enfant" and "Sneak Preview." Disney artists have sketched and sculpted the Disney exclusive pieces. Martin oversees all carvings on all pieces.

Limited edition box figurines bear the signatures of their creators. Peter's pieces may be signed or stamped with PC, P. Calvesbert or Peter Calvesbert. His signature varies so dramatically that even his bank manager once asked that he sign his name numerous times to verify his identity. David Lawrence uses the monogram

DL to sign his pieces. Martin Perry may use MRP, M. Perry or Martin R. Perry. Monique Baldwin uses M Baldwin or the monogram MB. Adam Binder uses AB, and Sherman Drackett signs SD.

Dates

Carving Dates

This is the date the artist's carving is finalised.

Release Dates

This is the date an item is offered for order to retailers.

Retirement Dates

If an item is not a limited or timed edition and has no retirement date, the item is an open edition as of the printing date of this book. Retirement dates represent the date the moulds were destroyed. However, pieces may be in another stage of production other than casting. Additionally, retired pieces may still be in distribution if stock exists.

Last Ship/Order Dates

The last ship date applies to limited editions and represents the date the last of the edition is shipped to retailers. The last order date applies to timed editions and represents the final day/month orders are accepted by Harmony Ball Company and Harmony International Ltd. for the item, unless extra stock remains.

Measurements

The dimensions stated for the items are the calibrated measurements in millimeters (Width x Depth x Height). The width and depth dimensions remain consistent, though the height may vary depending on the amount of time spent grinding down the base in the linishing process.

Hallmarks

Harmony Kingdom hallmarks contain quite a bit of information. They tell you the year the piece was produced, the year (and sometimes month) the piece was carved, who the artist is and the edition.

The Crown Stamp denotes the year of production. While the crown remains consistent, the icon at the top of the crown changes from year to year. The location of the stamp also aids in determining the age of the box. The stamp was placed on the base from July 1995 through autumn 1996, and on the bottom of the lid from autumn 1996 onward. If your box has no crown stamp it usually means it was produced before July 1995.

Year of Production Hallmark Stamp denotes year piece produced.

1995 AND 1996	= CROWN WITH TREBLE CLEF
1997	= CROWN WITH HEART
1998	= CROWN WITH 5 POINT STAR
1999	= CROWN WITH HALF MOON
2000	= CROWN WITH DOUBLE DIAMOND/DOUBLE M
2001	= CROWN WITH SMILEY FACE
2002	= CROWN WITH PEACE SYMBOL

Year of Creation Hallmark denotes year carving of piece completed.

1995	= APPLE/BOMB (AN HOMAGE TO OKLAHOMA CITY TRAGEDY)
1996	= DIAMOND/COFFIN (CORINNA & MARTIN ATTENDED HBC'S NEW YEAR'S EVE PARTY AND AWOKE EARLY ON JANUARY 1, 1996 FOR A SPECIAL TOUR OF THE FRANKLIN COUNTY MORGUE ARRANGED BY AN HBC EMPLOYEE)
1997	= HEART (EXCITEMENT OVER LORD BYRON'S INTRODUCTION AS HE SEARCHES FOR TRUE LOVE)
1998	= STAR (PETER CARVED STARS INTO "SNEAK PREVIEW" WHICH WAS THE FIRST BOX TO BE PRODUCED IN 1998)
1999	= HALF MOON (DEPICTS THE EVE OF THE MILLENNIUM. BEGAN AS A MOON AND A STAR BUT THE STAR DID NOT HOLD UP IN THE CASTING PROCESS. SEE "PARADE OF GIFTS" FOR EXAMPLE OF HALF MOON WITH STAR.)
2000	= DOUBLE DIAMOND/DOUBLE M (TWO CAPITAL LETTER M'S IN MIRROR IMAGE FORM A DOUBLE DIAMOND SHAPE. M IS THE ROMAN NUMERAL FOR 1000, SO MM = 2000.)
2001	= SMILEY FACE (REFERENCES THE SMILEY FACES, OR "EMOTICONS" USED TO SHOW EMOTION ON THE WORLD WIDE WEB.)
2002	= PEACE SYMBOL (HOPEFULNESS FOR WORLD PEACE.)

The carved hallmarks on the box figurines are generally on the exterior bottom of the pieces but sometimes are found on the lid. The original pieces did not contain hallmarks. The copyright symbol was implemented in 1994. Other hallmarks followed in mid-1995. Hallmarks do not follow a set sequence and are not listed sequentially in the "Secrets Revealed" portion of the reference guide.

Date	Hallmark Introduced
SEPTEMBER 1993	FIRST APPEARANCE OF PC ON EXTERIOR ("SHELL GAME")
DECEMBER 1993	FIRST APPEARANCE OF PC IN INTERIOR ("DAY DREAMER")
SEPTEMBER 1994	FIRST APPEARANCE OF HBC'S TREBLE CLEF LOGO IN INTERIOR AND COPYRIGHT ©
MAY 1995	FOUR HALLMARKS APPEAR ON EXTERIOR OF PIECE: 1. APPLE FOR 1995 "YEAR OF CREATION" 2. © FOR COPYRIGHT OR HBC'S TREBLE CLEF LOGO 3. CLOCK FACE REPRESENTS MONTH CARVING COMPLETED. FOR A PERIOD OF TIME, CLOCK IS A MIRROR IMAGE. CLOCK MAY HAVE HANDS OR DOTS. 4. PETER'S MARK WHICH LOOKS LIKE A SNAKE THROUGH A STAFF (AS IF P & C ENTWINED)
JULY 1995	CROWN STAMP INTRODUCED ON BOTTOM OF FIGURINE ("SWEET SERENADE")

December 1995	Snake no longer used. PC appears ("Beak to Beak"). Other artist initials begin to appear.
January 1996	Diamond for 1996 "year of creation"
September 1996	Label appears on base with "Harmony Kingdom, Made in England," box name, and copyright. Crown stamp moves to bottom of lid.
January 1997	Heart for 1997 "year of creation" Edition/Version number hallmark replaces Carving Month: 1 = first 3000 boxes, 2 = second 3000, etc. (Edition number may appear on pre-1997 carvings if release date after 1996.) Some limited editions only have edition number "1" since they are individually numbered. Others have no edition number. Both © and HBC logo now used. Top centre of crown stamp modified, replacing treble clef with heart denoting 1997 as production year.
January 1998	Star for 1998 "year of creation" Top centre of crown stamp modified, replacing heart with five-pointed star denoting 1998 as production year.
January 1999	Moon for 1999 "year of creation" Top centre of crown stamp modified, replacing star with half moon denoting 1999 as production year. Edition/Version number replaced with infinity symbol after first 5,000 pieces produced.
January 2000	Double Diamond/Double M's for 2000 "year of creation" Top centre of crown stamp modified, replacing moon with double diamond denoting 2000 as production year.
January 2001	Smiley face for 2001 "year of creation" Top centre of crown stamp modified, replacing double diamond with smiley face denoting 2001 as production year.
January 2002	Peace symbol for 2002 "year of creation" Top centre of crown stamp modified, replacing smiley face with peace symbol denoting 2002 as production year.

Issue Price

Issue prices in the U.S. have remained constant since 1994 and in the U.K. since 1998. The following table lists price codes that appear in the appendix. Each code represents the U.S. Dollar and Pound Sterling suggested retail price for each piece. Please note the U.K. prices include the 17.5% Value Added Tax (VAT).

Price Code	US Dollar	Pound Sterling
P01	$ 17.50	£ 11.95
P02	$ 20.00	£ 15.00
P03	$ 29.50	£ 19.95
P04	$ 35.00	£ 24.95
P05	$ 38.50	£ 25.95
P06	$ 45.00	£ 29.50
P07	$ 49.00	£ 33.95
P08	$ 55.00	£ 39.95
P09	$ 65.00	£ 49.50
P10	$ 70.00	£ 41.50
P11	$ 75.00	£ 58.95
P12	$ 80.00	£ 70.50
P13	$ 90.00	£ 64.95
P14	$ 95.00	£ 69.95
P15	$100.00	£ 64.95
P16	$120.00	£ 86.95
P17	$150.00	£ 99.95
P18	$175.00	£117.50
P19	$225.00	£152.95
P20	$250.00	£187.95
P21	$400.00	£258.50
P22	$500.00	£381.00
P23	$600.00	£425.00
P24	$650.00	N/A
P25	$890.00	£693.50
P26	$25.00	£17.95
P27	$28.00	£21.25
P28	$30.00	£19.95
P29	$40.00	£28.95
P30	$46.00	N/A
P31	$49.50	£39.95
P32	$52.00	N/A
P33	$54.00	N/A
P34	$56.00	N/A
P35	$58.50	N/A
P36	$72.00	N/A
P39	$85.00	N/A
P40	$200.00	N/A
P41	$270.00	£199.95
P42	$12.00	£9.95
P43	$50.00	N/A
P44	N/A	£75.00

Secrets Revealed

TREASURE JESTS
SMALL

Algenon
Item No.: TJCA8
Artist: PC
Size: 45x55x83
Status: Retired
Carving Date: 97
Release Date: Jan 98
Retired Date: Apr 2002
Issue Size: 27,048

This box figurine is based on Peter's kitten, Algy. Here Algy gets into trouble while chasing a bird, upsetting a flowerpot full of bulbs. The mouse is upside down under a leaf near Algy's paw. On Version 1, the inside of the box depicts Peter in a bubble bath with his rubber ducky. Inside Version 2 there are three balls of wool and a pair of knitting needles. The inscription on the lid, "ZOE BAIN," refers to an old girlfriend of Peter's with whom he had lost touch. Peter inscribes, "July 3 Where R U? →" (the arrow pointing to Peter's e-mail address) in hopes that Zoe might see his message and contact him. The e-mail address was removed on Version 2. Other inscriptions include "LG" (which stands for "Little Ginger," Algy's formal name), and I2E1 (which means "Italy 2, England, 1," the sweepstake score at the HK UK office before the qualifying football game for the World Cup. (The result was a draw, and England got through to the next round.) The hallmarks include ©, heart, HBC logo, ed.#, and Pc.

All Angles Covered
Item No.: TJME
Artist: PC
Size: 50x50x57
Status: Retired
Carving Date: 94
Release Date: Sep 94
Retired Date: Oct 2000
Issue Size: 22,330

This box figurine features meerkats, African sentries, known for establishing lookout posts and digging burrows in the sand for their food. HK assists them by supplying binoculars, a bucket, and a spade. The mouse can be found on the lid, peeking out between the meerkats' shoulders. Being an early piece, there are no markings or inner carvings. Interior hallmarks include HBC logo.

All Ears

Item No.: TJRA
Artist: PC
Size: 61x33x44
Status: Retired
Carving Date: 93
Release Date: Dec 93
Retired Date: Dec 96
Issue Size: 6668

A very early piece, this inquisitive bunny rabbit stands alone and does not incorporate an inner carving, a hidden mouse, inscriptions, or any hallmarks.

All Tied Up

Item No.: TJSN
Artist: PC
Size: 50x51x34
Status: Retired
Carving Date: 93
Release Date: Sep 93
Retired Date: Dec 96
Issue Size: 4566

This box figurine, a pile of entwined snakes, is one of the first that featured Peter's trademark mouse. What a terrifying place for the mouse to make his debut - between coils of snakes! There are no inscriptions, inner carving, or hallmarks. Peter left his initials on the back of a rattler at the base and P.C. can be found in some interiors.

Antipasto

Item No.: TJAE
Artist: PC
Size: 42x65x64
Status: Retired
Carving Date: 97
Release Date: Jan 98
Retired Date: Apr 99
Issue Size: 13,369

This box figurine features two adult anteaters and one youngster attempting a feast, but the nest of ants they seek is a force to be reckoned with. Seventeen ants fight back with hand grenades and a mousetrap. The mouse is in the small hollow of the tree trunk on the lid. The inside of the box reveals the anteaters' family cookbook, complete with gourmet ant recipes, hence the title "Antipasto." Inscriptions include "Leaf Futters Rule," carved on the tree, which should have read "Cutters," but Peter's knife slipped. (Leaf Cutter is a type of ant). "Good Luck Kimberly" refers to an HK collector who was expecting a baby at the time of carving. "40x" refers to the fact that anteaters' sense of smell is 40 times greater that of humans. Hallmarks include ©, heart, HBC logo, ed.#, and Pc.

Harmony Kingdom Box Details

Aria Amorosa
Item No.: TJES
Artist: PC
Size: 49x72x75
Status: Retired
Carving Date: 97
Release Date: Jan 98
Retired Date: Jul 98
Issue Size: 9530

This box figurine depicts two seals, lovingly entwined, mouths open in song. A plimsol line with numerical markings runs down the belly of one of them, a representation of the amount of oil that can be extracted from an elephant seal. Peter carved the cigarette lighter under the other seal's flipper after a beach-combing trip in North Wales where he found the beach littered with plastic lighters. Peter's mouse looks out startled from under another flipper. The inspiration for the rat carved inside was a topical news item that Peter misheard on the radio at the time of carving: the "monster rat" catastrophe. It turns out that it was the "Montserrat catastrophe," a volcano threatening to erupt in the Caribbean. Hallmarks include ©, heart, HBC logo, ed.#, and Pc, with "P. Calvesbert" on the base.

Artful Dodger
Item No.: TJH08
Artist: PC
Size: 58x46x71
Status: Open
Carving Date: 01
Release Date: Jan 02

The Golden Retriever is one of the most popular pets in America, beloved for its friendly good-natured disposition. And who can resist those sad eyes? This intelligent pup artfully pretends that he has not yet been fed by concealing a heap of kibble behind the upturned bowl. While Master Carver Peter Calvesbert was working on this piece, he purchased a new computer with Microsoft XP installed on it, and immediately returned to working on the old computer since the new one has taken to crashing. In England the term "dog's breakfast" refers to anything that is something of mess, so Peter has carved "XP" on the inside of the dog bowl. The suggestion for this box figurine came from the winner of a Harmony Kingdom contest, Cyndra Henry, whose name is inscribed on the interior. The artist's signature mouse peeps out from under the golden's shaggy fur. Hallmarks are located on the back of the bowl and include ©, smiley face, HBC logo, ed.#, and Pc.

At Arm's Length

Item No.: TJOC
Artist.: PC
Size: 42x41x58
Status: Retired
Carving Date: 93
Release Date: Sep 93
Retired Date: Jun 96
Issue Size: 2029

An elegant octopus is the subject of this box figurine. The mouse peaks out from behind one of the tentacles. There are no inner carvings or inscriptions. Interior hallmarks include P or Pc.

At The Hop

Item No.: TJRA2
Artist: PC
Size: 49x47x56
Status: Retired
Carving Date: 95
Release Date: Nov 95
Retired Date: Apr 02
Issue Size: 25,850

A group of gentle bunnies pile on top of one another in neat rows. This piece was inspired by Japanese netsuke and is therefore more symmetrical than other box figurines. The mouse is hidden between two bunnies' hind legs and later a carrot was added. There are no inner carvings or inscriptions. Interior hallmarks include the HBC logo, and P. Calvesbert is inscribed on the base.

Baby Boomer

Item No.: TJKA
Artist: PC
Size: 61x61x71
Status: Retired
Carving Date: 97
Release Date: Jan 98
Retired Date: Apr 99
Issue Size: 16,615

This box figurine features 4 adult kangaroos, 7 babies, and Noel Wiggins tucked in a pouch wearing one of his Harmony Ball ties. Noel wears glasses in most of the pieces and sunglasses in a small quantity. The mouse keeps a low profile tucked away to Noel's right. The ubiquitous tin can litter appears again. The interior of Version 1 has a baby kangaroo sleeping with its teddy bear. The interior of Version 2 contains a pair of boxing gloves. Inscriptions include "MOB," a generic term for kangaroos; "Blue Flier," a female kangaroo with a blue grey coat; and "Boomer," a male kangaroo. The inscription on the inside of the rim is a dedication to HK's former Australian distributor, Henrik. The inscription "Griff's Last Purr" around the base is a dedication to the Perry family cat, Griff, who died 22.7.97 at age 18. Hallmarks include ©, heart, HBC logo, ed.#, and Pc.

Baby On Board

Item No.: TJAR
Artist: PC
Size: 69x42x45
Status: Retired
Carving Date: 93
Release Date: Dec 93
Retired Date: Dec 97
Issue Size: 13,217

This is one of three mother and baby boxes that Peter carved during 1993. Peter was drawn by the texture possibilities of the armadillo, and enjoyed putting in the bands and scales. Notice that the mother is 6-banded, and the baby 3-banded, to show that the baby is half of his mother. The baby is atop the mother rather than snuggled underneath to provide a handle for the lid. The mouse does not appear on this piece, nor do any inner carvings or inscriptions. The only hallmark is PC below the tail.

Back Scratch

Item No.: TJCA2
Artist: PC
Size: 59x34x46
Status: Retired
Carving Date: 93
Release Date: Dec 93
Retired Date: Jan 95
Issue Size: 554

This humorous feline box figurine is an early piece and does not incorporate the hidden mouse, inscriptions, inner carving, or hallmarks. This is one of the rarest and most sought after pieces.

Bad to the Bone

Item No.: TJHO7
Artist: PC
Size: 44x60x70
Status: Open
Carving Date: 01
Release Date: May 01

This mixed breed dog of questionable heritage jealously guards everything he owns. Quite the collector, he has amassed an enormous pile of bones, tins of dog food, and even an old boot. And this bad boy's been to the butcher's lately, judging from the telltale string of sausages hanging from his jowls. Within the pile of bones are two of his favourite videos: "100 Best Cat Chases" and the sequel "Cat Chase 2." "S.F." engraved on the Frisbee stands for Samuel Frederick, the name of Peter and Andrea Calvesbert's son. The signature mouse shelters inside the boot. The Version One interior features an understandably frightened feline. The Version Infinity shows a telephone, Cockney rhyming for "dog and bone." Hallmarks include ©, smiley face, HBC logo, ed.#, and Pc.

Page 42   Harmony Kingdom Box Details

Bamboozled

Item No.: TJPA
Artist: PC
Size: 51x64x67
Status: Open
Carving Date: 97
Release Date: Jun 97

This piece's subject matter is a serious one, as Peter was in a serious frame of mind contemplating the near extinction of the Giant Panda. The tombstone inside inscribed "1000 to Save" and the "1000" carved on a bamboo shoot refers to what scientists believed was the number of giant pandas remaining in the mountains of China at the time of carving. (This number later changed to "1006" when six more pandas were discovered.) Not only are pandas threatened by poaching, but by the deforestation of the bamboo forests where they live. Bamboo, being the panda's staple diet, is essential to its survival. Nonetheless, in this box figurine, the panda shares his bamboo with the mouse. On Version 1, the bamboo shoots were tinted yellow and the leaves green. Version 2 was left untinted, except for the black of the Panda. Some mould changes were made to reduce rejects during production, which included widening the space between the Panda's arms, and bringing two leaves closer together. Hallmarks include ©, heart, HBC logo, ed.#, and Pc.

Beak To Beak

Item No.: TJLB
Artist: PC
Size: 56x41x57
Status: Retired
Carving Date: 95
Release Date: Dec 95
Retired Date: Dec 97
Issue Size: 12,422

Created as a Valentine's Day piece for 1996, this piece features two lovebirds nestled cozily on a bench. Even Peter's signature mouse has a mate for the holiday. Inscribed on the bench is "PC loves AR" (Peter Calvesbert and Andrea Riley), "MP loves CP" (Martin and Corinna Perry), "RM loves MH" (Ruth McDonald and Mike Horne, two close friends of Peter's), "BC loves FL" (Peter's brother and his girlfriend), and the anonymous "Trace loves..." with a series of initials for her string of lovers. The piece also contains a slew of other lovers: amorous hedgehogs, snakes, mice, and even a lonely little rabbit. "I love SA" refers to South Africa, where Peter and Andrea honeymooned in October 1995. "MUFC" stands for Manchester United Football Club. "HK Rules" refers to Harmony Kingdom and "Noel" for Noel Wiggins. Peter's obsession with the Mazda MX5 ("MXV") sports car is compared to the then new MGF he wanted. Carved on the back of the bench is "Sticky + Tonkin P.I.P." which immortalises Ruth and Mike's pets who both tragically died on the same day. "P.I.P." means "play in peace." The two cans reflect Peter's concern about littering. Inside is the HBC logo. Some pieces have 1995 on the back of the bench while most have 1996. Hallmarks include apple, clock face with month 11, HBC logo, and Pc.

Harmony Kingdom Box Details

Beau Brummell
Item No.: TJH05
Artist: PC
Size: 57x51x70
Status: Open
Carving Date: 00
Release Date: Jun 00

A dandified poodle holds a set electric clippers and glares, as if to threaten the next person who tries to clip his curly fur. The poodle's dense coat is nature's way of keeping the dog dry while in the water. Poodles were originally bred to hunt and clipping was done for good reasons. The pompom on the tail provided a way to lift them from the water and hair was kept around the front and back to protect the chest and kidneys. Now that the poodle is mainly kept as a household pet, the patterns seem merely fashionable. "Beau Brummell" is named for the famous trend setter of the English Regency. The code that appears around the base of the Version 1 is the same as that on "Signing Line," and only the key word is different but can be guessed. All the clues to solving the cipher appear on "Signing Line," and the only clue Peter provides is that the deciphered message is his opinion on the docking of dogs' ears and tails. On the Version Infinity, the code has been removed. The mouse hangs on to the cord between the poodle's front paws. Hallmarks include ©, double diamond, HBC logo, ed.#, and Pc.

Blue Heaven
Item No.: TJD02
Artist: PC
Size: 57x51x83
Status: Open
Carving Date: 01
Release Date: Jan 02

The dolphins' method of fishing served as the inspiration for this box figurine: the dolphins surround their chosen dinner. Here the fish, and Peter's signature mouse, are seen making a desperate bid for freedom. The Version One edition features six bottle-nosed dolphins and one "dolphin-nosed" bottle, and the interior depicts a group of fish plotting their escape. For the Infinity Version, the bottle is replaced by a seventh dolphin and the interior shows the frogman, whose flippers are on the exterior of the box. Hallmarks include ©, smiley face, HBC logo, ed.#, and Pc.

Braganza
Item No.: TJDLCA4
Artist: DL
Size: 76x46x71
Status: Open
Carving Date: 02
Release Date: May 02

David Lawrence tells a story about his grandmother, born in an age very different from our own. Neighbors looked out for each other and there was no need to lock the doors. The one time her faith in human nature was shaken was the after-

PAGE 44   Harmony Kingdom Box Details

noon she brought a friend over for tea. As she entered the kitchen, she heard a rustling in the cupboard containing the teapot in which she kept her "housekeeping" money. Fearing felony, she armed herself with a rolling pin. The rustling was caused by no more than the family cat chasing a mouse. The teapot fell earthward and shattered, the mouse went free, the cat was disgruntled and the ladies had tea from a teabag. The pattern on the sides of the teapot reveals the artist's trademark acorn. The teapot contains two heart-shaped teabags, a modern invention abhorred by loose leaf aficionados, including David's grandmother. Hallmarks are also inside and include ©, peace sign, HBC logo, and DL.

Brean Sands
Item No.: TJCB2
Artist: PC
Size: 66x50x48
Status: Open
Carving Date: 96
Release Date: Jun 96

This is the third crab box figurine which features a clever crustacean coaxing a timid minnow from its coral reef hideaway. The crab almost has his prey, using a slice of bread as bait. On this same baited claw our crustacean friend sports a wristwatch. The mouse hides amid the coral on the back of the piece, near a minnow. The words "Brean Sands" are inscribed on the back of the crab's shell, referring to the name of a beach in England where Peter and his family vacationed over twenty years ago. Initially, "Brean Sands" was designed to have an empty interior, though few were actually produced this way. One hundred pieces depict a hand inside, and the remaining pieces have a treasure chest within. In September 1996 a few hundred pieces were produced in white, some of which went to the U.S. but were mostly sold in the U.K. Hallmarks include diamond, clock face with month 2, HBC logo, and Pc.

Cannery Row
Item No.: TJCA12
Artist: PC
Size: 51x76x64
Status: Open
Carving Date: 00
Release Date: Jun 00

Two kittens frolic in a large cardboard box, better than any expensive cat toy! Maybe it's the faint scent of tuna lingering on the old box that has attracted the frisky felines. Inscribed on the box lid is the phrase "River Severn Tuna." The River Severn is a former favourite fishing spot of Peter's, and about the unlikeliest place on earth you'd ever find a tuna. A dead bird with its feet in the air reminds us that although cats are loveable and cuddly creatures, they have predatory instincts as well. The kittens on Version 1 and Version Infinity are different colours (grey in Version 1 and orange in Version Infinity). In addition, Version 1 features an extra mouse peeping out of a hole chewed in the side of the box. A name change occurred as well between the two versions. Version 1 is named "Tony's Tabbies II" and Version Infinity "Cannery Row." Hallmarks include ©, double diamond, HBC logo, ed.#, and Pc.

Harmony Kingdom Box Details

Catch A Lot
Item No.: TJWH4
Artist: PC
Size: 78x42x61
Status: Retired
Carving Date: 98
Release Date: Jun 98
Retired Date: Apr 99
Issue Size: 17,876

This box figurine features a whaling boat named "Cachalot" (French for sperm whale), and five fisherman (4 on board and 1 overboard). Inside Version 1 Jonah saws his way from the whale's mouth into the hull of the boat. Inside Version 2 a swarm of tourist boats rush to get the first sighting of a whale. A third version in the Infinity Edition depicts a dog on the roof of the wheelhouse sporting a slicker to protect him from the rain. NCP stands for National Car Parks. The mouse is tucked inside a life preserver. Hallmarks include ©, star, HBC logo, ed.#, and Pc.

Caw Of The Wild
Item No.: TJBB
Artist: PC
Size: 68x59x87
Status: Open
Carving Date: 99
Release Date: Jun 99

What do http://www70.pair.com/robn-jays and our lovely crested blue jay have in common? Both are colourful and have admirers throughout the world. Peter sculpted "Caw of the Wild" in honour of Rob and Jay, the duo who create the aforementioned infamous website full of rumors and gossip about Harmony Kingdom. "20 MAR" commemorates the epic 19-day flight around the world or the Breitling-Orbiter 3 hot air balloon and the "Sod It" expletive inside Version Infinity refers to British entrepreneur Richard Branson's failed attempt. "17 3 99" is the date English entertainer Rod Hull fell from his roof to his death. Peter fondly remembers Rob and his puppet Emu from his childhood years. "To Rob" appears inside Version 1 as the bird itself commemorates Jay. Hallmarks include ©, HBC logo, ed.#, 99, and Pc.

Changing Of The Guard
Item No.: TJCH
Artist: PC
Size: 68x50x60
Status: Retired
Carving Date: 96
Release Date: Jun 96
Retired Date: Jun 02
Issue Size: 26,523

A favourite of Peter's because of its challenging texture, this box figurine depicts three scaly chameleons, each bearing an inscription: "USA," "HK," "PC," and "KAY" (Antiquark's General Manager) hidden in reptile scales. The inside of this piece reveals a little snail but was initially empty. There was no mouse on this figurine until it was later added beside the chameleon with USA on its back. Hallmarks include diamond, clock face with month 4, HBC logo, and Pc.

Close Shave
Item No.: TJHE3
Artist: PC
Size: 55x58x62
Status: Retired
Carving Date: 96
Release Date: Jun 96
Retired Date: Oct 98
Issue Size: 10,913

Hedgehogs run rampant in the Cotswolds, much like squirrels in New Hampshire and armadillos in Texas, and they are prone to suffer the same fate in their attempt to cross roadways. This box figurine depicts a near miss. All four hedgehogs nestle atop a bed of leaves, scattered with trinkets and rubbish. The mouse is hiding beneath a leaf near the worm on the base. The tyre of the car that swerved to miss the lucky, shaven fellow is found within the box. A few prototypes show the hedgehogs eating worms. These were removed or covered with leaves on the production pieces. Hallmarks include diamond, clock face with month 2, HBC logo, and Pc.

Cookie's Jar
Item No.: TJCA11
Artist: PC
Size: 45x46x84
Status: Open
Carving Date: 99
Release Date: Jan 00

Cats humour nearly everyone with their inventive mischief making. Peter has never seen a cat in a goldfish bowl, but he says that if he were of the feline race he would frequent this form of watering hole. Here, this kitty is none too successful as yet another fish escapes from his clutches. The interior of Version 1 features chocolate cookies, which are as much a temptation to us humans as goldfish are to cats. Version Infinity contains two plucky survivors lying low in an aquarium treasure chest, waiting for the cat to get bored or full. Peter's signature mouse has chosen an interesting hiding place. Hallmarks include ©, moon, HBC logo, ed.#, and Pc.

Harmony Kingdom Box Details

Croc Pot

Item No.: TJAL2
Artist: PC
Size: 66x44x65
Status: Retired
Carving Date: 97
Release Date: Jan 98
Retired Date: Oct 00
Issue Size: 19,204

This pair of crocodiles rest leisurely in their boat with a zebra leg as a paddle, having finished a large meal. Litter around and inside the boat provides clues to the morsels that they have just eaten. The mouse is hiding near the boat's missing rudder. Within the box are a peace sign, fish skeletons, footprints of a wading bird, and a hamburger box with "M" inscribed on it. After being contacted by McDonald's, the "M" inside Version 1 was changed to "HK" due to potential trademark confusion. Coincidentally, the name of the box is not unlike the name of McDonald's founder, Ray Kroc. "Cool cider," "docile orc," and "cod recoil" are anagrams for "crocodile." Hallmarks include ©, heart, HBC logo, ed.#, and Pc.

Damnable Plot

Item No.: TJBV
Artist: PC
Size: 54x56x59
Status: Retired
Carving Date: 95
Release Date: Jan 95
Retired Date: Apr 99
Issue Size: 16,257

Five busy beavers appear on this box figurine. One of the beavers crushes a discarded beer can; another has a bundle of dynamite clenched in its teeth, planning the "damnable plot." The mouse is tucked underneath this devious beaver. Inscribed on the base of this box are Peter's initials and the date of completion, January 26, 1995. This date is not present on later models due to mould deterioration. "35 Today" was inscribed in the box because Peter finished it on his birthday. Underneath the chin of the seated beaver is another message: "FRED, DDC, -20". Peter, an avid golfer, wrote the message in homage to Fred Couples, who scored 20 under at the Dubai Desert Classic Golf Tournament. Some of the early boxes had "Claire" and "Luka" inscribed on the tail of the top beaver, referring to a girl Peter admired from afar, and her dog, Luka. The reference was later removed. On one of the beaver's feet are the numbers 6 and 7. These stand for the shoe sizes of the beaver (one foot is bigger than the other.) Interior hallmarks include © and HBC logo.

Day Dreamer

Item No.: TJPO
Artist: PC
Size: 71x36x36
Status: Retired
Carving Date: 93
Release Date: Dec 93
Retired Date: Jun 96
Issue Size: 4247

This pensive pony box figurine is a very early piece and does not incorporate the hidden mouse, an inner carving, or any hallmarks, except for P.C. or P. Calvesbert inside.

Dead Ringer

Item No.: TJHO3
Artist: PC
Size: 59x71x63
Status: Open
Carving Date: 98
Release Date: Jan 99

This is Peter's first Small Treasure Jest with two lids. The papa and pup have just taken over delivery of the morning post. The postman's hat (ER. Elizabeth Regina) is based on the hat that Peter's father wore when he worked for the Royal Mail. Peter heard many a story of his father's bravery in delivering Her Majesty's mail. However, this poor postman has failed to continue on his round. Amongst the scattered and chewed letters is one addressed to Sherman, R&D department, Wimberley Mills (one of Martin's residential carvers) and another to President Clinton, White House, Washington. And are those letters to Monica Lewinsky, Santa at the North Pole, Lucy Genic (for hallucinogenic), and Reader's Digest? Peter's mouse lurks under the mailbag with his own fan mail. In Edition 1, Peter has included references to the week's news; there was a change to UK law that will allow a dog with a passport to travel abroad without quarantine restrictions. The key and registration number belong to Peter's long awaited new car, a Puma. The Infinity Version contains Winston Churchill, known as the bulldog. Hallmarks include ©, star, HBC logo, ed.#, and PC.

Harmony Kingdom Box Details

Den Mothers
Item No.: TJWO
Artist: PC
Size: 51x57x51
Status: Retired
Carving Date: 95
Release Date: Jan 95
Retired Date: Dec 96
Issue Size: 6264

This group of adult and baby wolves originally contained paw prints and the inscription "I ❤ her" on the inside. There is no hidden mouse or inner carving. Hallmarks include "JAN 95" for the carving date and Pc, with interior © and HBC logo.

Dog Days
Item No.: TJHO
Artist: PC
Size: 59x49x56
Status: Retired
Carving Date: 94
Release Date: Sep 94
Retired Date: Jan 01
Issue Size: 28,438

This hound dog box figurine is an early piece and does not incorporate the hidden mouse, inner carving, or any hallmarks. It pre-dates the arrival of Peter's beloved dog, Murphy. Interior hallmarks include © and HBC logo.

Down Under
Item No.: TJPL
Artist: PC
Size: 54x53x56
Status: Retired
Carving Date: 96
Release Date: Jun 97
Retirement Date: Apr 99
Issue Size: 12,851

Peter inscribed "Platypus" to help identify this furry-bodied mammal with webbed feet and poisonous spur claws. Human activity is again evidenced by the recurring tin can motif. The mouse is accompanied by a computer "mouse" to celebrate the purchase of Peter's first computer. Inside the box are 3 platypus eggs. The inscription "Where's Bob?" is a friendly reference to HK's Bob McKinlay, a man so busy and on the move, one is never quite sure where to find him. At the April 1998 ICE Show held in Edison, New Jersey, one hundred collectors were invited to paint their own Version during the first HK painting seminar. Hallmarks include ©, diamond, HBC logo, ed.#, and Pc.

Driver's Seat

Item No.: TJZE
Artist: PC
Size: 40x62x80
Status: Retired
Carving Date: 97
Release Date: Jun 97
Retired Date: Apr 02
Issue Size: 15,468

Peter loves to watch TV wildlife documentaries, and in this piece, he turns the table by giving the zebra the chance to dominate its predator. Here the zebra sits firmly upon a lioness that has Swiss Army knife claws, a bandage from a previous wound, and a pierced tongue. Under the front leg of the zebra, the mouse makes a full appearance, baring paws, stomach, bottom and tail as he mirrors the zebra's courage. Around the base of the lid is the Latin inscription, "Mites possidebunt terram" meaning "The meek shall inherit the earth." Due to production difficulties, the area between the neck and chin were filled in on Version 2. Also the base of the lid was deepened to increase stability. There is no inner carving except for HBC logo. Hallmarks include ©, heart, HBC logo, ed.#, and Pc.

Ed's Safari

Item No.: TJSA
Artist: PC
Size: 55x54x53
Status: Open
Carving Date: 95
Release Date: Mar 95

In this chaotic box figurine, a safari jeep lies trapped under the enormous bellies of elephants. A turtle is flattened beneath one of the pachyderm's feet. Vultures greedily leer over the carcass, waiting for the elephant to move his foot. A safari member has brought his golf clubs and is squashed between two of the enormous elephants. The mouse is peering out from among the elephants' legs. On the back of the safari bus is inscribed "49'S WIN," referring to the San Francisco 49ers winning the Super Bowl that year. "The Big Day 30-9-95" is Peter and Andrea's proposed wedding day. There is no inner carving. Hallmarks include PC and "95" on the rim, and an interior © and HBC logo.

Ed's Safari II

Item No.: TJSA2
Artist: PC
Size: 76x51x64
Status: Open
Carving Date: 98
Release Date: Jun 98

In this box figurine, the safari animals are on the roof of the bus, trying to thwart the tourists' binoculars and cameras. In Version 1 Peter has commandeered Ed's safari tour and poor Ed is tied up inside the box. In Version 2, Ed has escaped and Peter is tied up inside. The third version shows Andrea in the driver's seat with Peter and Ed tied up inside. The bus has been put up "For Sale." This version also mentions Andrea's employer, *The Evershaw Journal*. The sign on the bus indicates the driver. The mouse hides within the vulture's wing. Hallmarks include ©, star, HBC logo, ed.#, and Pc..

Ed's Safari III
Item No.: TJSA3
Artist: PC
Size: 59x61x84
Status: Retired
Carving Date: 99
Release Date: Jan 00
Retired Date: Apr 02
Issue Size: 11,147

Ed's safari bus must have travelled back in time, as the tour has become lunch for a dinosaur. On the underside of the bus is DYOUTHINKHESAURUS? Also inscribed on the bus is "Ed's Ferrari." Since a new vehicle will be needed, it may as well be a classy coach. The plate on the bus has number 6262, referring to one of Peter's friends, whose birthday is 6th February 1962. Always in the midst of the excitement, Mad Murphy is hiding on the front grill. Within Version 1 a frightened turtle abandons his suitcase in his attempt to flee the dinosaur's giant tongue. Version Infinity features an elephant that has fallen off a ladder. Hallmarks include ©, moon, HBC logo, ed.#, and Pc.

Family Tree
Item No.: TJKO
Artist: PC
Size: 56x55x61
Status: Retired
Carving Date: 94
Release Date: Nov 94
Retired Date: Apr 00
Issue Size: 13,343

These cute koalas curl around one another in this box figurine. The mouse tucks himself under a koala's bottom end. This early piece does not incorporate an inner carving, any inscriptions, or hallmarks except for the interior © and HBC logo.

Faux Paw
Item No.: TJLI
Artist: PC
Size: 62x65x59
Status: Retired
Carving Date: 97
Release Date: Jun 97
Retired Date: Sep 99
Issue Size: 16,572

Five lionesses and one lion slumber in a relaxed group, unaware that a sleepwalking antelope has wandered into their midst. The mouse is hidden in the lion's mane. Savanna grass, a snakeskin, and lion footprints are carved on the inside of the figurine. Inscribed on the lip of the lid is the warning "THE DANGER OF SLEEPWALKING." The inscription "Martha's Son" refers to a racehorse on which Peter bet during the local Cheltenham Gold Cup Week. Carved into the bottom rim of the base are the initials "HB" and an image of a comet to commemorate the Hale Bopp Comet of 1997. The little house is the one that Peter and Andrea almost bought while he was working on this piece. Hallmarks include ©, heart, HBC logo, ed.#, and Pc.

Flight of Fancy

Item No.: TJB12
Artist: PC
Size: 48x33x83
Status: Open
Carving Date: 02
Release Date: May 02

Hornbills are famous for their unusual nesting habits. When Mr. and Mrs. decide its time for baby hornbills, the mother chooses a natural nesting cavity and then is sealed inside with a mixture mud and water, leaving a small slit for air and food. Dad's job is to keep mom happy and well fed and his mate and chicks are completely dependent upon him at this time – if he is hunted or dies, the entire family will most likely not survive. This private couple tacked up a "Do not disturb" sign on their tree. In case of pregnancy cravings, bags of crisps and chocolate bars abound. "Cotswold Wildlife Park" inscribed on a branch refers to a park where Great Indian Hornbills live. "Cuckoo 17.4.02" refers to the date that Peter Calvesbert observed a cuckoo, back in England after migrating. The artist's signature mouse checks out the view from the nesting cavity. The Version One interior shows the gear used by a keeper to retrieve a feather (which now has a place of pride in Peter Calvesbert's studio). The infinity version interior shows hatching eggs. Hallmarks include ©, peace sign, HBC logo, ed.#, and Pc.

Forty Winks

Item No.: TJHE
Artist: PC
Size: 51x39x41
Status: Retired
Carving Date: 92
Release Date: Mar 92
Retired Date: Dec 96
Issue Size: 5385

The sleepy hedgehog rests on his back in this first small box figurine carved by Peter. Because it is such an early piece, it does not incorporate the hidden mouse, an inner carving, inscriptions, or any hallmarks.

Foul Play
Item No.: TJSK
Artist: PC
Size: 57x64x64
Status: Open
Carving Date: 98
Release Date: Jan 99

Three skunks guard their "olFactory," armed with a canister of air freshener. Their neighbour, the rabbit, has donned his daily apparel: a gas mask. The unfortunate porcupine with his low tech defense (a clothes peg), has succumbed to the awful stench. Even the snake has failed to slither away in time. Peter's mouse must be holding his breath. And why the Australian skink? Well, he thought he was going to star in a Harmony Kingdom box figurine and is appalled and embarrassed at his error. How could he confuse "skink" with "skunk?" Is Australian English so different from American English or British English? "I love Plum" is a reference to a military store on an island off the East Coast of the United States. Inside Edition 1 there is a young skunk reading from a recipe book and mixing ingredients for the skunk pong in a cauldron. The inscription around the cauldron refers to the official term for the skunk's smelly fluid, "mercaptan." Scattered around the pot are two tins of baked beans (57 variety), salt and pepper, a bat wing, eyeballs, fish and more secret ingredients. The Infinity Version has old sneakers. Hallmarks include ©, star, HBC logo, ed.#, and Pc.

Friends In High Places
Item No.: TJGI
Artist: PC
Size: 55x45x87
Status: Open
Carving Date: 96
Release Date: Jan 97

During Peter's honeymoon in Africa, the majesty and grace of its creatures inspired him to sculpt this elegant piece. In this box figurine, the giraffes have stripped the trees of their leaves so that there is no shade for the lion cubs. However, the giraffes know the cubs have full bellies and are no threat, and allow them to take cover from the fierce sun, a moment of harmony in the animal kingdom. The initial 500 pieces have the mouse under the chin of a giraffe. During the moulding process the mouse became nearly unrecognisable, so it was moved between the lion's paws. A South African cent is carved within, commemorating Peter and Andrea's honeymoon. Hallmarks include ©, diamond, HBC logo, ed.#, and Pc.

Fur Ball
Item No.: TJCA3
Artist: PC
Size: 54x55x61
Status: Open
Carving Date: 95
Release Date: Apr 95

In this box figurine the group of cats stare off into space, apparently unaware that a mouse is hiding right in middle of them. Markings include "PC" and "2/95" (carving date), which is near the hind leg of the white cat but may not have been reproduced due to the wearing of moulds. Interior hallmarks include © and HBC logo.

Fuss Pot
Item No.: TJHO4
Artist: PC
Size: 58x44x61
Status: Retired
Carving Date: 99
Release Date: Jan 00
Retired Date: Feb 02
Issue Size: 10,234

Although the design is clean and simple, there is the usual HK touch of humour with the tub of moisturiser. Do cosmetic manufacturers test their wrinkle creams on Shar-peis? These odd looking dogs survived a brush with extinction and strangely enough must have a black tongue if they are to be successful show dogs (a pink tongue is an instant disqualification). Inside the box is some liquorice, so our Shar-pei can have a black tongue whenever it is needed. What would they eat to keep themselves so wrinkled? Peter figures it's raisins. Finally, everyone knows the adage about dogs and their owners looking alike, so the name of a British comedic actor named Sid James made it into the interior of the box. He starred in most of the "Carry On" films and had a very wrinkled, but happy, face. Hallmarks include ©, moon, HBC logo, ed.#, and Pc.

Gateau
Item No.: TJDLCA2
Artist: DL
Size: 56x56x71
Status: Open
Carving Date: 02
Release Date: May 02

Surprise, surprise! "Gateau" celebrates the return of David Lawrence to Harmony Kingdom and the coincidences that lead to his reunion with Martin Perry. It was about the time of his daughter Rose's birthday in February 2002 when the two crossed paths at the Spring Fair in Birmingham. And the final prototype of this delightful box figurine was approved around the time of younger daughter Katie's third birthday. The artist's trademark acorn makes a surprise appearance as the interior carving. Hallmarks are found on the interior and include ©, peace sign, HBC logo, and DL.

Gertrude

Item No.: TJDLCA3
Artist: DL
Size: 48x36x86
Status: Open
Carving Date: 02
Release Date: May 02

This beautiful carved stein is inspired by a vessel belonging to artist David Lawrence. It is one of the few containers not to be eroded, distorted or decayed by "Penfold's Old Peculiar," a strong brew with a specific gravity of 1057 degrees. Two dates on the stein – 1995 and 2002 – are the two dates when David started carving for Harmony Kingdom: his first appearance and the time of his resurrection. Two drinking greetings are engraved around the bottom: "Raise a cup of kindness" (borrowed from Robert Burns) and "Wassail! Wassail!" (an Old Norse word meaning "Be whole"). Hidden inside the stein is a hop, the fruit responsible for the pungent flavoring of most English real ales. Hallmarks include ©, peace sign, HBC logo, and DL.

Group Therapy

Item No.: TJAA
Artist: PC
Size: 46x54x72
Status: Retired
Carving Date: 94
Release Date: Nov 94
Retired Date: Dec 96
Issue Size: 3170

Try to find all seven ants hidden on this aardvark box figurine, one of Peter's personal favourites. The mouse is poking his nose out into the open. There is no inner carving or inscriptions. Interior hallmarks include © and HBC logo.

Hammin' It Up

Item No.: TJPI
Artist: PC
Size: 47x46x40
Status: Retired
Carving Date: 93
Release Date: Sep 93
Retired Date: Dec 96
Issue Size: 13,217

This pig pile box figurine is a very early piece and does not incorporate the hidden mouse, an inner carving, inscriptions, or hallmarks.

Hide-and-Seek
Item No.: TJRH
Artist: PC
Size: 36x86x66
Status: Open
Carving Date: 02
Release Date: May 02

The Javan is the rarest rhinoceros species, with an estimated 50 remaining in the wild – and none in zoos. Small and with a single horn, the Javan rhino lives a solitary life in the jungles of southeast Asia. In addition to the artist's signature mouse, five unidentified creatures hide in the undergrowth. "P.C." is inscribed on the box twice. Inside the Version One a rhino contemplates extinction. The Version Infinity interior shows a rhino "charging" (as in "two dollars please"). Hallmarks include ©, peace sign, HBC logo, ed.#, and Pc.

Hog Heaven
Item No.: TJPI2
Artist: PC
Size: 70x50x64
Status: Retired
Carving Date: 96
Release Date: Jun 96
Retired Date: Oct 00
Issue Size: 26,018

This is the third box figurine depicting pigs. The pigs on the first 1400 figurines were painted ivory, pink, and brown. The next 4200 were left unpainted. In May 1997, the original colouration was re-introduced in response to collectors' feedback. Inside the box figurine is the pigs' favourite fruit, an apple, but a small number have been found empty. "Blue 20.4.96," etched inside a pig's ear, marks the arrival of a new member to the Calvesbert family, Andrea's horse, Soldier Blue. Inscribed along the top rim of the box is the alphanumeric code "2125" for Babe, the pig made famous first by a local English children's writer, and then on the big screen. There was no mouse in the early pieces, but the mouse was later added in 1997. Hallmarks include ©, diamond, clock face with month 4, interior HBC logo, and Pc.

Horse Play
Item No.: TJSE
Artist: PC
Size: 47x46x69
Status: Retired
Carving Date: 94
Release Date: Jan 95
Retired Date: Jun 96
Issue Size: 1907

This box figurine features a merry-go-round of lovely seahorses. Inscribed on a piece of seaweed is "DORMY" – a hotel by the Broadway Golf Club. The horseshoe on the base is for luck. There is no inner carving or mouse. Interior hallmarks include © and HBC logo.

Harmony Kingdom Box Details

In Fine Feather
Item No.: TJPU
Artist: PC
Size: 58x57x73
Status: Retired
Carving Date: 97
Release Date: Jan 97
Retired Date: Oct 00
Issue Size: 20,038

The puffins on this box figurine are feeling frisky because it's mating season, hence their bright beaks. The mouse is peaking out from underneath a puffin. Inside is a sand eel whose tail is curled in the shape of a heart. The rosette refers to Andrea's horse winning the Best Horse in Show in summer 1996. Inscription "1 May 2002" is to remind Peter that on this date he can claim his money back on a set of VAS golf clubs that he bought in 1996. Hallmarks include ©, heart, HBC logo, ed.#, and Pc.

Inside Joke
Item No.: TJMO
Artist: PC
Size: 54x45x58
Status: Retired
Carving Date: 94
Release Date: Sep 94
Retired Date: Apr 00
Issue Size: 17,561

Here three monkeys are sharing an inside joke. Could it be that there is no mouse on this box figurine and they imagine collectors searching for it? There are no inscriptions or inner carvings except for © and HBC logo.

It's A Fine Day
Item No.: TJHI
Artist: PC
Size: 61x33x48 or 59x33x47
Status: Retired
Carving Date: 93
Release Date: Dec 93
Retired Date: Jun 96
Issue Size: 4916

This box figurine depicts a gazing single hippo. The mouse is located between the hippo's front feet. This piece does not incorporate inscriptions, inner carving, or hallmarks.

Jersey Belles
Item No.: TJCO
Artist: PC
Size: 56x54x54
Status: Retired
Carving Date: 95
Release Date: Aug 95
Retired Date: Sep 99
Issue Size: 13,768

Cows that grazed in the fields behind Peter's family home in Colwall inspired these two Jersey cows. The mouse is located at the base by the milk cans. The sign to Colwall Church refers to Peter's planned wedding to Andrea in September 1995. Inscribed on the upright of the fence is "PC loves MX5," which refers to the Mazda sports cars that Peter loves. The tag hanging on the ear with "47" should have been a "48" for the address of a house Peter and Andrea were considering purchasing. Hallmarks include apple, clock face with month 8, HBC logo, and snake/staff for PC.

Jonah's Hideaway
Item No.: TJWH
Artist: PC
Size: 55x33x44
Status: Retired
Carving Date: 93
Release Date: Dec 93
Retired Date: Jun 96
Issue Size: 7342

"Jonah's Hideaway" was the very first box figurine to feature an inner carving. Inside is a resting Jonah with shirtsleeves rolled up. There are no inscriptions, hallmark, or mouse.

King of the Hill
Item No.: TJPG
Artist: PC
Size: 48x63x76
Status: Fixed Ed
Carving Date: 01
Release Date: Oct 01
Issue Size: 4000

The pangolin is a tree-dwelling mammal, covered with scales somewhat resembling an armadillo's. Like the armadillo, the pangolin rolls itself into a tight ball to defend against predators. The pangolin spends its days eating termites with its ten-inch long tongue. One of the termites waves a white flag in surrender. Also found on the mound is "No. 8," which Peter Calvesbert chose at random for the termites' house number. On the interior is the queen termite surrounded by a few of her many youngsters. The numbers "36K" and "50" refer to the queen's ability to lay up to 36,000 eggs a day each day for 50 years. She has a book of baby names to aid her in naming that huge brood. Peter's signature mouse is located in the bend of the pangolin's tail. Limited to an edition of 4000 signed pieces worldwide (3600 Americas). Hallmarks include ©, smiley face, HBC logo, and Pc.

Harmony Kingdom Box Details

Kit & Caboodle

Item No.: TJCA14
Artist: PC
Size: 63x63x82
Status: Open
Carving Date: 01
Release Date: May 01

Fourteen kittens are packed into a basket like sardines. Their expressions show what they think about this situation. The signature mouse is hidden on top of a kitten's head; or should that be under the top kitten's bottom? Inside the Version 1, a horde of mice are packed in even tighter than sardines. The Version Infinity interior features a smug cat with room to move, relaxing in luxury. Hallmarks include ©, smiley face, HBC logo, ed.#, and Pc.

Leatherneck's Lounge

Item No.: TJIG
Artist: PC
Size: 57x70x76
Status: Retired
Carving Date: 00
Release Date: Jun 01
Retired Date: Jun 02
Issue Size: 8200

The wonderful texture of the iguanas' skin hides small messages in raised bumps. "LPZ" stands for Lincoln Park Zoo. Peter's first close-up encounter with one of the leathery lizards was at the International Collectibles Expo in Rosemont in 1998, when some animals from the Zoo visited HK's booth with their keeper, Jaime. "2000" marks the millennium and "Iggy" is a nickname for "iguana." Collector Christopher Daly sent Peter a picture of his pet iguana "Sneaker," who whips the family dog Max with his long green tail. An inscription under one of the branches reads "Hi Sneaker." Also on the tree is carved "Toy 2," a reference to the funniest movie Peter's ever seen, "Toy Story 2." The mouse is hidden inside one of the hollow branches and one of his legs can be seen poking out through a hole in the branch. Within both Version 1 and Version ∞ is an iguana head, looking strangely like a mythical dragon or dinosaur. Note the mysterious mould variation on the exterior of Version 1 (addition of a bird). Hallmarks include ©, double diamond, HBC logo, ed.#, and Pc.

Let's Do Lunch

Item No.: TJVU
Artist: PC
Size: 46x40x46
Status: Retired
Carving Date: 94
Release Date: Sep 94
Retired Date: Jan 95
Issue Size: 1269

Some vicious vultures hover over the carcass of a lamb, with salt and peppershakers lying nearby. This piece does not incorporate the hidden mouse, inscriptions, inner carving, or hallmarks.

Harmony Kingdom Box Details

Liberty And Justice
Item No.: TJEA
Artist: PC
Size: 64x45x80
Status: Retired
Carving Date: 96
Release Date: Jun 96
Retired Date: Mar 02
Issue Size: 13,992

This box figurine features a majestic eagle with her baby eaglets. The mouse is located in the eggshell over the hallmarks. Inside is a fish. There are no inscriptions. Hallmarks include ©, diamond, mirror image clock face with month 7, HBC logo, and Pc.

Life's A Picnic
Item No.: TJBE
Artist: PC
Size: 50x57x50
Status: Retired
Carving Date: 94
Release Date: Jan 95
Retired Date: Oct 98
Issue Size: 17,842

These three bears have fished their fill, and by the look on their faces, couldn't eat another thing. The mouse peeks out from behind one of the rocks. Inscribed inside the top rim are the numbers "8, 44 and 16," and under a fish's chin, "30," as well as a "27" on a rock. These were Peter's favourite lottery numbers at the time of carving. (The sixth number was variable.) There is no inner carving. Inside is HBC logo and ©. Hallmarks include "Nov. 94" and "PC" located on a rock near the base.

Look Before You Leap
Item No.: TJFR4
Artist: PC
Size: 55x50x72
Status: Open
Carving Date: 01
Release Date: Jan 02

Two frogs wait for a third to jump off a leaf. On the Version One edition, the pair of tricksters have tied a piece of string to their companion's leg and are waiting for the fun to start. One carries a camera to capture the ensuing disaster. For the Infinity Version, the rope and camera have been removed. The mouse can be found under a frog's leg. Hallmarks include ©, smiley face, HBC logo, ed.#, and Pc.

Love Seat
Item No.: TJWA
Artist: PC
Size: 58x43x57
Status: Retired
Carving Date: 94
Release Date: Nov 94
Retired Date: Dec 97
Issue Size: 12,745

Having finished a game of noughts and crosses, Wal begins to inscribe his loved one's name while she affectionately refers to him as "Blubber Box." The mouse is peeking out between the folds of skin. This box figurine was especially popular during Valentine's Day due to the plump subjects' curious romantic coupling. The base on this piece varies in size by 1/4". Those with deeper bases have P.C. inscribed on them. There is no inner carving. Interior hallmarks include HBC logo and ©.

Major's Mousers
Item No.: TJCA4
Artist: PC
Size: 73x72x78
Status: Retired
Carving Date: 95
Release Date: May 95
Retired Date: Jun 97
Issue Size: 9372

These five senior citizen cats were originally conceived as a Harmony Ball chiming sphere holder with optional kitten lid. Spot the likeness of former Prime Minister John Major. Even the mouse, located between the heads of two cats, looks as if he should move into The House of Lords. Some of the early moulds had the inscription "DroPclaws 4" under the striped kitten, a reference to a legal clause opposed by the Labour Party. The retirement of this box figurine was announced one month prior to John Major's "retirement." The interior is empty, except for HBC logo. Hallmarks include 3/95 and P.C.

Menage A Trois
Item No.: TJFR3
Artist: PC
Size: 57x45x71
Status: Open
Carving Date: 98
Release Date: Jun 98

This box figurine features three amourous tree frogs. Inside Version 1 are two bottles of French wine, bread, cheese, and grapes. The Infinity Version contains a parrot passed out on his back, claws in the air. The mouse is tucked inside a frog's arm. Hallmarks include ©, star, HBC logo, ed.#, and Pc.

Mud Bath

Item No.: TJBO
Artist: PC
Size: 73x46x54
Status: Retired
Carving Date: 95
Release Date: Apr 95
Retired Date: Jun 97
Issue Size: 3958

These gentle gents are at their favourite hangout, "The Swamp." The mouse is hidden in one of the boar's ears. Another clue that this is an original: the inscription "An Original PC" on the base of the box. Above this is a sign reading, "Pete's Shed - 2014 miles." This is the distance between Peter's studio shed and HK corporate headquarters in Columbus, Ohio. Below that is the date "2 Feb 95" which is the completion date for carving. Interior hallmarks include © and HBC logo.

Murphy's Last Stand

Item No.: TJPB
Artist: PC
Size: 60x49x62
Status: Retired
Carving Date: 97
Release Date: Jun 97
Retired Date: Oct 97
Issue Size: 10,168

Having followed their friend Murphy on a mad adventure to the North Pole, the two penguins are trying to push the polar bear off Murphy, who is trapped underneath as he scrambles to pick up his keys. Murphy last appeared in "Holding Court" smoking a cigarette. Oblivious to the excitement is a young penguin asleep on the magnetic pole on top of the polar bear's back, which handily serves as the lid handle. The mouse is dangerously close to the bear's bared teeth. Inside are Murphy's four beer bottles. Look for the hidden inscription, "JC 1875," a reference to the oldest woman in the world, Jeannie Calmont, celebrating her 122nd birthday in France at the time of carving. "Benson 9" on the rim refers to a 9-year-old horse that Peter sometimes borrows to ride with Andrea. Hallmarks include ©, heart, HBC logo, ed.#, and Pc.

Harmony Kingdom Box Details

Neighborhood Watch
Item No.: TJRF
Artist: PC
Size: 45x46x57
Status: Retired
Carving Date: 94
Release Date: Oct 94
Retired Date: Jun 97
Issue Size: 8837

This micro rainforest encapsulates Peter's environmental concerns. This jungle habitat is home to fifteen creatures. Nestled atop the rainforest are an elephant and several macaws, joined below by an alligator, snake, and a group of mischievous primates. Standing at the base of the box is a man, chainsaw in hand, ready to begin deforestation. Near the giraffe, Peter displays what he thinks of those who destroy the forests. Colouration on this piece was very light until late 1996 when more colour was added. The mouse is not present. There is no inner carving. The only marking is "PC" on the base below the swinging primate. Interior hallmarks include © and HBC logo.

Nic Nac Paddy Whack
Release Date: TJHO2
Artist: PC
Size: 62x50x67
Status: Retired
Carving Date: 96
Release Date: Jun 96
Retired Date: Nov 01
Issue Size: 33,624

This group of four dogs has raided the artist's dustbin (trash can) outside his house at number 48. One wears a collar and another dangles a chain leash, suggesting that he has just escaped from his owner. The mouse is located in the discarded bones. The Ringmaster's boots can be found inside, sometimes the left boot and other times the right. The first 1446 pieces had a heavily painted red dog (until August 1996), after which the colour was subdued. The name of the piece has had multiple spellings. Hallmarks include ©, diamond, mirror image clock face with month 7, HBC logo, and Pc.

Night Shift
Item No.: TJOP
Artist: PC
Size: 44x70x67
Status: Fixed Ed
Carving Date: 01
Release Date: Oct 01
Issue Size: 4000

The peculiar opossum has many unusual characteristics, including a prehensile tail, opposable thumbs on its hind feet, immunity to many venomous snakes, and a pouch to carry babies in. Although the female may have as many as 25 young in a litter, she only has nipples for thirteen. The inscription 13ULS stands for "13 unlucky for some," referring to the baby 'possums who may not be lucky enough to

PAGE 64 *Harmony Kingdom Box Details*

be fed. "KG" in a circle pays tribute to Karen Gilbert, House of Lords Dealer. On the sides of the opossum's neck are carved "Sep.01," the date the model was created, and "PF," "Pete's Favourite." The interior shows an opossum's head surrounded by sweet potatoes, inspired by a recipe Peter came across in his research. The mouse peeks out of a branch in the log. Limited to an edition of 4000 signed pieces worldwide (3600 Americas). Hallmarks include ©, smiley face, HBC logo, and Pc.

Of The Same Stripe
Item No.: TJTI
Artist: PC
Size: 69x41x48
Status: Retired
Carving Date: 93
Release Date: Sep 93
Retired Date: Jan 01
Issue Size: 38,218

This is the first mother and baby box figurine in the Small Treasure Jest Series. As in many of Peter's earlier pieces, it does not incorporate the hidden mouse, inscriptions, inner carving, or hallmarks.

Old Gladstone
Item No.: TJDLCA
Artist: DL
Size: 61x51x66
Status: Open
Carving Date: 02
Release Date: May 02

One Sunday, at the end of his rounds, father came in with a twinkle in his eyes, carrying his battered old doctor's "Gladstone bag" with more care than usual. He unfastened the catch, releasing a tiny meow, and then from the dark interior, the tiniest of kittens emerged. The funny thing was that in time he became father's cat rather than ours. "Old Gladstone," as he became known, always stayed by my father's side of an evening, and, in later years, would often be seen out with him on his rounds. They've grown a bit old and deaf together, and father has now got himself a smart new case, so Gladstone can keep snug in the bag from whence he had once sprung. On the interior, Gladstone gets a fish served on one of the doctor's kidney dishes. Hallmarks are found on the interior and include ©, peace sign, HBC logo, and DL.

Package Tour
Item No.: TJCM
Artist: PC
Size: 55x52x67
Status: Open
Carving Date: 98
Release Date: Jan 99

"It was the straw that broke the camel's back" served as inspiration for this box figurine. The nomad offering Sahara trips, wiping the camel spit from his eye, should not be worrying about straws breaking his camel's back. The camel is so loaded up with stuff -- including the kitchen sink -- that there is no room for the toy box, suitcases, or any tourists. One suitcase bears the names "River Nile, Luxor" and "Sin City" (a reference to HK's "Sin City" not USA's Las Vegas). The other bears the inscription "Dangar 1 Moorcroft 4"; this commemorates an evening in August 98 at the first UK collectors show when Nick Dangar of Harmony International had an evening on the town with four lovely women from Moorcroft Pottery. It is said that it is easier for a camel to pass through the eye of a needle than it is for a rich man to go to heaven. This biblical quote is referred to in the newspaper headlines: "Rich Man Enters Heaven," and "Huge Needle Found." Meanwhile on the other side of the figurine near the discarded tin can lays a needle. Peter's mouse, complete with very long tail, and cockatiel, Spike, take shelter from the scorching sun beneath the camel's neck. "For CD" on the end of a blanket roll is in memoriam to Carol Dixon who, with her husband, Les, was an early collector of Harmony Kingdom. "TE" on a blanket refers to Lawrence of Arabia. In the interior of Edition 1, Lawrence of Suburbia lies resting in costume. Could Peter be referring to his fellow artist David Lawrence, who counts Morris Dancing amongst his passions? Inside the Infinity Version is a map and pair of slippers. Hallmarks include ©, star, HBC logo, ed.#, and Pc.

Pas de Deux
Item No.: TJPA2
Artist: PC
Size: 61x48x71
Status: Open
Carving Date: 02
Release Date: May 02

This smaller cousin of the giant panda, the red panda resembles a raccoon. Two red pandas, named Nissan and Micra, live at the Cotswold Wildlife Park in England, and their names are inscribed on the branches. A wasp near the base pays homage to the hundreds of wasps nearby when Peter Calvesbert visited them last summer. The mouse is located between two leaves. Fed up that the giant panda gets all the attention, these two red pandas have chained one up out of the way on the interior of Version One. A red panda is held hostage inside the interior of Version Infinity. Hallmarks include ©, peace sign, HBC logo, ed.#, and Pc.

Peace Summit
Item No.: TJWO2
Artist: PC
Size: 69x50x76
Status: Open
Carving Date: 98
Release Date: Jan 99

A wolf and a beaver are nose to nose in tense negotiation in this box figurine. The beaver is ready to pull the pin on a hand-grenade to protect her young brood inside the tree trunk with "Alphas Rule" graffiti. The leaders of a wolf pack are known as Alphas, so we know who is responsible for the graffiti. There are two sets of mouse footprints in the snow leading to the tree where Peter's signature mouse can be seen peering out of a hole in the trunk. The drawing of Alexis is a reference to Noel's niece who helped edit the reference guide and "Queen's Courier" newsletters. Inside are four squirrels staking their lives on the outcome of the negotiations. The Infinity Version has Little Red Riding Hood's hat and cape added to the exterior of the box. Hallmarks include ©, star, HBC logo, ed.#, and Pc.

Pecking Order
Item No.: TJBM
Artist: PC
Size: 71x66x52
Status: Open
Carving Date: 99
Release Date: Jun 99

This box figurine defies the expression "three's a crowd." The unlikely trio rests peacefully, with the mouse nestled between the cat's paws and a dog protecting his two friends. Inside Version 1 are Mad Murphy's favourite possessions: a teddy bear, guitar, stereo, pin-up poster, Pungu magazine (children's cartoon character), bicycle pump, after shave and hot water bottle. The anagram on Murphy's pillow unscrambles to spell Subaru Forester, the new car that Peter had just purchased. Murphy himself is seen emerging from the piece. Tubs the turtle replaced Murphy in the Infinity Version, and the interior portrays a mouse reading a "Beware of the Log" sign. Thinking this is a mistake, he changes it to "Beware of the Dog," whereupon he is flattened by a log. Hallmarks include ©, moon, HBC logo, ed.#, and Pc.

Petty Teddies
Item No.: TJTB
Artist: PC
Size: 64x58x69
Status: Open
Carving Date: 98
Release Date: Jan 99

This box figurine stars two Harmony Kingdom dogs: the Perry's Alfie and Peter's Murphy. It represents the fantasy world of these fast friends who meet every Wednesday at Wimberley Mills and wreak havoc as they dash around the studio fighting over balls, sticks and toys. Murphy cannot be left alone with soft toys. It is, after all, a dog's natural instinct to tear up small furry things! Possibly that's why Peter's mouse has found a secure hiding spot. This piece does contain some disturbing images and should only be viewed by a "mature" audience. One teddy has a knife in its back and another is smoking. Up until March 1999 the name of this piece was "Perished Teddies." It was changed due to its similarity to another collectible. Inside Version 1 is a beheaded doll looking vaguely familiar. The Infinity Version portrays Peter lying amidst torn up teddy bears. Hallmarks include ©, star, HBC logo, ed.#, and Pc.

Photo Finish
Item No.: TJMA2
Artist: PC
Size: 83x45x70
Status: Retired
Carving Date: 96
Release Date: Jan 97
Retired Date: Apr 00
Issue Size: 14,196

This box figurine has numerous references to famous racehorses. Under the hoof of one horse is a snail, which is a reference to the horse Escargot. The words "grease" and "tniap" refer to Grease Paint, a horse that used to run regularly in the Grand National. The cigar between the hind legs is in honour of the famous racer, Cigar. Early versions had black goggles on the jockeys. The mouse is between the elbows of the jockeys. Inside is a horseshoe. Hallmarks include ©, diamond, HBC logo, ed.#, and Pc.

Pink Paradise

Item No.: TJFL
Artist: PC
Size: 60x59x74
Status: Retired
Carving Date: 96
Release Date: Jun 96
Retired Date: Oct 00
Issue Size: 19,394

This box figurine is from Peter's golf-crazed days. Even the necks of the flamingos are reminiscent of golf clubs. Inside is the bent golf putter of Greg Norman (Australian professional golfer) who had just been defeated by Nick Faldo (British) in the US Open. Look for the anagram on the rim of the base referring to the German outsider that Peter hoped would win, Alexander Cejka. The mouse is hiding behind a flamingo neck. The first two thousand flamingos had black beaks, but due to the number of black smudges that were occurring, the painting specification was changed in September 1996 to untinted beaks. Hallmarks include diamond, clock face with month 4, HBC logo, and Pc.

Planet Dustbin

Item No.: TJPD
Artist: PC
Size: 48x44x76
Status: Retired
Carving Date: 01
Release Date: Jul 01
Retired Date: Nov 01
Issue Size: 2230

A departure from Peter's usual animal Treasure Jests, this Box Figurine epitomizes how Peter feels we humans treat our planet: just like a dustbin. The "No Fish" sign in the North Atlantic indicates the over-fishing of the seas and the inability of oil tankers to stay the right way up. Under one handle are the numbers "25" and "4" to point a finger at the country that contains 4% of the world's population but reportedly produces 25% of the world's greenhouse gases. The letter K inscribed on Japan marks the city of Kyoto. On a happier note the whale fluke near the tip of South Africa reminds Peter of his honeymoon and his first sighting of southern right whales. The polar bears on the lid and the penguins on the base are a reminder that the bears are found in the Arctic and the penguins in the Antarctic. The lid is a unique screw top. On the interior the signature mouse is buried by a pile of cans. Hallmarks include ©, smiley face, HBC logo, and Pc.

Play School
Item No.: TJFI2
Artist: PC
Size: 58x42x43
Status: Retired
Carving Date: 94
Release Date: Sep 94
Retired Date: Apr 98
Issue Size: 15,753

This box figurine features a school of playful fish. Peter's tin can is present. The mouse is peaking out above the base by the conger eel. There is no inner carving or any inscriptions. Inside is HBC logo.

Pongo's Palm
Item No.: TJOR2
Artist: PC
Size: 57x51x76
Status: Open
Carving Date: 00
Release Date: Dec 00

A young orangutan shelters from the rain under a broad green leaf. Carved into the underside of the leaf are the words "Borneo" and "Sumatra." These two Indonesian islands are the only places in the world where orangutans are still found in their natural habitat. On both versions the mouse also waits out the rain under a leaf. The following code appears on the base of Version 1: RQBHHYAQDR-FLHMSHBW. The keyword is "Harmony Kingdom" and the type of animal on the box. The code is removed from Version Infinity and is replaced by the cryptic carving "NBIII." This stands for Notah Begay III, Peter's 50-1 bet for the winner of the 2000 British Open Golf Championship. The interiors of both versions portray orangutan faces. Hallmarks include ©, double diamond, HBC logo, ed.#, and Pc.

Potty Time
Item No.: TJCA15
Artist: PC
Size: 67x51x80
Status: Open
Carving Date: 01
Release Date: Jan 02

This box figurine is the concept of Robin Davis, winner of the House of Peers' 2001 Design A Jest Contest. A group of kittens have discovered a new toy: a toilet. The back of the bathroom fixture is inscribed with the name of its legendary inventor, Thomas Crapper. A newspaper, essential reading, can be seen tucked down the back of the loo. The mouse, including a rare view of his bottom, is hidden away in the tissue. On the lid is the inscription AD4 NYY3, referring to the Arizona Diamondback's four games to three win over the New York Yankees in the 2001 World Series. The interior of the Version One shows two alligators, in reference to the urban myths of alligators breeding in the sewers. The Version Infinity interior shows another cat in the bowl in place of the alligators. Hallmarks include ©, smiley face, HBC logo, ed.#, and Pc.

Harmony Kingdom Box Details

Powder Room
Item No.: TJCA13
Artist: PC
Size: 57x63x76
Status: Open
Carving Date: 01
Release Date: May 01

Three kittens are desperate to use the litter tray, even though room is tight and privacy is obviously scarce. As is the tradition in men's toilets, a burning cigarette is balanced precariously on the edge of the box. One of the kittens evidently expects to be in the loo for some time, as he has taken the newspaper crossword with him. On his collar is a tag with the letter "M." His companion behind him looks somewhat distressed as the third kitten successfully unravels an entire roll of tissue. Don't squeeze the mouse! On the interior of Version 1 someone (not unlike Pete) sinks into another "bog." One sign advertises a building lot for sale. Another nearby sign indicates the reason for the sale. The Version Infinity shows a cat using a "human restroom." Hallmarks include ©, smiley face, HBC logo, ed.#, and Pc.

Princely Thoughts
Item No.: TJFR
Artist: PC
Size: 59x44x31
Status: Retired
Carving Date: 92
Release Date: Apr 92
Retired Date: Jun 96
Issue Size: 9682

This single toad box figurine is the second small box carved by Peter. This very early piece does not incorporate the hidden mouse, inscriptions, inner carving, or hallmarks. Some early versions of this piece have a hollow space inside the lid to accommodate the Harmony Ball chiming sphere, which came with the piece when originally released by Harmony Kingdom.

Puddle Huddle
Item No.: TJTO
Artist: PC
Size: 67x67x47
Status: Retired
Carving Date: 95
Release Date: May 95
Retired Date: Jun 02
Issue Size: 29,583

Outside Peter's studio shed toads are plentiful, especially during springtime. Here six huddle together. One wears a ring and another a watch to remind Peter of his upcoming wedding, while a third toad proudly shows off his new tattoo. The mouse seems trapped under the bully of the group, while the fate of the dragonfly is left unresolved. Hallmarks include apple, mirror image clock face with month 7, HBC logo, and Pc.

Harmony Kingdom Box Details

Purrfect Friends
Item No.: TJCA
Artist: PC
Size: 52x55x50
Status: Retired
Carving Date: 94
Release Date: Sep 94
Retired Date: Nov 01
Issue Size: 53,078

There are no inscriptions on this cat box figurine, but there are two mice. The first is between the hind legs of the white cat and the second is under the belly of the brown cat. There is no inner carving. Interior hallmarks include © and HBC logo.

Reminiscence
Item No.: TJEL
Artist: PC
Size: 39x60x49
Status: Retired
Carving Date: 93
Release Date: Sep 93
Retired Date: Dec 96
Issue Size: 15,957

This early box figurine, depicting a solitary elephant, has no hallmarks, inscriptions, or inner carving. Peter's mouse is found between the pachyderm's hind legs.

Rocky's Raiders
Item No.: TJRC
Artist: PC
Size: 60x57x61
Status: Retired
Carving Date: 97
Release Date: Jan 98
Retired Date: Mar 02
Issue Size: 16,497

Here we've caught Rocky raccoon and his three mates in the midst of a robbery. Having ransacked a house for valuables, they make their escape through the garden. Unfortunately, they are delayed by the antics of Tubs the Turtle who is hanging onto one raccoon's ear. Another raccoon will have to rescue the youngest member of the gang who is stuck inside a tree trunk. Rocky himself is tempted by a bottle of champagne that Peter and Andrea had saved from their South African honeymoon. Peter's mouse hides in another tree trunk. Inside the box are the stolen items: camera, watch, ring, necklace, pen, and bag of money. The first raccoon that Peter saw was in Chicago in June 1997, but in order to study them closely he visited an animal sanctuary close to his home where Rocky, Penny, and Mouse were the resident raccoons. Peter also remembers another resident, Yogi, the copabari. "Little Den" is the new home that Peter and Andrea were buying at the time. Hallmarks include © (not on first edition of 3000), heart, HBC logo, ed.#, and Pc.

Rumble Seat
Item No.: TJCA5
Artist: PC
Size: 66x61x72
Status: Open
Carving Date: 96
Release Date: Jun 96

There is no need to search for the mouse on this piece; there are 15 mice scattered about the six friendly felines who lounge on an antique chair. Inside the box lies a slice of Swiss cheese. When the lid is removed, you will find the inscription "Dr 3 20.5.96." This is a reference to the death of British actor Jon Pertwee, who was the third actor to play Doctor Who in the widely popular British sci-fi television show by the same name. The chairs have undergone numerous colouration changes. The first 66 chairs were brown, the next 446 were green, after which the rest were painted yellow. Hallmarks include ©, diamond, clock face with month 5, HBC logo, and Pc.

Saint Or Sinner
Item No.: TJDR
Artist: PC
Size: 63x63x76
Status: Open
Carving Date: 00
Release Date: Dec 00

This box figurine is the second dragon portrayal carved by Peter in year 2000, the first being a NetsUKe. Peter's seeming obsession with the dragon is due to 2000 being the Year of the Dragon. While in the Far East, dragons are symbols of good luck and health; they also have a fiery side and command lightning and storms. Since dragon tattoos seem to be all the rage among the human set, this dragon sports a tattoo on his right arm that looks suspiciously like the artist. A very brave mouse has left footprints all around the base and takes refuge under the fire-breather's arm. The interior of Version 1 depicts the skeleton of St. George, the Christian martyr and patron of England, who, according to legend, slew a fearsome dragon. Inside Version Infinity you'll find St. George, with the St. George cross on his chest plate. Hallmarks include ©, double diamond, HBC logo, ed.#, and Pc.

School's Out
Item No.: TJFI
Artist: PC
Size: 59x37x56
Status: Retired
Carving Date: 93
Release Date: Sep 93
Retired Date: Apr 99
Issue Size: 33,230

This box figurine features a school of fish, one swimming upside down. Peter's tin can is present, and the mouse swims along with his aquatic friends. One variation occurred in October 1994 when more rocks were added to thicken the base. There is no inner carving or inscription.

Harmony Kingdom Box Details

Scotland Yard
Item No.: TJH06
Artist: PC
Size: 51x63x70
Status: Open
Carving Date: 01
Release Date: May 01

Three terriers stand nose to tail in a circle of canine cuddliness. Each one of their dog tags bears a secret inscription. One collar reads "Albert.crepe.vest," which is an anagram for "Peter Calvesbert." The initials "J.K.P.W." on the tag stand for Jack Kofi Perry Wiggins, the son of Harmony Kingdom co-founder Noel Wiggins. Little Jack was born in February 2001. One Scottie Dog hopes to remember the 43rd president of the United States is George W. Bush by carrying the number "43" on his tag. The last dog wears her heart on her collar: "I ❤ H" stands for "I love Harmony." The Version 1 interior shows a little Scottie perusing a catalogue of bones and doggie beds. The interior of the Infinity Version shows a big Scottie Dog's head. Hallmarks include ©, smiley face, HBC logo, ed.#, and Pc.

Shell Game
Item No.: TJTU
Artist: PC
Size: 47x57x52
Status: Retired
Carving Date: 93
Release Date: Sep 93
Retired Date: Sep 01
Issue Size: 41,793

This box figurine features a stack of playful turtles. Luggage straps wrap around the turtles' shells. The mouse is located under the turtle that wears a pendant. Originally only PC appeared on the turtle's pendant, but later © and HBC logo were added as interior hallmarks.

Side Steppin'
Item No.: TJCB
Artist: MP
Size: 71x50x21
Status: Retired
Carving Date: 92
Release Date: Jan 93
Retired Date: Dec 96
Issue Size: 6813

This single crab box figurine is a very early piece and does not incorporate the hidden mouse, inscriptions, inner carving, or hallmarks. One variation exists, where a rock was added between the crab's claws.

Sleepy Hollow
Item No.: TJLE
Artist: PC
Size: 64x47x48
Status: Retired
Carving Date: 96
Release Date: Jan 97
Retired Date: Sep 01
Issue Size: 19,357

Peter's tribute to big cats catches a mother leopard and three cubs in the intense African heat settling down for a siesta. However, as mothers know, there is always one offspring who refuses to co-operate: one youngster sleeps in the hollow trunk of a log, another lies idly chewing a branch and the third just wants to play. Peter's mouse is having a nap in a hole in the log. Inside is a scroll with the message "Save Me," a reminder to preserve the species. Hallmarks include ©, diamond, HBC logo, ed.#, and Pc.

Slow Dance
Item No.: TJTU4
Artist: PC
Size: 57x51x89
Status: Open
Carving Date: 00
Release Date: Dec 00

A mere two hours before the carving demonstration at Clair de Lune Convention 2000, Harmony Kingdom's second multi-day convention held in Lake Geneva, Wisconsin, Peter still had no idea what he would carve. As he wandered around the marina, inspiration struck when he sighted his first snapping turtle. The turtles on "Slow Dance" are kitted out in Roaring Twenties style to commemorate the convention's 1920's theme and swing dance competition. The lady looks elegant in her plume and feather boa, but her long necklace seems to have come undone. Pearls roll underfoot along with the key to room 664, the room Peter shared with Adam Binder at the event. The gent sloshes his drink on his dance partner while Peter's signature mouse hides out in a hole in his hat. The turtles on Version 1 have competition numbers pinned to their backs: "1" on the male and "22" on the female. Prior to the convention, Peter attended a history-making New York Yankees vs. Boston Red Sox game where the Red Sox suffered their largest ever defeat (22-1). The interior of Version 1 portrays a baby turtle and more loose pearls. The competition numbers are removed from Version Infinity, and the interior is a close up of a snapping turtle's face. Hallmarks include ©, double diamond, HBC logo, ed.#, and Pc.

Special Delivery
Item No.: TJST
Artist: DL
Size: 79x60x78
Status: Retired
Carving Date: 99
Release Date: Jan 00
Retired Date: Aug 01
Issue Size: 8951

The arrival of the stork suggests the existence of some mysterious and miraculously neat delivery service: a couple of wing flaps and "Oh look - a baby!" In some countries "the event" takes place under a gooseberry bush, in others in a cabbage patch or under a rhubarb bush. If only the everyday epic were really like the avian scene of grace and calm! Looking around this touching arrival you will find numerous related objects: the spring green cloth indicates the freshness and hopefulness of new life, and the box of cigars inside the Version 1 are traditional announcements of the new arrival. The teddy bear and soft blanket on the Infinity Version interior are of course necessities when welcoming Baby home. Hallmarks include ©, moon, HBC logo, ed.#, DL and eye.

Splashdown
Item No.: TJWH3
Artist: PC
Size: 69x54x78
Status: Retired
Carving Date: 97
Release Date: Jun 97
Retired Date: Mar 02
Issue Size: 15,275

Peter's first close up sighting of whales was on a visit to Cape Cod in June 1996 with the Perry family after the Rosemont International Collectibles Exhibition. Some pieces include the mouse on the whale's left fin; others have no mouse. Within this box figurine is the HBC logo, a mermaid's tail disappearing into the depths, and a fish jumping the waves. "Deep Blue" is inscribed in the lid, and "I hate Ninevah" faintly inscribed inside. Due to production difficulties, the base was redesigned to shorten the waves. Hallmarks include ©, heart, HBC logo, ed.#, and Pc.

Sunday Swim
Item No.: TJDO
Artist: PC
Size: 47x63x53
Status: Open
Carving Date: 94
Release Date: Nov 94

This box figurine featuring six playful dolphins is based on the famous Irish dolphin, Funghi, who swims in the Dingle Bay in the Republic of Ireland. It is reported that Funghi and his friends love to swim with people. There is no inner carving, inscriptions, or mouse. Interior hallmarks include © and HBC logo.

Swamp Song
Item No.: TJAL
Artist: PC
Size: 46x46x58
Status: Retired
Carving Date: 93
Release Date: Dec 93
Retired Date: Dec 97
Issue Size: 16,540

This box figurine, featuring three dancing alligators, is a very early piece and does not incorporate the hidden mouse, inscriptions, inner carving, or hallmarks.

Sweet Serenade
Item No.: TJHU
Artist: PC
Size: 66x49x54
Status: Open
Carving Date: 95
Release Date: Jul 95

This box figurine features a solitary hummingbird with a blooming flower. The mouse is on the base near the flower's stem. This was the first piece with the year of production date stamp and standardised hallmarks. Hallmarks include apple, clock face with month 4, HBC logo, and snake/staff for PC.

Sweet Spot
Item No.: TJLE2
Artist: PC
Size: 51x76x46
Status: Open
Carving Date: 02
Release Date: May 02

The beautiful dark-brown coat of the clouded leopard, spangled with spots, stripes and blotches, makes this big cat a target for hunters. It's much safer to be in a zoo – but also very boring lying on a fiberglass rock. This leopard still clutches his ticket to the zoo, although he may be somewhat disenchanted with the visit. The bird skull on the rock shows the leopard's preferred prey. Peter's mouse peeks out of a crevice. The interior of the Version One shows two birds. Inside the Version Infinity is a leopard in the trees, dreaming. Hallmarks include ©, peace sign, HBC logo, ed.#, and Pc.

Teacher's Pet
Item No.: TJBI
Artist: PC
Size: 52x42x56
Status: Retired
Carving Date: 94
Release Date: Sep 94
Retired Date: Jun 97
Issue Size: 7182

Her class of twelve surrounds the wise old owl, some vying for her attention, others distinctly bored, others up to mischief. Peter's pet parrot, Spike, has been sent along to join the classroom in the hope of improving his limited but raucous vocabulary. Spike can be seen peering out from behind a wing looking decidedly cheeky. This is also the shoebill's first appearance, who later starred in his own solo box. Peter's mouse would not have stood a chance had he appeared here. Interior hallmarks include ©, HBC logo, and P.C.

The Great Escape
Item No.: TJBP
Artist: PC
Size: 63x51x78
Status: Open
Carving Date: 99
Release Date: Jun 99

Three caged parrots are busy at work planning their escape. Peter's signature mouse is an unwitting accomplice as he performs for onlookers, distracting attention away from the soon-to-be fugitive birds. Peter says that he always wanted a parrot but that his pet cockatiel, Spike, would have nothing of it. Before the arrival of Peter's cat, Algy, Spike had free run of the house. Though he is now caged for his own safety, he still struts about Peter's studio shed. The dismembered fingers refer to what happens when one is tempted to pet a parrot. A file and more fingers are inside Version 1. The Infinity Version contains a book entitled "The Great Escape." Hallmarks include ©, 99, HBC logo, ed.#, and Pc.

The Great Escape II
Item No.: TJLO
Artist: PC
Size: 77x70x74
Status: Open
Carving Date: 00
Release Date: Jun 01

Three Maine lobsters, reddened from the boiling water, have decided that they are not enjoying the sauna. They've knocked the lid off the pot and are bursting forth, tentacles waving in anger. The mouse hides out under one of the lobster's bulging eyes. Within Version 1 Peter and his rubber ducky are swirling in a whirlpool. Is that a shark fin ominously circling? The Infinity version features what Peter calls "Lobster and Finger Soup" inside. Hallmarks include ©, double diamond, HBC logo, ed.#, and Pc.

The Last Laugh
Item No.: TJBD
Artist: PC
Size: 73x59x92
Status: Open
Carving Date: 99
Release Date: Jun 99

You may not be familiar with the odd looking dodo. Perhaps it's because the last sighting of this now extinct species was in 1681, as seen on the gravestone. A passenger pigeon, once one of the most numerous birds on the planet, carves the epitaph. Little does he realise that he too will soon be extinct. "Martha 29 1914" pays homage to the last passenger pigeon that died in the Cincinnati Zoo. "Ireland?" refers to Peter's possible relocation to Ireland and "Felix" commemorates the horse of Peter's wife, Andrea. The tin can and human footprint signify man's role in earth's ecological crisis. Peter's mouse is nestled in the wing of the pigeon. Inside Version 1, the dodo bluntly tells a cat to go away. Cats and dogs ate dodo eggs and were partly responsible for their extinction. The interior of the Infinity Version contains gravestones of other animals with their dates of extinction. Hallmarks include ©, 99, HBC logo, ed.#, and Pc.

Tin Cat
Item No.: TJSH
Artist: PC
Size: 56x57x62
Status: Retired
Carving Date: 96
Release Date: Jun 96
Retired Date: Apr 98
Issue Size: 14,436

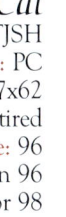

This box figurine features three menacing sharks circling a shipwreck. The unfortunate diver, having discovered a treasure chest, is now trapped inside. The remains of another diver lie beneath the hull. Peter's mouse appears inside the barrel on the deck. The name of the boat, "Tincat I," is an anagram for Titanic. The boat was painted brown on the first 990, after which it was changed to a natural bleached colour. In September 1996, the sharks' fins and tails were shortened slightly. Hallmarks include ©, diamond, clock face with month 4, HBC logo, and Pc.

Harmony Kingdom Box Details

Tongue And Cheek
Item No.: TJFR2
Artist: PC
Size: 50x50x50
Status: Open
Carving Date: 94
Release Date: Nov 94

These three handsome frogs are sitting beside their pool spawning new ideas. Smooth skinned, except for their bellies, and still glistening from their last dip, the most languid has allowed his tongue to drop right down to his elegant toes as he leans back in the sun. The other two pose displaying their fine, flexible form. Even the mouse is posing, wedged between two bare cheeks. There are no inscriptions or inner carvings. Interior hallmarks include © and HBC logo.

Tony's Tabbies
Item No.: TJCA7
Artist: PC
Size: 52x63x79
Status: Open
Carving Date: 97
Release Date: Jun 97

This youthful group of cats contrasts to the older, more staid cats of "Major's Mousers," whose retirement was announced April 1997 shortly before that of John Major, former Prime Minister. "May 1 97" and "Blair Wins" refer to the landslide victory for Tony Blair and the Labour party in the UK General Election in May 1997. Peter had spotted the first cuckoo of the season and a grass snake while working on this piece, thus their incorporation. The tin can appears again, and Peter insists that this is the first time the mouse has shown his bottom. Inside a cat uses the walls of the box as a scratching post. Hallmarks include ©, heart, HBC logo, ed.#, and Pc.

Too Much Of A Good Thing
Item No.: TJMC
Artist: PC
Size: 48x48x58
Status: Retired
Carving Date: 94
Release Date: Nov 94
Retired Date: Sep 99
Issue Size: 15,631

This cat received more than it wished for with fifty-five intertwined mice, precluding the need for Peter's signature mouse. The box figurine is based on Corinna and Martin's ancient cat, Griff, who was a hopeless mouse catcher. Interior hallmarks include © and HBC logo.

Top Banana
Item No.: TJOR
Artist: PC
Size: 45x55x51
Status: Retired
Carving Date: 93
Release Date: Sep 93
Retired Date: Dec 96
Issue Size: 1499

This box figurine depicts an orangutan holding a banana. The length of the banana varies based on the production mould used. The mouse is between the orangutan's legs. There are no hallmarks, inscriptions, or inner carvings.

Topsy Turvy
Item No.: TJEL4
Artist: PC
Size: 70x44x76
Status: Open
Carving Date: 01
Release Date: Jan 02

Africa is a wild place, not exactly smooth pavement, so surely elephants must trip occasionally. Master Carver Peter Calvesbert's luck is such that if he were camping in someplace like, say, Kenya, an elephant would probably trip over him in the night. This improbable, inelegant scene is complete with Peter's teddy and cricket bat (which every Englishman reportedly keeps near the bed in case of intruders). A tortoise can be seen sprinting to safety as the elephant topples over. The signature mouse is out of harm's way under the pillow. Inscribed around the lid are the words "Ross Lodge Please," referring to a new home that Peter and his wife Andrea hoped to acquire at auction. The interior shows a baby elephant. For the Infinity Version, a tree trunk replaces Peter in his sleeping bag. Hallmarks include ©, smiley face, HBC logo, ed.#, and Pc.

Trumpeters' Ball
Item No.: TJEL2
Artist: PC
Size: 65x60x66
Status: Open
Carving Date: 96
Release Date: Jun 96

This group of raucous elephants circles one another in this box figurine. The mouse is on an elephant's knee. Inside the box lies a tusk. An extra trunk was sighted on the early boxes between the elephant's legs, just over the hallmarks. The trunk was removed due to production considerations in August 1996. A variety of colour variations exist on this piece: the first 1090 were painted yellow and grey until early August, 1996; the next 460 had no colouring at all, after which two of the elephants in the piece were couloured grey. Hallmarks include ©, diamond, HBC logo, clock face with month 4, ed.#, and Pc.

Harmony Kingdom Box Details

Trunk Show
Item No.: TJCR
Artist: PC
Size: 44x45x64
Status: Retired
Carving Date: 93
Release Date: Dec 93
Retired Date: Dec 96
Issue Size: 6467

Six crows used to hang about in a noisy gaggle in the trees near Peter's studio shed. Two of them are hiding inside, one upside down in a trunk, another squinting through a hole. Peter's poor mouse, hiding in the tree trunk, will find little peace with this raucous crowd. "P&A" is inscribed around a heart. There is no inner carving or hallmarks.

Turdus Felidae
Item No.: TJBR
Artist: PC
Size: 49x55x89
Status: Open
Carving Date: 99
Release Date: Jun 99

A robin has caught a mouse in its wings as it sits atop a cat that also has caught a mouse. This piece is the companion piece to "Caw of the Wild" and honors HK collectors Rob and Jay. On the lid you can find Rob & Jay's email so that you can respond to their question "Got any rumours?" The interior of Version 1 contains "To Jay" while the Infinity Version contains two robin eggs and a ball of yarn. Hallmarks include ©, 99, HBC logo, ed.#, and Pc.

Unbridled And Groomed
Item No.: TJMA
Artist: PC
Size: 60x63x52
Status: Retired
Carving Date: 95
Release Date: May 95
Retired Date: Oct 98
Issue Size: 20,382

Peter sculpted this box for Andrea, who loves horses. The mouse is on the base between the horse's legs. The only inscription is "PC 95" on the base. Interior hallmarks include © and HBC logo.

Unexpected Arrival

Item No.: TJPE
Artist: PC
Size: 51x46x35
Status: Retired
Carving Date: 94
Release Date: Sep 94
Retired Date: Apr 00
Issue Size: 23,513

This triumvirate of penguins portrays the males of the species incubating the eggs while the females have ventured off to gather food. Two of the penguins are decked in either bow or traditional necktie. The third has lost his in a state of shock.

Apparently the missus has been calling on someone outside her species, as a baby alligator hatches from the egg. Originally, this box figurine had no markings except for "PC 94" found on the base. The mouse was later added under a wing, as was the © and HBC logo.

Untouchable

Item No.: TJHE2
Artist: PC
Size: 60x36x40
Status: Retired
Carving Date: 94
Release Date: Sep 94
Retired Date: Jan 95
Issue Size: 1889

This single standing hedgehog box figurine is a very early piece and does not incorporate the hidden mouse, inscriptions, inner carving, or hallmarks.

Up To Scratch

Item No.: TJBA
Artist: PC
Size: 57x51x95
Status: Open
Carving Date: 00
Release Date: Dec 00

Peter loves to carve what he calls the "weird and wonderful" animals of the world. The intriguing peculiarity of the baboon is his remarkable facial colouring, not to mention his bright blue and red bottom, surely eye-catching to the lady baboons! Out of a sense of decorum, Peter included only the baboon's colourful face. Peter's initials appear within the long, curving fingers of the baboon's hand. The mouse hides out under a shaggy thigh. Those collectors still searching for a "Back Scratch" will find one in miniature on the interior of Version 1. Version Infinity contains a back scratcher to help the baboon get to those hard to reach places. Hallmarks include ©, double diamond, HBC logo, ed.#, and Pc.

Whale Of A Time
Item No.: TJWH2
Artist: PC
Size: 60x49x64
Status: Retired
Carving Date: 96
Release Date: Jan 97
Retired Date: Oct 98
Issue Size: 15,154

The whales are breaching the waves, one carrying Peter's mouse in its fin. Near the mouse is a corked bottle with a message from a lost sailor. Inside the box is a mermaid, playing the harp. There are no inscriptions. Hallmarks include ©, diamond, HBC logo, ed.#, and Pc.

When Nature Calls
Item No.: TJPB2
Artist: PC
Size: 68x59x50
Status: Retired
Carving Date: 98
Release Date: Jan 99
Retired Date: Feb 02
Issue Size: 18,440

At the time of the creation of "Murphy's Last Stand," Peter had actually created two rough polar bear box figurines. "When Nature Calls" was put on the back burner as he preferred to develop "Murphy's Last Stand." In 1998, Peter took another look at the embryonic "When Nature Calls" and felt inspired to continue with its creation. Here, the Polar Bear is in a happier frame of mind as he patiently waits for the occupant of the igloo to come out of the ice tunnel. Little does the polar bear realise that the English explorer, having sensed the danger outside, is creating another escape route by removing an ice brick. Murphy and friend, in exile at the North Pole, are ready to aid and abet the man's escape. But who will help Peter's mouse? The seal is not happy to have had his breathing hole built over and is checking out the igloo for food pickings. Murphy has left his mark leaving his name in "Yellow Snow." Version 1 has a man starting to peek out the back of the igloo; his head appearing in Version Infinity. Hallmarks include ©, star, HBC logo, ed.#, and Pc.

Who'd A Thought
Item No.: TJOW
Artist: MP
Size: 58x43x40
Status: Retired
Carving Date: 90
Release Date: Jan 93
Retired Date: Jan 95
Issue Size: 935

This single owl box figurine is a very early piece and does not incorporate the hidden mouse, inscriptions, inner carving or hallmarks. This is one of the rarest and most sought after pieces.

Wise Guys
Item No.: TJOW2
Artist: PC
Size: 55x54x52
Status: Retired
Carving Date: 94
Release Date: Jan 95
Retired Date: Oct 00
Issue Size: 24,392

These three rowdies have become the consummate "Good Fellas" of the collection. The leader of this gang of renegade owls sports shoes and a necktie. His "birdie" guards stand close by. One of them holds proof of what happens when you arrive without an appointment. The mouse is nailed to the wing of one owl. Carved on the base is the inscription "P.C. Xmas- 94" referring to the time of this box's inception. There is no inner carving. Inside is HBC logo.

Wishful Thinking
Item No.: TJTU2
Artist: PC
Size: 42x60x74
Status: Retired
Carving Date: 97
Release Date: Jan 98
Retired Date: Sep 99
Issue Size: 17,170

The inspiration for this box figurine was Traddles, the Perry's pet tortoise. Here, Titan the tortoise celebrates his 150th birthday. The mouse peeks out above the "Good Luck Son" card. When the lid is removed, the interior cavity is shaped like a bassinet. Could the birthday turtle be planning a family? At the time that Peter was carving this piece, the space probe, Cassini, was launched on a scientific mission to Saturn. It uses the gravity of planets to propel itself towards its final destination going from planet to planet, hence the inscription inside the first edition, VVEJGA, meaning Venus, Earth, Jupiter Gravity Assisted. Version 1 also has the date and time that the space probe will reach Saturn – 8:30 July 1 2004. Inside Version 2 are a pair of running shoes. The interior lid is inscribed with the name of the astronomer who discovered Saturn's largest moon Titan in 1655. Other variations include a screw, a partial screw, or a cigarette lighter under the table. Hallmarks include ©, heart, HBC logo, ed.#, and Pc.

Harmony Kingdom Box Details

TREASURE JESTS
Large

Awaiting A Kiss
Item No.: TJLFR
Artist: PC
Size: 110x79x57
Status: Open
Carving Date: 91
Release Date: Mar 91

This toad box figurine is a very early piece and does not incorporate the hidden mouse, inscriptions, inner carving, or hallmarks. An early version has a square hole in the lid and a corresponding knob on the base.

Drake's Fancy
Item No.: TJLDU4
Artist: PC
Size: 107x56x64
Status: Retired
Carving Date: 90
Release Date: Oct 90
Retired Date: Apr 99
Issue Size: 5508

This mandarin duck box figurine is a very early piece and does not incorporate the hidden mouse, inscriptions, or hallmarks. Originally the inside was empty. A treble clef was added on the tail feathers when an egg was placed inside in 1996.

Holding Court
Item No.: TJLPE
Artist: PC
Size: 135x102x81
Status: Retired
Carving Date: 95
Release Date: Apr 95
Retired Date: May 01
Issue Size: 6,423

Holding Court is the first non-box figurine by Harmony Kingdom. This piece features seventeen birds and graffiti galore. Most of the writing refers to different species of penguins: "Chinstraps have big heads," "Kings eat yellow snow," "Gentoos do it every year," "Emperor posers," "Rockhoppers rule," "Gentoos have snow balls." In the upper left hand corner of the fence is a heart with the initials "PC" and "AR". Also on this fence is a "Wanted" poster for Mad Murphy, who makes his first appearance here. There is no mouse. "Holding Court" was originally distributed to dealers as a display stand for brochures, but due to requests from collectors, the piece was made available for resale. The first 334 had no frontal plaque, after which "Harmony Kingdom" was added to the mould. Hallmarks include © and HBC logo.

Page 86 Harmony Kingdom Box Details

Horn A' Plenty
Item No.: TJLRH
Artist: PC
Size: 131x74x79
Status: Retired
Carving Date: 91
Release Date: Oct 91
Retired Date: Dec 97
Issue Size: 6910

This single rhino box figurine is a very early piece and does not incorporate the hidden mouse, inner carving, or hallmarks. Some of the earliest pieces have "SAC" under the top of the rhino's jaw.

Journey Home
Item No.: TJLFI
Artist: PC
Size: 125x70x70
Status: Retired
Carving Date: 91
Release Date: Mar 91
Retired Date: Sep 99
Issue Size: 7011

This fish box figurine is a very early piece and does not incorporate the hidden mouse, inscriptions, inner carving, or hallmarks. The HBC logo was added to this piece in 1996.

Keeping Current
Item No.: TJLDU3
Artist: PC
Size: 112x60x81
Status: Retired
Carving Date: 90
Release Date: Oct 90
Retired Date: Oct 98
Issue Size: 4488

This smew duck box figurine is a very early piece and does not incorporate the hidden mouse, inscriptions, or hallmarks. This piece may come with or without a cracked egg inside. When the egg was added in 1996, the treble clef was placed on the cracked egg, rather than on the tail of the duck, like the other large duck pieces.

Harmony Kingdom Box Details

On A Roll
Item No.: TJLDO
Artist: PC
Size: 117x60x83
Status: Retired
Carving Date: 92
Release Date: Sep 92
Retired Date: Apr 00
Issue Size: 8723

This box figurine, featuring a single dolphin riding the waves, is a very early piece and does not incorporate the hidden mouse, inscriptions, inner carving, or hallmarks.

One Step Ahead
Item No.: TJLTU
Artist: PC
Size: 108x66x56
Status: Retired
Carving Date: 93
Release Date: Jan 94
Retired Date: Sep 99
Issue Size: 7309

This early box figurine of a lone turtle does not incorporate the hidden mouse, inscriptions, inner carving, or hallmarks. However, the artist's emerging style can be seen in the sly expression on the turtle's face, the Mr. T medallion, and the fashionable belt cinching the shell in place.

Pen Pals
Item No.: TJLPI
Artist: PC
Size: 103x73x76
Status: Retired
Carving Date: 91
Release Date: Mar 91
Retired Date: Apr 00
Issue Size: 9734

An early version of this pig box figurine had "SAC" between the legs of the small pig. Today, only the "C" remains. The mouse appears in full at the gate and predates the signature mouse added to Peter's work a year and a half later.

Pondering
Item No.: TJLDU
Artist: PC
Size: 115x56x68
Status: Retired
Carving Date: 90
Release Date: Oct 90
Retired Date: Jun 97
Issue Size: 3918

This ruddy duck box figurine is a very early piece and does not incorporate the hidden mouse or hallmarks. It may come with or without an interior egg (some cracked, some not cracked). The earliest moulds had "SAC." This was eventually removed, and in September 1996, the HBC logo was added under the duck's tail.

Pride And Joy
Item No.: TJLTI
Artist: PC
Size: 142x72x89
Status: Retired
Carving Date: 93
Release Date: Feb 93
Retired Date: Oct 98
Issue Size: 12,102

This single tiger box figurine is a very early piece and does not incorporate the hidden mouse, inner carving, or hallmarks. This was the first box to feature a mother and baby. On the lip of the base is "A, P and 93." On the lid under the cub's head, the "A" and "P" appear again, plus an "M" and "X", which represent the car of Peter's dreams.

Quiet Waters
Item No.: TJLDU2
Artist: PC
Size: 101x57x63
Status: Retired
Carving Date: 90
Release Date: Oct 90
Retired Date: Sep 99
Issue Size: 3518

This tufted duck box figurine is a very early piece and does not incorporate the hidden mouse or any hallmarks. Originally there was no interior egg, and "ZOE" was inscribed under the tail. When the egg was added, "ZOE" was replaced with the HBC logo.

Standing Guard
Item No.: TJLWO
Artist: PC
Size: 123x53x93
Status: Retired
Carving Date: 93
Release Date: Dec 93
Retired Date: Jun 97
Issue Size: 3646

This mother wolf with pups is a very early piece and does not incorporate inscriptions, inner carving, or hallmarks. The mouse is under one of the baby wolves.

Step Aside
Item No.: TJLCB
Artist: MP
Size: 141x88x50
Status: Retired
Carving Date: 90
Release Date: May 93
Retired Date: May 01
Issue Size: 8759

This single crab box figurine is a very early piece and does not incorporate the hidden mouse, inscriptions, inner carving, or hallmarks. Martin moulded this piece from the shell of an actual crab that he found in Scotland.

Straight From The Hip
Item No.: TJLHI
Artist: PC
Size: 130x86x73
Status: Retired
Carving Date: 91
Release Date: Oct 91
Retired Date: Apr 00
Issue Size: 6989

This single hippo box figurine is a very early piece and does not incorporate the hidden mouse, inscriptions, inner carving, or hallmarks.

Sunnyside Up
Item No.: TJLHE
Artist: PC
Size: 92x72x55
Status: Retired
Carving Date: 91
Release Date: Mar 91
Retired Date: May 01
Issue Size: 8998

This single hedgehog box figurine is a very early piece and does not incorporate the hidden mouse, inscriptions, inner carving, or hallmarks.

Tally Ho!
Item No.: TJLFH
Artist: DL
Size: 98x85x73
Status: Open
Carving Date: 98
Release Date: Jun 99

A cunning fox dashes to his home beneath the earth, with bloodthirsty hounds in close pursuit. A cannon is poised at the entrance, and from the score board on the interior wall you can see that this is not the first time that the hounds have been outfoxed. Another clue to the fox's success is the broken spade that belongs to the "earthstopper." An earthstopper is a hunter who stops up the fox's "front door" while the fox is out on his nocturnal rambles, preventing re-entry the next morning. "Taunton 7 miles" points you in the direction of The Rising Sun, David's favourite pub. David throws you off by hiding Peter's mouse behind the sign. In the foliage is a barrel marked "TDMM" which stands for Taunton Deane Morris Men, a group of folk dancers, of which David is a member. The interior of Version 1 is the fox's home complete with a fireplace. It differs from the Infinity Version in that the fox has a box of the finest fried chicken awaiting his return. Hallmarks include ©, star, HBC logo, ed.#, and DL.

Tea For Two
Item No.: TJLWA
Artist: PC
Size: 93x73x80
Status: Retired
Carving Date: 91
Release Date: Mar 91
Retired Date: Apr 99
Issue Size: 6772

This walrus box figurine is a very early piece and does not incorporate the hidden mouse, inner carving, or hallmarks. "ZOE," a girlfriend from Peter's youthful days, is inscribed under a fin on some.

Terra Incognita
Item No.: TJLMA
Artist: DL
Size: 115x87x81
Status: Open
Carving Date: 97
Release Date: Jun 97

This group of five wild horses was sculpted in celebration of the spirit of both wild horses and frontier people. The horses are bursting through a fence as they break down a "No Trespassing" sign. "Terra Incognita" is inscribed on the base. Inside are a raccoon, a riding boot, a blanket, and a Trilby hat with a 10/6d price ticket from Alice in Wonderland's Mad Hatter. A hidden cooking pot is found under the interior hat's screw top lid. Hallmarks include ©, heart, HBC logo, ed.#, and DL.

TREASURE JESTS
Rather Large

Rather Large Friends
Item No.: TJRLCA
Artist: PC
Size: 105x107x95
Status: Retired
Carving Date: 95
Release Date: Feb 96
Retired Date: Oct 98
Issue Size: 9350

Rather Large Friends is an enlarged version of the Small Treasure Jest "Purrfect Friends." Hallmarks include apple, clock face with month 10, HBC logo, and Pc.

Rather Large Hop
Item No.: TJRLRA
Artist: PC
Size: 105x102x105
Status: Retired
Carving Date: 95
Release Date: Feb 96
Retired Date: Oct 98
Issue Size: 4330

Rather Large Hop is an enlarged version of the Small Treasure Jest "At The Hop." Hallmarks include apple, HBC logo, clock face with month 11 and Pc. On some of the pieces, Andrea's car registration is inscribed on the rim.

Rather Large Huddle
Item No.: TJRLTO
Artist: PC
Size: 134x122x96
Status: Retired
Carving Date: 95
Release Date: Feb 96
Retired Date: Oct 98
Issue Size: 5423

Rather Large Huddle is an enlarged version of the Small Treasure Jest "Puddle Huddle." Hallmarks include apple, clock face with month 10, HBC logo, and Pc.

Rather Large Safari
Item No.: TJRLSA
Artist: PC
Size: 111x100x102
Status: Retired
Carving Date: 95
Release Date: Feb 96
Retired Date: Oct 98
Issue Size: 6692

Rather Large Safari is an enlarged version of the Small Treasure Jest "Ed's Safari."

Hallmarks include apple, clock face with month 11, HBC logo, and Pc.

TREASURE JESTS
Extra Large

Primordial Soup
Item No.: TJXXLTU
Artist: PC
Size: 140x129x140
Status: Retired
Carving Date: 95
Release Date: Dec 95
Retired Date: Apr 99
Issue Size: 7542

This box figurine is based on the Iroquois creation myth in which Great Turtle invites his fellow turtles to dive to the bottom of the sea in order to gather earth to place upon his back. This piece is covered with hundreds of turtles, one wearing a ribbon reading, "Linford," for the British athlete Linford Christie, and another a pendant with, "ZH," for Zoe Heller, a famous British Journalist. "NOEL," for Noel Wiggins, is carved into a turtle shell. The mouse can be found on the top of the box, near the turtle that has unique taste in jewellery. Inside the box figurine is the planet Saturn, stars, a crescent moon, comet, a large turtle shell with number "48" (Peter's address), and footprints leading to a manhole. Hallmarks include apple, clock face with month 12, HBC logo, and Pc.

PARADOXICALS

Paradise Found
Item No.: TJPPF
Artist: PC
Size: 52x53x56
Status: Retired
Carving Date: 95
Release Date: Oct 95
Retired Date: Dec 97
Issue Size: 7628

This box figurine is a trio of not-so-angelic angels. The first angel, wearing a Mercedes Benz logo pendant, gives his cohort a "hot-wing," while his victim stifles a giggle. The moulting angel is holding a newspaper, "The Guardian (Angel)," and seems to look very much like Peter. The mouse can be found by looking directly down at the top of the box. The interior depicts a map of Africa where Peter and Andrea honeymooned. On the lid is the question, "FLY?" The answer to this question can also be found: "OK." The date, 2.8.95 is when this final decision had been made. Inside is HBC logo.

Paradise Lost
Item No.: TJPPL
Artist: PC
Size: 55x49x59
Status: Retired
Carving Date: 95
Release Date: Oct 95
Retired Date: Apr 98
Issue Size: 9855

This is the second box figurine in the Paradoxicals Series, the companion piece to "Paradise Found." Three demons with wings, horns, hands, hairy legs, claws and scaly tails sit back to back above the flames of Hell. One leans on his elbows and sticks his tongue out, another is holding a one-eyed skull and appears to have been bitten by the skull. The third seems spooked by the spook he is holding. At the time of carving, Peter had been browsing through a book on the artist Pieter Brueghel and seems to have been more influenced by his paintings than by the gargoyle stone carvings of English churches. Hallmarks on the base include P Calvesbert and 95. Inside is HBC logo.

HI-JINX

Antarctic Antics
Item No.: TJXLPE
Artist: PC
Size: 97x98x100
Status: Retired
Carving Date: 94
Release Date: Aug 94
Retired Date: Oct 98
Issue Size: 3291

This box figurine is the second piece in the Hi-Jinx series. It depicts David Attenborough ("DA"), a well-known naturalist, interviewing penguins. Overwhelmed by thirty penguins, the photographer, soundman, and narrator seem to be reaching the end of their patience as the animals take over. The narrator is holding the mouth of one penguin shut so he can talk, while a bird picks his pocket. The parka-clad soundman has made a friend who has found an interesting place to warm up. The mouse is nestled on the backpack where a penguin is perched. Inside are eight eggs. The inside of the soundman's hat reads "buy me" and "Antiquark." Other birds include one wearing medals of honour, one taking pictures, another dressed in goggles, scarf, and waist coat, another holding a water bottle, and one smoking a cigar. The "ALR" on the hot water bottle stands for Andrea Louise Riley (Peter's wife). The hallmarks on the base include ©, No. 2, Antiquark, and PC 94 U.K.

Hold That Line
Item No.: TJXLFO
Artist: PC
Size: 92x92x103
Status: Retired
Carving Date: 94
Release Date: Aug 94
Retired Date: Oct 98
Issue Size: 4740

This box figurine is the first in the Hi-Jinx series. Sixteen teammates vie for possession of a fumbled football, located inside the box. Mixed in with the mayhem are a rhino, a boa constrictor, Peter's teddy bear, Rosie, and the mouse on the very top of the box. Other curiosities include a pair of dentures, the linebacker holding daisies, a bonus mouse squashed beneath the shoe of one of the players, and the star player, Martin Perry, in the #1 jersey (or is it ex-Chicago Bears player William "The Refrigerator" Perry?). Look for the hidden Super Bowl results: Dallas Cowboys 30, Buffalo Bills 13. The hallmarks on the base include ©, No. 1, Antiquark, and PC 94 U.K.

Mad Dogs And Englishmen
Item No.: TJXLHO
Artist: PC
Size: 91x86x111
Status: Retired
Carving Date: 94
Release Date: Nov 94
Retired Date: Oct 98
Issue Size: 4625

This fairly typical scene on an English village green depicts six men, twenty-one dogs, and one shell-shocked cat perched atop this pile of pandemonium. The mouse is behind the head of the Englishman who is saving the cat. "No. 3" denotes that this is the third piece in the Hi Jinx series. Other notables include a giant bone inside the box, a bulldog with "Love" and "Hate" tattooed across his knuckles, and a bonus mouse inscribed on the side of the base of the box. The hallmarks on the base include ©, No. 3, Antiquark, and PC 94 U.K.

Open Mike
Item No.: TJXLBA
Artist: PC
Size: 98x95x88
Status: Retired
Carving Date: 95
Release Date: Feb 95
Retired Date: Oct 98
Issue Size: 3032

"Crow's Nest" is Harmony Kingdom's eclectic band of musicians. Aside from the band members you'll find Murphy, Peter's faithful canine companion, and an elephant which is hidden behind the pigtailed fan. The drummer bears a striking resemblance to Peter. Turn the box upside down to see a little smiley face under all the hair of the lead guitar player. His speaker bears the artist's initials. Note the brassiere tastefully draped over one of the bass drums. There are two mice: one between the base drums and another squished on the sole of the female vocalist's shoe. Inside the box lies a cat, whose paws are clamped over her ears in order to drown out the cacophony. The hallmarks on the base include ©, Antiquark, and PC 95 U.K.

THE GARDEN PARTY

Baroness Trotter
Item No.: TJZPI
Artist: PC
Size: 28x36x46
Status: Retired
Carving Date: 95
Release Date: Jan 96
Retired Date: May 01
Issue Size: 14,781

The mouse lies upside down between the pig's front legs. Hallmarks include PC and HBC logo inside.

Count Belfry
Item No.: TJZBA
Artist: DL
Size: 29x27x54
Status: Retired
Carving Date: 96
Release Date: Jan 97
Retired Date: Sep 99
Issue Size: 6978

Hallmarks include ©, HBC logo, and M.

Courtiers At Rest
Item No.: TJZTU
Artist: PC
Size: 34x33x46
Status: Retired
Carving Date: 95
Release Date: Jan 96
Retired Date: May 01
Issue Size: 17,095

Hallmarks include PC 96. The mouse is hiding under a turtle's shell.

Duc De Lyon
Item No.: TJZLI
Artist: DL
Size: 30x35x50
Status: Retired
Carving Date: 96
Release Date: Jan 97
Retired Date: Sep 99
Issue Size: 7220

Hallmarks include ©, HBC logo, and M.

Earl Of Oswald
Item No.: TJZEL
Artist: DL
Size: 31x34x47
Status: Retired
Carving Date: 96
Release Date: Jan 97
Retired Date: Sep 99
Issue Size: 9253

Hallmarks include ©, HBC logo, and M.

Garden Prince
Item No.: TJZFR
Artist: PC
Size: 29x28x48
Status: Retired
Carving Date: 95
Release Date: Jan 96
Retired Date: Nov 01
Issue Size: 13,033

Hallmarks include HBC logo on ball in crown. Inside is HBC logo.

Ladies In Waiting
Item No.: TJZCA
Artist: PC
Size: 31x29x47
Status: Retired
Carving Date: 96
Release Date: Jan 96
Retired Date: Nov 01
Issue Size: 26,493

Hallmarks include HBC logo inside and PC 96 near base.

Lord Busby
Item No.: TJZBE
Artist: DL
Size: 31x27x49
Status: Retired
Carving Date: 96
Release Date: Jan 97
Retired Date: Apr 99
Issue Size: 7274

Hallmarks include ©, HBC logo, and M.

Major Parker
Item No.: TJZMO
Artist: DL
Size: 29x33x48
Status: Retired
Carving Date: 96
Release Date: Jan 97
Retired Date: Sep 99
Issue Size: 6262

Hallmarks include ©, HBC logo, and M.

Marquis De Blanc
Item No.: TJZRA
Artist: DL
Size: 27x35x51
Status: Retired
Carving Date: 96
Release Date: Jan 97
Retired Date: Sep 99
Issue Size: 9222

Hallmarks include ©, HBC logo, and M.

Royal Flotilla
Item No.: TJZFI
Artist: PC
Size: 36x25x50
Status: Retired
Carving Date: 95
Release Date: Jan 96
Retired Date: Apr 98
Issue Size: 11,488

Hallmarks include diamond (despite 95 carve date), mirror image clock face with month 2, and PC. Inside is HBC logo.

Yeoman Of The Guard
Item No.: TJZOW
Artist: PC
Size: 26x25x30
Status: Retired
Carving Date: 95
Release Date: Jan 96
Retired Date: May 01
Issue Size: 13,145

Hallmarks include apple, HBC logo, clock face with month 11 and PC. The mouse is located between the owl's feet. Inside is HBC logo.

TREASURE JESTS
Mini

Catch As Catch Can
Item No.: TJCA10
Artist: PC
Size: 60x32x59
Status: Open
Carving Date: 99
Release Date: Jan 00

The mouse, hanging on the can's handle, shows a rare view of his tail and bottom.

Khepera's Castle
Item No.: TJDB
Artist: PC
Size: 48x48x54
Status: Retired
Carving Date: 01
Release Date: May 01
Retired Date: Nov 01
Issue Size: 3458

There is no mouse. The scarab beetle is a symbol of the Egyptian god Khepera. There were multiple color variations, all signed by Martin Perry, consisting of ten boxes each of five colors.

Midas Touch
Item No.: TJFI3
Artist: PC
Size: 64x32x64
Status: Open
Carving Date: 00
Release Date: Dec 00

Possible baby names for Peter's first child, "Jodie" and "Sam" appear on the fins.

The mouse peeks out from between two aquatic plants.

Moggy Bag
Item No.: TJCA9
Artist: PC
Size: 48x33x61
Status: Open
Carving Date: 99
Release Date: Jan 00

The mouse is in the kitten's paw. On the interior is a carving of fish bones.

Harmony Kingdom Box Details

Orange Crush
Item No.: TJT12
Artist: PC
Size: 47x39x59
Status: Open
Carving Date: 00
Release Date: Jun 00

The mouse appears as either the second or third claw on the left rear paw.

Pot Sticker
Item No.: TJHE4
Artist: PC
Size: 42x42x62
Status: Retired
Carving Date: 99
Release Date: Jan 00
Retired Date: Mar 00
Issue Size: 7844

The mouse hides under a leaf.

Stuffed Shirt
Item No.: TJCA16
Artist: PC
Size: 46x41x56
Status: Open
Carving Date: 01
Release Date: Jan 02

The mouse is in the t-shirt with the kittens. 200 "Stuffed Shirt" have "World Tour" on the t-shirt. These 200 variations are randomly found in the first 3600 produced (the version pictured, with "UK" and "USA" on the shirt). For all pieces made after 3600, the t-shirt is blank.

The Good Race
Item No.: TJTU3
Artist: PC
Size: 54x38x39
Status: Open
Carving Date: 99
Release Date: Jan 00

The mouse is under the turtle's knee. "P.C." is inscribed on the front of the shell.

Trunk Call
Item No.: TJEL3
Artist: PC
Size: 54x30x60
Status: Open
Carving Date: 99
Release Date: Jan 00

Under an elephant's rump is a dangerous place for a mouse!

ROLY POLYS

Alfred
Item No.: TJRPFR2
Artist: AB
Size: 44x38x51
Status: Open
Carving Date: 01
Release Date: Mar 01

Interior carving is a pair of lips. 360 Hard Body versions worldwide. Named after a movie director.

Benny
Item No.: TJRPHE
Artist: AB
Size: 38x38x38
Status: Retired
Carving Date: 00
Release Date: Mar 01
Retired Date: Sep 01
Issue Size: 4175

Interior carving is a beetle. 570 Hard Body versions worldwide. Named for a comedian.

Bones
Item No.: TJRPHSK
Artist: AB
Size: 38x41x41
Status: Retired
Carving Date: 01
Release Date: Jul 01
Retired Date: Sep 02
Issue Size: Not Available

Interior carving is a bone. 345 Hard Body versions worldwide.

Boris
Item No.: TJRPHMU
Artist: AB
Size: 38x44x44
Status: Fixed Ed
Carving Date: 01
Release Date: May 02
Issue Size: 2500

No Hard Bodies were made. Named for an actor of films in the 1950's and 1960's.

Botero
Item No.: TJRPTU
Artist: AB
Size: 44x45x38
Status: Retired
Carving Date: 00
Release Date: May 00
Retired Date: Sep 00
Issue Size: 10,343

There is no interior carving. 835 Hard Body versions worldwide. Named for an artist.

Brando
Item No.: TJRPHO
Artist: AB
Size: 40x42x40
Status: Retired
Carving Date: 00
Release Date: May 00
Retired Date: Sep 00
Issue Size: 10,299

There is no interior carving. 440 Hard Body versions worldwide. Named for an actor.

Candy
Item No.: TJRPBE
Artist: AB
Size: 62x65x59
Status: Fixed Ed
Carving Date: 00
Release Date: Sep 00
Issue Size: 2000

Interior carving is a honeycomb and a maple leaf. Named for a comedian. Canadian exclusive.

Cass
Item No.: TJRPCA3
Artist: AB
Size: 38x44x44
Status: Open
Carving Date: 00
Release Date: Nov 00

Interior carving is a picture of a wind-up toy mouse. 790 Hard Body versions worldwide. Named for a singer.

Chaney
Item No.: TJRPHGE
Artist: AB
Size: 38x44x44
Status: Fixed Ed
Carving Date: 01
Release Date: May 02
Issue Size: 2000

This Roly Poly was made only as a Hard Body. Named for an actor.

Costello
Item No.: TJRPCR
Artist: AB
Size: 44x38x38
Status: Retired
Carving Date: 00
Release Date: Mar 01
Retired Date: Sep 01
Issue Size: 4424

Interior carving is the astrological symbol for Cancer. 790 Hard Body versions worldwide. Named for an actor.

Curly
Item No.: TJRPPI
Artist: AB
Size: 40x46x41
Status: Retired
Carving Date: 00
Release Date: May 00
Retired Date: Feb 02
Issue Size: 11,661

There is no interior carving. 968 Hard Body versions worldwide. Named for an actor.

Cyril
Item No.: TJRPSE
Artist: AB
Size: 38x44x44
Status: Open
Carving Date: 00
Release Date: Nov 00

Interior carving is a fish. 790 Hard Body versions worldwide. Named for a British politician.

Divine
Item No.: TJRPFR
Artist: AB
Size: 41x41x38
Status: Open
Carving Date: 00
Release Date: May 00

There is no interior carving. 1354 Hard Body versions worldwide. Named for an actor.

Dizzie
Item No.: TJRPMO
Artist: AB
Size: 42x40x43
Status: Retired
Carving Date: 00
Release Date: May 00
Retired Date: Sep 00
Issue Size: 10,290

There is no interior carving. 960 Hard Body versions worldwide. Named for a musician.

Dom
Item No.: TJRPMA
Artist: AB
Size: 39x48x43
Status: Retired
Carving Date: 00
Release Date: May 00
Retired Date: Jun 02
Issue Size: 11,778

There is no interior carving. 420 Hard Body versions worldwide. Named for an actor.

Elvis
Item No.: TJRPCA4
Artist: AB
Size: 38x38x51
Status: Open
Carving Date: 01
Release Date: Mar 01

Interior carving is a fish. 910 Hard Body versions worldwide. Named for a singer.

Fats
Item No.: TJRPFI2
Artist: AB
Size: 38x44x44
Status: Open
Carving Date: 00
Release Date: Nov 00

Interior carving is a hook and "CDL 2000." 900 Hard Body versions worldwide. Named for a musician.

Fergie
Item No.: TJRPRA
Artist: AB
Size: 40x43x39
Status: Retired
Carving Date: 00
Release Date: May 00
Retired Date: Oct 00
Issue Size: 10,331

There is no interior carving. 548 Hard Body versions worldwide. Named for a royal personage.

Frankie
Item No.: TJRPHFR
Artist: AB
Size: 38x44x44
Status: Fixed Ed
Carving Date: 01
Release Date: May 02
Issue Size: 2500

No Hard Bodies were produced. Named for a ghoulish fictional character.

Garcia
Item No.: TJRPLI
Artist: AB
Size: 38x38x44
Status: Retired
Carving Date: 00
Release Date: May 01
Retired Date: Feb 02
Issue Size: 4551

Interior carving is a crown. Named for a musician. 790 Hard Body versions worldwide.

Page 106   Harmony Kingdom Box Details

Gleason
Item No.: TJRPGO
Artist: AB
Size: 38x44x44
Status: Open
Carving Date: 00
Release Date: Nov 00

Interior carving is a pair of underwear. Named for an actor. 790 Hard Body versions were created.

Hardy
Item No.: TJRPBU
Artist: AB
Size: 38x44x44
Status: Retired
Carving Date: 00
Release Date: Nov 00
Retired Date: Aug 01
Issue Size: 5714

Interior carving of teacup and saucer. Named for an actor. 680 Hard Body versions were created.

Henry
Item No.: TJRPHI
Artist: AB
Size: 38x44x44
Status: Retired
Carving Date: 00
Release Date: Nov 00
Retired Date: Aug 01
Issue Size: 5715

A picture of grass is carved on the interior. Named for King Henry VIII. 550 Hard Body versions were created.

Hilda
Item No.: TJRPHWI
Artist: AB
Size: 41x47x41
Status: Retired
Carving Date: 01
Release Date: Jul 01
Retired Date: Sep 02
Issue Size: Not Available

A cauldron is carved on the interior. There were 575 Hard Bodies issued (500 US, 75 UK).

Hitchcock
Item No.: TJRPHCA
Artist: AB
Size: 38x41x44
Status: Retired
Carving Date: 01
Release Date: Jul 01
Retired Date: Sep 02
Issue Size: Not available

Interior carving is stars. 690 Hard Bodies worldwide. Named for a movie director.

Jabba
Item No.: TJRPHGE
Artist: AB
Size: 38x44x44
Status: Fixed Ed
Carving Date: 01
Release Date: May 02
Issue Size: 500

This Roly Poly is available only as a Hard Body. 500 were made. Named for a movie character.

Kennedy
Item No.: TJRPELD
Artist: AB
Size: 62x65x58
Status: Fixed Ed
Carving Date: 00
Release Date: Dec 00
Last Ship Date: Dec 00
Issue Size: 250

With so much talk about counting and recounting in the year 2000 presidential election, Harmony Kingdom decided to do a hand recount of Roly Polys inventory. Much to our surprise we found a very rare Roly Poly hiding in a few of the "Louis" the elephant gift boxes. No, it's not a pregnant chad or Votomatic. It's "Kennedy!" "Kennedy" is a Hard Body donkey.

Somehow this symbol of the Democratic party overturned the election of GOP elephants and infiltrated a Harmony Kingdom shipment. Rather than interfere with the Supreme Court Justices' schedules, a lottery was held to determine which HK dealers will receive "Kennedy." Maybe we should call this group of dealers our Electoral College!

Liz
Item No.: TJRPEA
Artist: AB
Size: 38x44x44
Status: Open
Carving Date: 00
Release Date: Nov 00

Interior carving is a feather. 680 Hard Body versions worldwide. Named for an actress.

Louis
Item No.: TJRPEL
Artist: AB
Size: 62x65x59
Status: Open
Carving Date: 00
Release Date: May 00

There is no interior carving. 1107 Hard Body versions worldwide. Named for a musician.

Mae
Item No.: TJRPDO
Artist: AB
Size: 30x47x42
Status: Retired
Carving Date: 00
Release Date: May 00
Retired Date: Sep 00
Issue Size: 10,321

There is no interior carving. 1329 Hard Body versions worldwide. Named for an actress.

Monica
Item No.: TJRPFI
Artist: AB
Size: 42x47x43
Status: Retired
Carving Date: 00
Release Date: May 00
Retired Date: Feb 01
Issue Size: 11,213

There is no interior carving. 745 Hard Body versions worldwide. Named for a Washington, DC, intern.

Mostel
Item No.: TJRPOW
Artist: AB
Size: 42x42x40
Status: Retired
Carving Date: 00
Release Date: May 00
Retired Date: Feb 01
Issue Size: 10,803

There is no interior carving. 1201 Hard Body versions worldwide. Named for an actor.

Orson
Item No.: TJRPOC
Artist: AB
Size: 38x44x44
Status: Open
Carving Date: 00
Release Date: Nov 00

Interior carving is a crab. 680 Hard Body versions worldwide. Named for an actor/director.

Ozzie
Item No.: TJRPHPU
Artist: AB
Size: 41x41x41
Status: Retired
Carving Date: 01
Release Date: Jul 01
Retired Date: Sep 02
Issue Size: Not Available

The interior features a drawing of a pie. Named for a singer. 690 Hard Bodies were issued (600 in the US, 90 in the UK).

Pavarotti
Item No.: TJRPPE
Artist: AB
Size: 38x44x44
Status: Open
Carving Date: 00
Release Date: Nov 00

Interior carving is of six small fish. 900 Hard Body versions worldwide. Named for a singer.

Roseanne

Item No.: TJRPRH
Artist: AB
Size: 38x44x44
Status: Retired
Carving Date: 00
Release Date: Nov 00
Retired Date: Aug 01
Issue Size: 5697

Interior carving is a pair of glasses. 900 Hard Body versions worldwide. Named for an actress.

Rosie

Item No.: TJRPCA
Artist: AB
Size: 62x65x59
Status: Retired
Carving Date: 00
Release Date: May 00
Retired Date: Sep 01
Issue Size: 12,265

There is no interior carving. 297 Hard Body versions worldwide. Named for a talkshow host.

Rush

Item No.: TJRPRO
Artist: AB
Size: 38x31x44
Status: Retired
Carving Date: 01
Release Date: Mar 01
Retired Date: Sep 01
Issue Size: 4133

The interior has a picture of a frightened worm. Named for a talk show host. 680 Hard Body versions worldwide.

Tony & George

Item No.: TJRPBB
Artist: AB
Size: 42x42x51
Status: Fixed Ed
Carving Date: 01
Release Date: Jan 02
Issue Size: 2002

This special two-sided Roly Poly symbolizes the staunch alliance between the US and the UK. Prime Minister Tony Blair appears on one side, with a Union Jack across his chest. On the other side is President George W. Bush and the Star Spangled Banner. Two color variations exist, a regular painted version and 200 vividly painted boxes. "Tony & George" was released exclusively in the US.

Harmony Kingdom Box Details

Victoria
Item No.: TJRPCA2
Artist: AB
Size: 38x44x44
Status: Open
Carving Date: 00
Release Date: Nov 00

Interior carving is a bird. 550 Hard Body versions worldwide. Named for Queen Victoria.

Winston
Item No.: TJRPHO2
Artist: AB
Size: 38x44x44
Status: Open
Carving Date: 00
Release Date: Nov 00

Interior carving is the Union Jack. 790 Hard Body versions worldwide. Named for Winston Churchill.

NetsUKe

Bush Baby
Item No.: TJNBU
Artist: PC
Size: 51x44x76
Status: Fixed Ed
Carving Date: 00
Release Date: Mar 01
Issue Size: 2500

"Bush Baby" is a solid body figurine similar in size to a Small Treasure Jest. Bush babies are endangered primates, and Peter Calvesbert's profound concern for these wide-eyed creatures is evident in every detail of his carving. Color variations exist. In the Americas, 1800 of the pieces have orange eyes and 200 have green eyes. In the UK, 450 "Bush Baby" have orange eyes and 50 have green eyes.

Finky
Item No.: TJNRO2
Artist: PC
Size: 38x51x57
Status: Open
Carving Date: 00
Release Date: Dec 00

The mouse is behind the berry.

Francis
Item No.: TJNEL
Artist: PC
Size: 57x57x57
Status: Retired
Carving Date: 99
Release Date: Jan 00
Retired Date: Jan 00
Issue Size: 1569

This figurine is a NetsUKe version of the Mini Treasure Jest "Trunk Call."

Georgie
Item No.: TJNDR
Artist: PC
Size: 44x44x58
Status: Open
Carving Date: 00
Release Date: Jun 00

The mouse tries to escape from under the dragon's coils.

Harry
Item No.: TJNRA
Artist: PC
Size: 58x27x42
Status: Retired
Carving Date: 99
Release Date: Jan 00
Retired Date: Sep 01
Issue Size: 7314

The mouse hangs on underneath an ear.

Nell
Item No.: TJNHO
Artist: PC
Size: 59x41x48
Status: Open
Carving Date: 99
Release Date: Jan 00

The mouse peers out from under an ear.

Ollie
Item No.: TJNOW
Artist: PC
Size: 33x37x58
Status: Open
Carving Date: 99
Release Date: Jan 00

Eluding capture, the mouse is safely tucked under a wing tip.

Sammy
Item No.: TJNRO
Artist: PC
Size: 32x51x64
Status: Open
Carving Date: 00
Release Date: Jun 00

No signature mouse appears on this piece.

Sid
Item No.: TJNSN
Artist: PC
Size: 44x51x63
Status: Open
Carving Date: 00
Release Date: Dec 00

The mouse puts in an appearance directly above the hallmarks.

Squee
Item No.: TJNDO
Artist: PC
Size: 63x26x57
Status: Open
Carving Date: 99
Release Date: Jan 00

The mouse is located under the rear fluke of the larger dolphin.

Tarka
Item No.: TJNOT
Artist: PC
Size: 56x39x41
Status: Open
Carving Date: 99
Release Date: Jan 00

The mouse stows away inside the shell.

Waddles
Item No.: TJNDU
Artist: PC
Size: 32x45x60
Status: Open
Carving Date: 99
Release Date: Jan 00

There is no mouse on this figurine. But there is a touch of artistic humor. Look for the faint "xxxk" inscription on the underside of the right wing.

Harmony Kingdom Box Details

Two By Two

Antony & Cleopatra
Item No.: TJ2NRA
Artist: AB
Size: 76x31x67
Status: Retired
Carving Date: 01
Release Date: Oct 01
Retired Date: Aug 02
Issue Size: 2622

Named for Cleopatra, queen of Egypt, and her famous Roman lover Mark Antony.

Barney & Betty
Item No.: TJ2NPI
Artist: AB
Size: 67x62x51
Status: Retired
Carving Date: 01
Release Date: Oct 01
Retired Date: Aug 02
Issue Size: 2614

Named for a cartoon couple.

Bonnie & Clyde
Item No.: TJ2NFR
Artist: AB
Size: 60x44x66
Status: Fixed Ed
Carving Date: 01
Release Date: Oct 01
Issue Size: 3000

Named for infamous American gangsters.

Franklin & Eleanor
Item No.: TJ2NOW
Artist: AB
Size: 73x41x57
Status: Retired
Carving Date: 01
Release Date: Oct 01
Retired Date: Aug 02
Issue Size: 2561

Named for President Franklin D. Roosevelt and Eleanor Roosevelt.

Harmony Kingdom Box Details

Marie & Pierre
Item No.: TJ2NCA
Artist: AB
Size: 83x63x51
Status: Retired
Carving Date: 01
Release Date: Oct 01
Retired Date: Aug 02
Issue Size: 2721

Named after scientist Marie Curie and her husband.

Ranier & Grace
Item No.: TJ2NDO
Artist: AB
Size: 92x63x76
Status: Retired
Carving Date: 01
Release Date: Oct 01
Retired Date: Aug 02
Issue Size: 2551

Named for Prince Ranier of Monaco and Grace Kelly.

Samson & Delilah
Item No.: TJ2NLL
Artist: AB
Size: 68x71x57
Status: Fixed Ed
Carving Date: 02
Release Date: Mar 02
Issue Size: 2000

Named after a Biblical couple.

Interchangeables

Bog Hopper
Item No.: TJIFR
Artist: AB
Size: 51x67x31
Status: Open
Carving Date: 01
Release Date: Oct 01

The Interchangeables are three-part boxes with a base, head and neck. The parts of one box can be exchanged with the parts of the other boxes, making your own creations.

Crack A Smile
Item No.: TJIAL
Artist: AB
Size: 51x89x32
Status: Open
Carving Date: 01
Release Date: Oct 01

The Interchangeables are three-part boxes with a base, head and neck. The parts of one box can be exchanged with the parts of the other boxes, making your own creations.

Hearts Content
Item No.: TJIEL
Artist: AB
Size: 38x67x51
Status: Open
Carving Date: 01
Release Date: Oct 01

The Interchangeables are three-part boxes with a base, head and neck. The parts of one box can be exchanged with the parts of the other boxes, making your own creations.

In The Know
Item No.: TJIHI
Artist: AB
Size: 38x63x41
Status: Open
Carving Date: 01
Release Date: Oct 01

The Interchangeables are three-part boxes with a base, head and neck. The parts of one box can be exchanged with the parts of the other boxes, making your own creations.

Harmony Kingdom Box Details

Lady Luck
Item No.: TJIDU
Artist: AB
Size: 44x70x38
Status: Fixed Ed
Carving Date: 01
Release Date: Oct 01
Edition Size: 3000

The Interchangeables are three-part boxes with a base, head and neck. The parts of one box can be exchanged with the parts of the other boxes, making your own creations.

Make A Wish
Item No.: TJIFI
Artist: AB
Size: 38x82x44
Status: Open
Carving Date: 01
Release Date: Oct 01

The Interchangeables are three-part boxes with a base, head and neck. The parts of one box can be exchanged with the parts of the other boxes, making your own creations.

Wedded Bliss
Item No.: TJITU
Artist: AB
Size: 44x70x41
Status: Open
Carving Date: 01
Release Date: Oct 01

The Interchangeables are three-part boxes with a base, head and neck. The parts of one box can be exchanged with the parts of the other boxes, making your own creations.

ANGELIQUE

Angelique™

Bon Chance
Item No.: ANBO
Artist: DL
Size: 54x51x64
Status: Retired
Carving Date: 96
Release Date: Jun 96
Retired Date: Jan 01
Issue Size: 6353

This box figurine is the first tooth fairy box produced by HK. The strange little goblin perches on an inscribed coin reading "Every good child deserves favour." Within the box is a tiny tooth with the message "new teeth for old." An early version has the acorn perched over the interior message. "Bon Chance" has had a variety of colour combinations that have not been recorded, except for the first 225 that were green and red without golden wings. Inspiration for this piece came from Richard Dadd, a late 19th century English painter in the fantasy tradition. Hallmarks include ©, diamond, mirror image clock face with month 7, HBC logo, and DL.

Fleur-de-lis
Item No.: ANFL
Artist: DL
Size: 32x51x76
Status: Retired
Carving Date: 96
Release Date: Jun 96
Retired Date: Apr 98
Issue Size: 7888

David's daughter, Rose, served as inspiration for this box figurine. "Rosalina de Lorenzo" appears on the angel's sash and "R" and "L" on her hair ribbon. Early pieces had "Rosalina de Lorenzo" on the neck of the lid. The first ninety pieces had a wing span of 1 3/4". The next version had a 1" wing span. Then in Spring 1998, a third version appeared with a wingspan of 1 3/8". Inside is a dove. Hallmarks include ©, diamond, clock face with month 5, HBC logo, and DL.

Gentil Homme
Item No.: ANGE
Artist: DL
Size: 36x56x65
Status: Retired
Carving Date: 96
Release Date: Jun 96
Retired Date: Apr 98
Issue Size: 6786

This is the only boy in the Angelique series. The Latin inscription on the quiver reads: Amor Vinci Omnia, (Love Conquers All). "Gentil Homme" offers you a heart, already pierced with one of his love arrows, on a tiny pillow. Inside the box is a peach. The artist's acorn is under cupid's left buttock. Hallmarks include ©, diamond, clock face with month 5, HBC logo, and DL.

Ingenue
Item No.: ANIN
Artist: DL
Size: 49x65x61
Status: Retired
Carving Date: 96
Release Date: Jun 96
Retired Date: Apr 98
Issue Size: 8062

The village doctor's daughter, Alexandra, served as inspiration for this box figurine. Her name appears on the sash around her waste. The acorn is located in the folds of her gown. Originally the robes were coloured. Later they were left uncoloured but the face was painted. Inside is a heart with wings. Hallmarks include ©, diamond, clock face with month 5, HBC logo, and DL.

Joie De Vivre
Item No.: ANJO
Artist: DL
Size: 62x52x65
Status: Retired
Carving Date: 96
Release Date: Jun 96
Retired Date: Apr 98
Issue Size: 8170

The artist's neighbour, Gabriella, whose name is written on the hem of her robes, was inspiration for this box figurine. A group of rabbits sit at her feet enjoying life, as her name suggests. David's signature acorn appears in the folds of her dress under her left wing. Inside is a butterfly. The first version (approximately 100 pieces) has coloured robes, the face looking down and "Gabriella" around the lid. The next version (approximately 125 pieces) has a colourless robe with a painted face. With the third version the mould was changed and the head was positioned upward. Hallmarks include ©, diamond, clock face with month 5, HBC logo, and DL.

LORD BYRON'S HARMONY GARDEN

Albatross
Item No.: HG4AL
Artist: MB
Size: 77x48x88
Status: Open
Carving Date: 99
Release Date: Jan 00

Piloting the Albatross aircraft, with nose pointed eastward, off Byron flies.

Hallmarks include ©, moon, HBC logo, ed.#, and eye.

Alpine Flower
Item No.: HG3AL
Artist: MB
Size: 80x72x74
Status: Open
Carving Date: 98
Release Date: Jan 99

Lord Byron takes to the Alps for a stint of skiing on the Alpine Flower Slopes.

Hallmarks include ©, star, HBC logo, ed.#, M, and eye.

Begonia
Item No.: HGBE
Artist: MP
Size: 61x65x77
Status: Retired
Carving Date: 97
Release Date: Jan 98
Retired Date: Apr 00
Issue Size: 11,772

Gordy the goalie spider challenges Lord Byron to a rousing game of soccer at the

Begonia Fields. Hallmarks include ©, heart, HBC logo, ed.#, and M.

Cactus

Item No.: HGCA
Artist: MP
Size: 78x68x59
Status: Retired
Carving Date: 97
Release Date: Jan 98
Retired Date: Apr 02
Issue Size: 16,480

Enchanted by the queen, Byron spends the day tending to her flowers in the Cactus Greenhouse. Hallmarks include ©, heart, HBC logo, ed.#, and M.

Carnation

Item No.: HG5CA
Artist: SD
Size: 63x63x44
Status: Open
Carving Date: 00
Release Date: Dec 00

Byron is too tired to fly so he makes his way to the bus station and decides on a southerly route. He arrives at a parade of Carnation covered floats in the Southwest, where he spots a mysterious, beautiful bug. He puts on his best bow tie and buys a corsage to impress her. But she disappears in the crowd. Hallmarks include ©, double diamond, HBC logo, ed.#, and S.

Cherry Blossom

Item No.: HG4CB
Artist: MB
Size: 72x62x70
Status: Open
Carving Date: 99
Release Date: Jan 00

Inside the Cherry Blossom teahouse, Lord Byron is welcomed with open arms by a Geishabug who sings, dances and recites poetry for Lord Byron. He is enamoured with his lovely hostess, and she with him, but Byron's transport awaits him. Hallmarks include ©, moon, HBC logo, ed.#, and eye.

Chrysanthemum

Item No.: HGCH
Artist: MP
Size: 65x55x66
Status: Retired
Carving Date: 96
Release Date: Jan 97
Retired Date: Jan 00
Issue Size: 15,854

Lord Byron is a very curious little lady bug and spends many hours in the Chrysanthemum Plant-a-tarium, gazing at the skies and sketching the strange life forms that he sees. 4,462 pieces were made in England. Hallmarks include ©, diamond, HBC logo, ed.#, and M.

Harmony Kingdom Box Details

Cranberry
Item No.: HGCR
Artist: MP
Size: 67x55x63
Status: Retired
Carving Date: 96
Release Date: Jan 97
Retired Date: Apr 99
Issue Size: 13,029

Lord Byron, suitcase in tow, rushes through the Cranberry Tracks on his way to work. 3,418 pieces were made in England. Hallmarks include ©, diamond, HBC logo, ed.#, and M.

Daisy
Item No.: HGDA
Artist: MP
Size: 58x52x55
Status: Retired
Carving Date: 96
Release Date: Jan 97
Retired Date: Sep 99
Issue Size: 15,599

Lord Byron relaxes at the Daisy Lounge, where he watches his favourite films. 3,905 pieces were made in England. Hallmarks include ©, diamond, HBC logo, ed.#, and M.

Daisy II
Item No.: HG5DA
Artist: SD
Size: 63x63x38
Status: Open
Carving Date: 00
Release Date: Dec 00

Reaching the Northeast, Byron spends a few evenings at the opera and reflects on his long and arduous search for love. Maybe it is time to head home. At the Daisy airport lounge, he absentmindedly plucks petals, while awaiting his flight. "She loves me, she loves me not..." Hallmarks include ©, double diamond, HBC logo, ed.#, and S.

Egyptian Rose
Item No.: HG4ER
Artist: MB
Size: 80x78x88
Status: Retired
Carving Date: 99
Release Date: Jan 00
Retired Date: Aug 01
Issue Size: 7472

A tribe of Bedouin locusts befriends Byron and takes him on a desert trek to the pyramids inside the Egyptian Rose. Here he discovers the unknown tomb of Tutanthamen, full of magnificent treasures and the mummy of the ant king. Hallmarks include ©, moon, HBC logo, ed.#, and eye.

Forget Me Not
Item No.: HGFM
Artist: MP
Size: 75x67x57
Status: Retired
Carving Date: 97
Release Date: Jan 98
Retired Date: Apr 00
Issue Size: 12,816

Lord Byron debates with Bergson the blue bug at the Forget Me Not Academy. Hallmarks include ©, heart, HBC logo, ed.#, and M.

Gardenia
Item No.: HGGA
Artist: MP
Size: 77x63x60
Status: Retired
Carving Date: 97
Release Date: Jan 98
Retired Date: Sep 99
Issue Size: 11,538

Lord Byron is taught the fine and dangerous art of fly-fishing by Roger the wormer in the Gardenia Straights. Hallmarks include ©, heart, HBC logo, ed.#, and M.

Gill
Item No.: HG3GI
Artist: MB
Size: 92x65x58
Status: Open
Carving Date: 98
Release Date: Jan 99

On the Rock of Gibraltar, Byron bids adieu to his friends and fans, and smiles for the shutterbug. He climbs aboard Gill, the Deep Sea Charter and sets sail to lands unknown. Hallmarks include ©, star, HBC logo, ed.#, M, and eye.

Harmony Kingdom Box Details

Grapes
Item No.: HG4GR
Artist: MB
Size: 97x80x44
Status: Open
Carving Date: 99
Release Date: Jan 00

From Egypt Lord Byron travels up the Mediterranean coast to Israel to worship at the wailing wall of Grapes. Byron becomes master of The Cabala. Hallmarks include ©, moon, HBC logo, ed.#, and eye.

Hibiscus
Item No.: HG5HI
Artist: SD
Size: 63x63x38
Status: Open
Carving Date: 00
Release Date: Dec 00

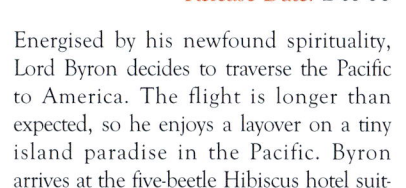

Energised by his newfound spirituality, Lord Byron decides to traverse the Pacific to America. The flight is longer than expected, so he enjoys a layover on a tiny island paradise in the Pacific. Byron arrives at the five-beetle Hibiscus hotel suitably decked out in native grass skirt and sunglasses, ready to relax on the beach and drink umbrella-festooned cocktails. After just a few days, he is ready to continue his adventures. Hallmarks include ©, double diamond, HBC logo, ed.#, and S.

Honeymoon Freesia
Item No.: HG6FR
Artist: SD
Size: 51x44x38
Status: Open
Carving Date: 01
Release Date: Oct 01

A romantic honeymoon follows the raucous wedding festivities. The quaint Freesia Hotel is the perfect setting for Byron and Annabella to begin their new life together. Lord Byron takes time to work on his memoirs, while Annabella composes poetry. Hallmarks include ©, smiley face, HBC logo, ed.#, and S.

Hops
Item No.: HG3HO
Artist: MB
Size: 61x63x81
Status: Open
Carving Date: 98
Release Date: Jan 99

What better place for apres-skiing than a German lodge? Lord Byron listens to patriotic songs in the Hops Bier Garten as Frauline Emmet serves him a frothy mug. Hallmarks include ©, star, HBC logo, ed.#, M, and eye.

Hot Pepper
Item No.: HG3HP
Artist: MB
Size: 83x80x83
Status: Retired
Carving Date: 98
Release Date: Jan 99
Retired Date: Nov 01
Issue Size: 11,765

After the Games, the Italian team invites Byron to their Hot Pepper Hideaway in Palermo. Failing to pay tribute to Caesar the local capo, Byron narrowly escapes with his spots intact. Hallmarks include ©, star, HBC logo, ed. #, M, and eye.

Hyacinth
Item No.: HGHY2
Artist: MP
Size: 62x55x67
Status: Retired
Carving Date: 96
Release Date: Jan 97
Retired Date: Sep 99
Issue Size: 16,335

Lord Byron is a member of the Hyacinth Gym and exercises daily. He claims to be able to bench press one hundred mustard seeds! 4,436 pieces were made in England. Hallmarks include ©, diamond, HBC logo, ed.#, and M.

Hydrangea
Item No.: HGHY
Artist: MP
Size: 78x59x47
Status: Retired
Carving Date: 96
Release Date: Jan 97
Retired Date: Sep 99
Issue Size: 14,451

Lord Byron is the proprietor of the Hydrangea Factory, where he makes miniature flower boxes. 4,156 pieces were made in England. Hallmarks include ©, diamond, HBC logo, ed.#, and M.

Iris
Item No.: HGIR
Artist: MP
Size: 58x46x79
Status: Open
Carving Date: 97
Release Date: Jan 98

Lord Byron jams with Cricket Charlie in the Iris Pub. Hallmarks include ©, heart, HBC logo, ed.#, and M.

Iris II
Item No.: HG5IR
Artist: SD
Size: 44x38x57
Status: Open
Carving Date: 00
Release Date: Dec 00

Travelling northward, Lord Byron stops over in the Mid-Atlantic states to visit some important historical landmarks. At the Iris memorial he throws down a blanket and abandons himself to the joys of a picnic feast, complete with delicious, enormous chocolate cupcakes. Hallmarks include ©, double diamond, HBC logo, ed.#, and M.

Lemon
Item No.: HG4LE
Artist: MB
Size: 71x56x74
Status: Open
Carving Date: 99
Release Date: Jan 00

Lord Byron is awakened from deep sleep by exotic sounds and realises that he's arrived at the Lemon souk in Morocco. Here he plays a cunning match of Parcheesi with a rug merchant. Lord Byron wins the game and the admiration of the locals. Hallmarks include ©, moon, HBC logo, ed.#, and eye.

Lily
Item No.: HG5LI
Artist: MP
Size: 63x63x51
Status: Open
Carving Date: 00
Release Date: Dec 00

Feeling more grounded, he heads Southeast and buys beach gear for a coastal holiday. Byron soaks up some rays on the Lily shoreline while he reads a book about fishing, friendship and the meaning of life by favourite author, Richard Brautigant. Even his feet get tanned! Hallmarks include ©, double diamond, HBC logo, ed.#, and M.

Lotus
Item No.: HG4LO
Artist: MB
Size: 94x86x63
Status: Open
Carving Date: 99
Release Date: Dec 00

Byron's pilgrimage still incomplete, he makes the 2000-mile journey up the Himalayas to meet the Daflea Lama inside the Lotus hideaway. Lord Byron becomes a tantric master and stows away inside a carton of cookies destined for a Japanese teahouse. Hallmarks include ©, moon, HBC logo, ed.#, and eye.

Marigold
Item No.: HG3MA
Artist: MB
Size: 72x74x75
Status: Open
Carving Date: 98
Release Date: Jan 99

Lord Byron plans a Venetian rendezvous with Legs, and the two talk of love, poetry, and the meaning of life in the grand Marigold Canal. Hallmarks include ©, star, HBC logo, ed.#, M, and eye.

Marsh Marigold
Item No.: HGMM
Artist: MP
Size: 58x62x67
Status: Retired
Carving Date: 96
Release Date: Jan 97
Retired Date: Sep 99
Issue Size: 14,315

Lord Byron whizzes around the Marsh Marigold Wall of Doom on his motorcycle. 3,661 pieces were made in England. Hallmarks include ©, diamond, HBC logo, ed.#, and M.

Miss Spider In Love
Item No.: HGMS
Artist: MB
Size: 95x63x102
Status: Open
Carving Date: 99
Release Date: Dec 00

Miss Spider and her suitor-turned-husband Holley snuggle on a loveseat in this romantic Box Figurine, based upon David Kirk's best selling children's book Miss Spider's Wedding. With its heartfelt inscription, "Of all the spiders in the world he chose to be with me," this sweet and unique sculpture is the perfect gift for that someone whom you fancy and for fans of Miss Spider. On the interior, Lord Byron hosts a tea party for some friends. Hallmarks include ©, moon, HBC logo, ed.#, eye, and C+K (for Calloway and Kirk).

Morning Glory
Item No.: HGMG
Artist: MP
Size: 66x50x82
Status: Retired
Carving Date: 96
Release Date: Jan 97
Retired Date: Apr 00
Issue Size: 14,386

Lord Byron approaches the front door of the Morning Glory but the lady of the house mistakes him for a door-to-door salesbug. 3,885 pieces were made in England. Hallmarks include ©, diamond, HBC logo, ed.#, and M.

Mother's Day Daffodil
Item No.: HG6DA
Artist: SD
Size: 57x57x38
Status: Open
Carving Date: 01
Release Date: Oct 01

Lord Byron carries a gift for his wife's first Mother's Day. Byron is happy to be settled and stable, but he knows that raising a family is bound to be his biggest adventure yet! Hallmarks include ©, smiley face, HBC logo, ed.#, and S.

New Baby Sweet Pea
Item No.: HG6SP
Artist: SD
Size: 57x44x44
Status: Open
Carving Date: 01
Release Date: Oct 01

After much anticipation and preparation, Lord Byron's first baby is born. Annabella proudly brings her child home from the Sweet Pea Hospital. Byron is in awe at the new little bug and the miracle and mystery of life. Hallmarks include ©, smiley face, HBC logo, ed.#, and S.

Orange
Item No.: HG3OR
Artist: MB
Size: 90x78x70
Status: Open
Carving Date: 98
Release Date: Jan 99

Lord Byron travels to Spain's Orange Arena where he courageously challenges and stunningly defeats Mighty Toro the beetle. Hallmarks include ©, star, HBC logo, ed.#, M, and eye.

Harmony Kingdom Box Details

Peace Lily
Item No.: HGPL
Artist: MP
Size: 53x47x72
Status: Open
Carving Date: 96
Release Date: Jan 97

A romantic by nature, Lord Byron is also a grand musician. From his music room in the Peace Lily, one can hear the sweet sorrowful sound of his pipe organ bellowing throughout Harmony Garden. 4,505 pieces were made in England. Hallmarks include ©, diamond, HBC logo, ed.#, and M.

Peony
Item No.: HGPE
Artist: MP
Size: 70x67x77
Status: Open
Carving Date: 97
Release Date: Jan 98

Queen Bee invites Lord Byron to sit for high tea in the Peony Palace where he is beeknighted. Hallmarks include ©, heart, HBC logo, ed.#, and M.

Pomegranate
Item No.: HG3PO
Artist: MB
Size: 92x80x66
Status: Open
Carving Date: 98
Release Date: Jan 99

In a stuporous state, Lord Byron remembers the Greek travel poster at the Double Pink Rose Roadside Cafe. Suddenly, he takes flight to the Pomegranate Hills of Athens where he is asked to carry the Olympic torch for all bugdom. Hallmarks include ©, star, HBC logo, ed.#, M, and eye.

Poppy
Item No.: HG4PO
Artist: MB
Size: 72x72x81
Status: Retired
Carving Date: 99
Release Date: Jan 00
Retired Date: Nov 01
Issue Size: 7629

Brimming with spirituality, Lord Byron catches a scarobvan to the Poppy mosque in Istanbul. Byron approaches TarrantAllah by reciting the sacred text of the Koran. Hallmarks include ©, moon, HBC logo, ed.#, and eye.

Rhododendron
Item No.: HGRH
Artist: MP
Size: 58x56x74
Status: Retired
Carving Date: 96
Release Date: Jan 97
Retired Date: Oct 99
Issue Size: 14,813

Lord Byron golfs at the Rhododendron Country Club. 4,034 pieces were made in England. Hallmarks include ©, diamond, HBC logo, ed.#, and M.

Rose
Item No.: HG5RO
Artist: MP
Size: 63x63x51
Status: Retired
Carving Date: 00
Release Date: Dec 00
Retired Date: Jun 02
Issue Size: 5397

Entering America through a bustling Northwestern port, Lord Byron stops off at the corporate headquarters of Micro Rose. Here he is given a personal tour by Chairman Pill Bug and the two spend the evening surfing the net. As dawn breaks, Byron sends a quick e-mail to Bumbles. Hallmarks include ©, double diamond, HBC logo, ed.#, and S.

Rose Bud
Item No.: HGRB
Artist: MB
Size: 68x66x64
Status: Open
Carving Date: 97
Release Date: Jan 98

Legs, the lovely caterpillar, woos Lord Byron back to her Rose Bud Abode. Hallmarks include ©, heart, HBC logo, ed.#, and M.

Snapdragon
Item No.: HGSN
Artist: MP
Size: 65x60x77
Status: Retired
Carving Date: 97
Release Date: Jan 98
Retired Date: Apr 00
Issue Size: 13,200

Summoning all his courage, Lord Byron leaps from the Snapdragon Cliffs into the tempestuous seas below. Hallmarks include ©, heart, HBC logo, ed.#, and M.

Harmony Kingdom Box Details

Snow Drop
Item No.: HGSD
Artist: MP
Size: 49x43x68
Status: Retired
Carving Date: 96
Release Date: Jan 97
Retired Date: Apr 99
Issue Size: 12,361

Although Lord Byron lives an active life, something is missing – a ladybug! On breezy spring mornings he sometimes picks up a hint of fragrant perfume and begins his flower-to-flower search. Is she in the Snow Drop? Alas, no one is inside. 3,845 pieces were made in England. Hallmarks include ©, diamond, HBC logo, ed.#, and M.

Sunflower
Item No.: HGSU
Artist: MP
Size: 68x65x67
Status: Retired
Carving Date: 97
Release Date: Jan 98
Retired Date: Apr 02
Issue Size: 16,543

Transformed into a butterfly, Legs tearfully sees Lord Byron off at the Sunflower Station. Hallmarks include ©, heart, HBC logo, ed.#, and M.

Sunflower II
Item No.: HG3SU
Artist: MB
Size: 75x61x72
Status: Retired
Carving Date: 98
Release Date: Jan 99
Retired Date: Feb 02
Issue Size: 12,701

Infused with artistic yearnings, Lord Byron slips away to the Sunflower Studio in the South of France where he unwittingly paints future masterpieces. Hallmarks include ©, star, HBC logo, ed.#, M, and eye.

Sunflower III
Item No.: HG5SU
Artist: SD
Size: 57x57x38
Status: Open
Carving Date: 00
Release Date: Dec 00

A little tired of the hustle and bustle, Lord Byron retreats to a Midwestern Sunflower farm. Working the land, tilling the soil, he gets back in touch with the earth's rhythms and simple values of hard work and dedication. Hallmarks include ©, double diamond, HBC logo, ed.#, and S.

Tulip
Item #: HG3TU
Artist: MB
Size: 72x70x82
Status: Retired
Carving Date: 98
Release Date: Jan 99
Retired Date: Feb 02
Issue Size: 14,581

In The Mushroom archives, Lord Byron is inspired by a book about Don Quixote. "I've never been where the windmill grows, with petals spinning when the breezes blow. To the Tulip Nether Lands I must go." There he plugs a leaky dam so a lovely windmill isn't over-watered. Hallmarks include ©, heart, HBC logo, ed.#, M, and eye.

Valentine Rose
Item No.: HG6RO
Artist: SD
Size: 63x57x44
Status: Open
Carving Date: 01
Release Date: Oct 01

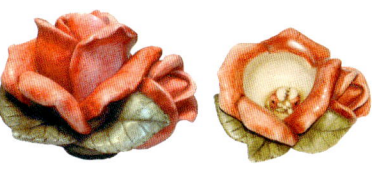

Weary and heart-sore, Lord Byron returns to his red rose cottage in the English countryside. After a period of seclusion, news of a Valentine's Day dance coaxes him out into village society. All the lady bugs vie to capture debonair LB's interest, but he dances all night with the beautiful, soulful Annabella. Hallmarks include ©, smiley face, HBC logo, ed.#, and S.

Wedding Lily
Item No.: HG6LI
Artist: SD
Size: 76x82x51
Status: Open
Carving Date: 01
Release Date: Oct 01

Byron and Annabella are nearly inseparable after the dance. Lord Byron has found his soul mate! Friends travel from near and far to attend the nuptials, which take place in the Lily Cathedral. Hallmarks include ©, smiley face, HBC logo, ed.#, and S.

CLAIR DE LUNE

Beauregard & Baby's Bed
Item No.: CLCB
Artist: JB
Size: 70x95x76
Status: Open
Carving Date: 00
Release Date: Dec 00

While Justine's prowling the Paris boulevards, Beauregard and Baby take their turn lounging on her opulent bed.

Marmalade & Mao Mao's Mirror
Item No.: CLCM
Artist: JB
Size: 89x89x89
Status: Open
Carving Date: 00
Release Date: Dec 00

Mao Mao has come upon a rococo mirror. Marmalade pokes around to share what's found in the hatboxes: a bonnet from several seasons ago and a 50 carat blue diamond on a necklace, rumored to have once been Marie Antoinette's.

Peezer, Paws & Po Po's Piano

Item No.: CLCP
Artist: JB
Size: 82x63x108
Status: Open
Carving Date: 00
Release Date: Dec 00

Lavishly carved with cherubs and scrollwork, the women of Clair de Lune cherish their antique upright piano and keep it in pristine condition despite its frequent use. During the wee morning hours, the household cats perform their own concerts.

Simba & Saffon's Settee

Item No.: CLCS
Artist: JB
Size: 108x51x76
Status: Open
Carving Date: 00
Release Date: Dec 00

When Kiki is out at one of her many art openings, Saffron and Simba take over her rooms at 20 rue Jacob.

Tartuffe & Teaser's Tub

Item No.: CLCT
Artist: JB
Size: 140x102x76
Status: Open
Carving Date: 00
Release Date: Dec 00

Think cats hate water? Wait until you see Colette's curious kitties!

Vix, Verne & Velvet's Vanity

Item No.: CLCD
Artist: JB
Size: 76x95x95
Status: Open
Carving Date: 00
Release Date: Dec 00

Each morning, Vix, Verne and Velvet watch their mistress Josephine ornament herself with the latest flapper fashions.

The trio decides to discover her beauty secrets by exploring the bedroom vanity.

Harmony Kingdom Box Details

HARMONY CIRCUS

The Arch
Item No.: HCAR
Artist: DL
Size: 145x59x172
Status: Retired
Carving Date: 96
Release Date: Apr 96
Retired Date: Jul 98
Issue Size: 734

The grand Circus Arch features Ionic columns, the Ball Brothers, two doves on its frieze, thick drapery, and two hidden compartments. Hallmarks include diamond, clock face with month 1, HBC logo, and DL.

The Audience
Item No.: HCAU
Artist: DL
Size: 109x80x112
Status: Retired
Carving Date: 95
Release Date: Apr 96
Retired Date: Jul 98
Issue Size: 1359

From top to bottom and left to right, the audience members include: Judge Lord Justice Stephen Floggam and Nippy, his pug; Lovely Joan; Chief Little Big Black White Crow's Paw; H.M. the Queen Elizabeth; the cake-eating Mary Antoinette; Noble Zephanid the Zulu; Rabid Roger the Robot; Tommy Turniphead the Musical Scarecrow; Mr. Lincoln; Frog Prince; Emperor Napoleon Boneyparts with his pet squirrel, Beezlebob; P.C. Norbert Chudleigh Wingfield; Grand Vizier, The Khazi of Puhole; and Mr. Moon. The interior portrays a drunken vicar. Hallmarks include apple, clock face with month 10, HBC logo, and DL.

Ball Brothers
Item No.: HCBA
Artist: DL
Size: 42x42x62
Status: Retired
Carving Date: 95
Release Date: Apr 96
Retired Date: Jul 98
Issue Size: 2608

As an advertising stunt to promote their flagging, cut-price, no frills, tatty holiday business, The Ball Brothers constructed a globe, sewed together three sea lion suits, and appeared outside their shop front to attract customers. So successful were they that they went on to assume their aquatic masquerade full time with The Harmony Circus. Hallmarks include apple, clock face month 9, HBC logo, and DL.

Beppo And Barney The Clowns
Item No.: HCCL
Artist: DL
Size: 52x68x66
Status: Retired
Carving Date: 95
Release Date: Apr 96
Retired Date: Jul 98
Issue Size: 2881

At an early age, Beppo and Barney inherited their father's funeral parlour business and were required for many years to adopt a serious and glum demeanor. One sunny spring afternoon the circus came to town, and the brothers put up the closed sign for good. The laughter and joy that had been repressed within them exploded in a vast display of creative mirth. Hallmarks include apple, clock face with month 6, HBC logo, and DL.

Circus Ring
Item No.: HCCR
Artist: DL
Size: 91x25x19
Status: Retired
Carving Date: 96
Release Date: Apr 96
Retired Date: Jul 98
Issue Size: 640

Philip Astley invented the circus ring in 1766 by training his horse to canter in a circle 13 meters in diameter at a constant speed, providing just the right amount of centrifugal force to achieve the most grace and balance. It was Astley's idea to intersperse physical feats with the antics of a clown, and it was one of Astley's riders who named the circus by using the Latin word for ring. The Harmony Circus Ring is made up of 12 individual components, one of which opens to reveal a hidden compartment. Hallmarks include diamond, clock face with month 2, HBC logo, and DL.

Harmony Kingdom Box Details

Clever Constantine
Item No.: HCCO
Artist: DL
Size: 50x41x71
Status: Retired
Carving Date: 96
Release Date: Apr 96
Retired Date: Jul 98
Issue Size: 1902

For a limited season each year, Otto Von Smirk and Clever Constantine take to the road with the Harmony Circus in an attempt to raise funds for their exotic explorations. Hallmarks include diamond, clock face with month 1, HBC logo, and DL.

Great Escapo
Item No.: HCES
Artist: DL
Size: 62x41x52
Status: Retired
Carving Date: 95
Release Date: Apr 96
Retired Date: Jul 98
Issue Size: 1733

Revolutionaries attempted to take the life of Prince Pangolin as they bound him with ropes and chains, forced him into a sack, and threw him into the icy waters of the Danube. What they didn't know was that the prince was none other than The Great Escapo. Hallmarks include apple, mirror image clock face with month 4, HBC logo, and DL.

Henry The Human Cannonball
Item No.: HCHE
Artist: DL
Size: 46x53x58
Status: Retired
Carving Date: 95
Release Date: Apr 96
Retired Date: Jul 98
Issue Size: 1886

Pioneering manned space flight long before the invention of rockets, the four Cannonball Brothers have appeared across the globe to great acclaim. Unfortunately, there is now but one of the Cannonball Brothers, Henry, remaining. Hallmarks include apple, clock face with month 6, HBC logo, and DL.

Il Bendi
Item No.: HCBE
Artist: DL
Size: 77x57x47
Status: Retired
Carving Date: 95
Release Date: Apr 96
Retired Date: Jul 98
Issue Size: 1468

It was whilst on a penny-pinching holiday in Milan, surveying his lunch (a tangled mass of spaghetti), that Il Bendi first had the idea for his act. Quadruple-jointed from birth, it took little effort for him to slip below his table, fold himself into a ball and roll silently out of the restaurant. Hallmarks include apple, clock face with month 6, HBC logo, and DL.

Lionel Loveless
Item No.: HCLI
Artist: DL
Size: 54x50x67
Status: Retired
Carving Date: 95
Release Date: Apr 96
Retired Date: Jul 98
Issue Size: 1983

Lionel's heart is bigger than his head as he publicly exhibits his love for all womankind by bending stout iron bars into lovelorn symbols of yearning. Hallmarks include apple, clock face with month 10, HBC logo, and DL.

Magician's Top Hat
Item No.: HCTO
Artist: DL
Size: 33x41x64
Status: Retired
Carving Date: 95
Release Date: Apr 96
Retired Date: Jul 98
Issue Size: 3154

During his youth, Il Magnifico the Magician worked on a construction site. To avoid going hungry, he took to carrying his sandwiches under his hard top hat. His greatest success of late has been the insertion of a small sperm whale into his topper. Hallmarks include apple, clock face with month 6, HBC logo, and DL.

Mr. Sediment's Superior Victuals
Item No.: HCSE
Artist: DL
Size: 64x39x64
Status: Retired
Carving Date: 96
Release Date: Apr 96
Retired Date: Jul 98
Issue Size: 1916

Mr. Sediment's Superior Victuals has been a byword for tasty quality within the pie and pastry world for more than two hundred years. He has something for everyone, from frogstoppers for the children, to a jar of gibblybit jam for Granny. Hallmarks include diamond, clock face with month 1, HBC logo, and DL.

Olde Time Carousel
Item No.: HCCA
Artist: DL
Size: 43x44x59
Status: Retired
Carving Date: 95
Release Date: Apr 96
Retired Date: Jul 98
Issue Size: 3322

His niece and nephew torment Uncle Posthumous. Watery eyed and desolate, he takes drastic measures and asks his coachman to retrieve the Olde Time Carousel from his attic. This will keep the terrible enfants occupied. Hallmarks include apple, mirror image clock face with month 4, HBC logo, and DL.

Pavareata
Item No.: HCPA
Artist: DL
Size: 52x56x62
Status: Retired
Carving Date: 95
Release Date: Apr 96
Retired Date: Jul 98
Issue Size: 3613

"I sing best when I am happy; I am happy when I have eaten well," says the industrial-sized internationally acclaimed soprano Pavareata. Hallmarks include apple, clock face with month 10, HBC logo, and DL.

Harmony Kingdom Box Details

The Ringmaster
Item No.: HCRI
Artist: DL
Size: 60x64x70
Status: Retired
Carving Date: 96
Release Date: Apr 96
Retired Date: Jul 98
Issue Size: 1649

"Roll up! Roll up! My lords, ladies and gentlemen, boys and girls, may I present, for your enjoyment and delight, the Harmony Circus!" An expectant hush falls upon the assembly. The Ringmaster feels a draught of cold air as his trousers fall about his ankles. The crowd roars its approval! Hallmarks include diamond, clock face with month 2, HBC logo, and DL.

Road Dogs
Item No.: HCRO
Artist: DL
Size: 40x60x67
Status: Retired
Carving Date: 95
Release Date: Apr 96
Retired Date: Jul 98
Issue Size: 3340

The first the Albion Brothers knew of their car's disappearance was the squeal of wheels as Turbot Terrier the Test Driver roared out of the factory gates on a lunchtime jaunt with his chums, Ratsnore and Fleascape. Down the hill and through the lanes, the reckless road dogs rambled until, swerving to avoid a house some fool had left in the middle of the road, there was a nasty crashing noise. Hallmarks include apple, mirror image clock face with month 4, HBC logo, and DL.

Suave St. John
Item No.: HCSU
Artist: DL
Size: 52x3x65
Status: Retired
Carving Date: 96
Release Date: Apr 96
Retired Date: Jul 98
Issue Size: 1744

Suave St. John has graced society with his charm and sophistication, moving with ease among the finest circles across the globe. When he was engaged for a tour with The Harmony Circus to display his ferocious physique, he found the proposition quite appealing. The nymphets of the dance and acrobatic troupe are found paying perpetual court in his caravan. Hallmarks include diamond, clock face with month 2, HBC logo, and DL.

Vlad The Impaler

Item No.: HCVL
Artist: DL
Size: 42x50x72
Status: Retired
Carving Date: 95
Release Date: Apr 96
Retired Date: Jul 98
Issue Size: 2538

Vlad, the swashbuckling, saber rattling Cossack, has for many years entertained the obscure European interior with his human-colander act. Brought to you now for the first time, after a lengthy stay in the best puncture repair clinic in Vladivostock, he attempts his greatest feat: he shall swallow the entire armoury of the Crimean Light Foot and Mouth Cavalry. Hallmarks include apple, clock face with month 9, HBC logo, and DL.

Winston The Lion Tamer

Item No.: HCWI
Artist: DL
Size: 47x74x68
Status: Retired
Carving Date: 95
Release Date: Apr 96
Retired Date: Jul 98
Issue Size: 2716

It is a little known fact that during the latter part of the Second World War, the British Premier, Winston Churchill, relaxed at moments of great personal stress by doing a spot of lion taming. Not content with thrashing the ungentlemanly cads Mussolini and Hitler, this lion of England would slip away from the Houses of Parliament to perform with the Harmony Circus. Hallmarks include apple, clock face with month 6, HBC logo, and DL.

Page 142 — *Harmony Kingdom Box Details*

TIMED EDITIONS
HOLIDAY

Beau Geste
Item No.: ANSE01
Artist: AB
Size: 44x32x86
Status: Ltd Time
Carving Date: 01
Release Date: May 01
Last Order Date: Dec 01
Issue Size: 3909

This curly-headed young angel is the guardian of pets, which is not as easy a job as one might think. A variety of animal angels assist, although some seem to be more of a hindrance than a help. Among Beau's companions are the slow but sure Tortoise; the shy, docile and calming Rabbit; and the very trusting and social Canary, who sits upon Cat's back. The Terrier is up to mischief, as is typical of the breed. Last but not least is the Mouse, who is perhaps responsible for the chewed string on Beau's harp. The Version One interior shows a heart and the Version Infinity interior shows a rose. Hallmarks include ©, smiley face, HBC logo, ed.#, and gecko.

Blue Moon
Item No.: TJSESN01
Artist: SD
Size: 76x70x102
Status: Ltd Time
Carving Date: 00
Release Date: May 01
Last Order Date: Dec 01
Issue Size: 4120

It's New Year's Day, 2001. A unique date such as 01-01-01 occurs only once in a blue moon, and something spectacular is bound to happen. Mr. Snow Man has awakened in a holly bush on the grounds at Wimberley Mills. But why is he wearing a spacesuit? Gazing around he attempts to bring his swirling, hazy thoughts and memories into focus. Just the evening before he was busy scruntinising stars through his telescope, watching to see if a millennium event would occur. Suddenly, his button eyes were blinded by a bright, flashing light. Memories of what happened afterward are vague and dim. Snow Man feels strongly, yet can't quite explain, that he was transported to another planet of peculiar beings, the Gonewilings. The aliens have even labelled his boots and stamped them S.M., so he must have told them his name. What else might he have told? The Version 1 interior features the spaceship on which he was abducted, and the Version Infinity shows the spaceships that brought him back. Hallmarks include ©, double diamond, HBC logo, ed.#, and S.

Harmony Kingdom Box Details

Bon Bon

Item No.: ANSE00B
Artist: DL
Size: 38x53x72
Status: Ltd Time
Carving Date: 99
Release Date: Jan 00
Last Order Date: Dec 00
Issue Size: 7881

A boy angel plays in his pyjamas and nightcap, resisting sleepiness and bedtime. This little drummer boy is excited and wide-awake on Christmas Eve. Inside Version 1 is a monkey, reminiscent of little boys' Christmas wishes: mechanised monkeys pounding tiny drums and bashing tin cymbals, and old-fashioned Sock Monkeys. The interior of the Infinity Version features a rattle with the gift tag "R to C." The rattle is a gift from Rose, David Lawrence's eldest daughter, to her new baby sister Catherine. Hallmarks include ©, moon, HBC logo, ed.#, and DL.

Bon Enfant

Item No.: TJ96AN
Artist: DL
Size: 80x35x41
Status: Ltd Time
Carving Date: 96
Release Date: Apr 96
Last Order Date: Dec 96
Issue Size: 8825

Bon Enfant is the 1996 holiday angel box figurine. There are three variations. Colouration on the first version of approximately 500 pieces includes an orange tunic, green wings, yellow hair, and gold applied to the tips of the wings and cuffs. The interior is empty. In the second version the tunic is green, the hair yellow, cuffs gold, and wings painted with gold, yellow, red, and green. The interior has a pillow with a heart and arrow. The third version has an uncoloured tunic, gold cuffs and wings, with pink on the lips and cheeks, with the same interior as the second version. The acorn is sometimes present at the angel's feet in the second and third versions. Hallmarks include diamond, clock face with month 2, HBC logo, and DL.

Celeste

Item No.: ANCE97
Artist: DL
Size: 52x63x95
Status: Ltd Time
Carving Date: 96
Release Date: Apr 97
Last Order Date: Dec 97
Issue Size: 15,054

Celeste, the star angel, was the 1997 holiday edition, with gold wings and gold five-pointed star. This same star was adopted as the 1998 hallmark and production stamp. With this piece David was influenced by the work of art nouveau artist Alphonse Mucha. "39" denotes that this was David's thirty-ninth piece that he carved. Hallmarks include ©, diamond, HBC logo, ed.#, DL, and 1997 in Roman numerals carved into the lid.

Chatelaine

Item No.: TJAN
Artist: DL
Size: 59x46x61
Status: Ltd Time
Carving Date: 95
Release Date: May 95
Last Order Date: Dec 95
Issue Size: 7988

Chatelaine was the first holiday edition, created for 1995. The "1" on the lid indicates that this was the first piece David carved. There is no acorn. Chatelaine may be clothed in an orange or green robe. Hallmarks include 4.95 (date carving completed) and DL.

Easy Slider

Item No.: TJSESN00
Artist: SD
Size: 51x102x102
Status: Ltd Time
Carving Date: 00
Release Date: Jun 00
Last Order Date: Dec 00
Issue Size: 7013

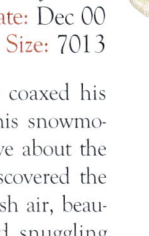

Sid the snowman has finally coaxed his girl Nancy to take a ride on his snowmobile. At first a tad apprehensive about the noisy machine, Nancy has discovered the joys of cruising in comfort: fresh air, beautiful scenery breezing by, and snuggling close to Sid. Sid quite possibly may be paying more attention to Nancy than to the road: a festive holly bush, unfortunate enough to be in the way, has been run over by the snowmobile. Within Version 1, Mad Murphy glides downhill on a makeshift sled of cardboard. Inside Version Infinity Wolfie, hatless and mittenless, curls up under his tail to keep warm. The hallmarks are located under the lid and include ©, double diamond, HBC logo, ed.#, and S.

Holy Roller

Item No.: TJSESA99
Artist: PC
Size: 80x97x58
Status: Ltd Time
Carving Date: 98
Release Date: May 99
Last Order Date: Nov 99
Issue Size: 9948

Santa has been struck on the head by an empty bottle of sherry, thrown by his wife after she discovered that he polished off its contents. It doesn't appear that he's learned his lesson as he clutches his bottle of "Old TNT." Santa's AA pin isn't doing much good, but Peter's signature mouse forgives him and snuggles up behind him. Take pity on poor Santa. He has to travel 221 million miles to visit the earth's 2 billion children at a speed of Mach 6395 and on roller-skates no less! Inside Version 1, Mad Murphy reads about these fascinating statistics. The interior of the Infinity Version portrays Santa playing with an undelivered toy, named after a famous drag racing track (Santa Pod) in England. Another secret found in both versions is a car advertisement: "For Sale MGBGT '77 18L White 1500 See Pete." Having purchased a new car, Peter thought to advertise his old car to all of his fans! Hallmarks include star, ©, HBC logo, ed.#, and Pc.

Holy Water

Item No.: TJSESA02
Artist: PC
Size: 76x55x76
Status: Ltd Time
Carving Date: 02
Release Date: May 02
Last Order Date: Dec 02
Issue Size: Not Available

After yet another busy Christmas, Santa settles into a well-deserved hot bath and the latest issue of a mind-broadening magazine, when he suddenly realizes he is no longer alone. One of the reindeer has joined him, but is soon summarily dispatched. Disgruntled at being expelled, the reindeer pulls the plug and drops it over the side. Around the bath are a pair of Santa's boxers, his toy boat and rubber duck, a loofah, and the book that every child wanted this Christmas, "Harry Potter." Santa saved himself a copy to find out what all the buzz was about. The words carved on the reindeer's hooves refer to Peter's son Sam turning one year old in February 2002. Versions One and Infinity differ in coloration only. The mouse stays dry between the book and the bathtub's clawed foot. Hallmarks include ©, peace sign, HBC logo, ed.#, and PC.

Jingle Bell Rock
Item No.: TJSESA98
Artist: PC
Size: 38x76x88
Status: Ltd Time
Carving Date: 98
Release Date: Apr 98
Last Order Date: Dec 98
Issue Size: 19,019

Santa is sound asleep in his rocking chair, with a magazine on his lap featuring the top-of-the line 1999 sleigh models. Underneath his rocker is a snoozing reindeer, assorted gifts and books with such titles as "Tyson The Wimp" (by Noel Wiggins), "Nawty Kids" and "Tax Avoidance." Peter's mouse is also asleep, amidst the books. "Nell Doggy Heaven" is inscribed behind Santa's head, a reference to the Perry's dog, who died while Peter was carving this piece. "Lord Lucan" on the gift tucked beneath Santa's rocker refers to a celebrated earl who in the 1960's allegedly murdered his children's nanny (mistaking her for his wife) and then mysteriously disappeared. Inside, wide eyed Mad Murphy gobbles up Santa's cookies. This is the first box figurine that incorporates movement into its design. Hallmarks include ©, star, HBC logo, ed.#, and Pc.

Joyeaux
Item No.: ANSE99C
Artist: DL
Size: 64x71x85
Status: Ltd Time
Carving Date: 98
Release Date: May 99
Last Order Date: Dec 99
Issue Size: 9941

Joyeaux is Noel's older sister and thus gets first bath. She sits drying off in a wicker chair, overseeing her brother's bath time antics, as two cats play cat and mouse around the chair. Snuggled tight in her towel, it will soon be time to climb the wooden hill to Bedfordshire. A mouse is tucked inside her slipper. Joyeaux's favourite doll that she has searched high and low for is hidden under the green chair in Version 1. Her brother's missing toys are found inside the natural wicker coloured chair in Version Infinity. Hallmarks include ©, star, HBC logo, ed.#, and DL.

King of the Road

Item No.: TJSESA00
Artist: PC
Size: 51x70x83
Status: Ltd Time
Carving Date: 99
Release Date: Jan 00
Last Order Date: Dec 00
Issue Size: 7280

For year 2000, Santa has adopted a speedier mode of transport. His motorcycle's license plate reads "HK4" in homage to the four Harmony Kingdom holiday Santas of years past. In order to comply with federal regulations he flies with a black box, which is found under the handlebars. The inscription "FS1E" is the name of Peter's first moped, a Yamaha FS1E, affectionately known as "Fizzy." "MG" stands for Moto Guzzi, Noel Wiggins' motorbike of choice. Mad Murphy checks all the tags on the gifts, looking for his present, but all he finds is one for "LY" - Lisa Yashon - co-owner of Harmony Kingdom. The "TY" tag stands for Thye Gn, proprietor of Cellini Fine Gifts, whom Peter met whilst in Portland, Oregon, during the spring of 1999 when he began thinking of the 2000 Santa. The Version 1 interior contains two cuddling petty teddies. Several mice have been added to the exterior and interior of Version Infinity. Hallmarks include ©, double diamond, HBC logo, ed.#, and PC.

Knackered Nick

Item No.: TJSESA01
Artist: PC
Size: 63x70x63
Status: Ltd Time
Carving Date: 01
Release Date: May 01
Last Order Date: Dec 01
Issue Size: 5281

Santa has finished his duties and has retired for a well deserved rest. His tee-shirt proudly proclaims this year's "World Tour." He also feels somewhat exhausted by what he's just read in the local paper "The Pole": the world population is growing by 78 million each year. Just think how much busier he'll be next year! "Y6B" in the headline is shorthand, similar to Y2K, and stands for "year six billion." One of Santa's reindeer is drafting a poorly spelled resignation letter after reading the same article. Another, seeing that Santa has pinned up a sock, slips a present in it. After all, someone has to deliver Santa's Christmas gifts. A leftover present, one of the ubiquitous singing fish, hangs on the footboard. Mince pies and a book on training reindeer are also in the bed. The jolly old elf has a side we haven't seen before: the barrel of a handgun pokes out from under the pillow and a pair of cuffs hang from a bedpost. The mouse peeks out from the stocking. The Version One interior contains letters to Santa and the newspaper headline reads "A. Binder Says Wasn't Me." The Version Infinity interior shows a stockpile of Christmas 2000's most popular gift, cell phones, and the newspaper headline reads "B. Clinton Says Wasn't Me." Hallmarks include ©, smiley face, HBC logo, ed.#, and PC.

La Gardienne

Item No.: ANSE98
Artist: DL
Size: 44x70x95
Status: Ltd Time
Carving Date: 98
Release Date: Apr 98
Last Order Date: Dec 98
Issue Size: 16,130

La Gardienne is the fourth holiday edition, created for 1998. This guardian angel with gilded wings and flowered headband gazes serenely at two doves that rest upon her arm. Inside is a nest with three tiny eggs. Hallmarks include ©, star, HBC logo, ed.#, and DL.

Nick Of Time

Item No.: TJSESA
Artist: PC
Size: 50x81x61
Status: Ltd Time
Carving Date: 95
Release Date: Apr 96
Last Order Date: Dec 96
Issue Size: 7804

The sleigh's runners have an A-Z book of the world to assist Santa in his work. On the back is a license plate with "NP" for North Pole and a snowball taillight. The reindeer under the sleigh is playing with a glove puppet, just as Peter did when he was a bored porcelain painter. "Evendine" and "80" refer to the local girls' school where his old girlfriend, Zoe Bain, attended in 1980. Doveridge House, Tong, is where she used to live. "Do not copy" is Peter's response to seeing illegal copies of his box figurines in South Africa. One mouse peeks out of Santa's sack and another is tucked into his right elbow. Inside are the HBC logo, a bottle of rum, and a mince pie. Hallmarks include apple, clock face with month 11, HBC logo, and Pc.

Noel

Item No.: ANSE99T
Artist: DL
Size: 53x100x66
Status: Ltd Time
Carving Date: 98
Release Date: May 99
Last Order Date: Dec 99
Issue Size: 9962

Noel is Joyeaux's little brother and thus gets second bath. While Joyeaux watches over her angelic sibling's bath time, Noel plays with his toy duck in his bubbly tub. But what lurks in the waters below? Version 1 contains a submerged rodent merrily rowing in a miniature boat inside and a green band around the bottom edge of the tub. The Infinity Version contains a sandy basin with starfish inside and no green rim outside. Hallmarks include ©, star, HBC logo, ed.#, and DL.

Harmony Kingdom Box Details

Pastille

Item No.: ANSE00G
Artist: DL
Size: 29x36x71
Status: Ltd Time
Carving Date: 99
Release Date: Jan 00
Last Order Date: Dec 00
Issue Size: 7895

A girl angel fresh from her bath snuggles in her robe on Christmas Eve. She cuddles her teddy bear close, whispering to her confidant her wishes for the next morning. The loyal dog and mug of cocoa under her chair keep her warm and cosy. The artist's signature acorn appears on her mug. On the inside of the piece, at the back, appear the numbers 15.21.9.5.99.3.55, referring to David Lawrence's new daughter, Catherine May, who was born at 3:21 May 9, 1999 and weighed 3.55 kg. In the interior of version 1 is the doll the angel dreams of as a gift. Version Infinity has a set of alphabet blocks inside. Hallmarks include ©, moon, HBC logo, ed.#, and DL.

Snowdonia Fields

Item No.: TJSESN99
Artist: MP
Size: 82x82x113
Status: Ltd Time
Carving Date: 99
Release Date: Sep 99
Last Order Date: Dec 00
Issue Size: 8598

This box figurine features a snowman, snow woman and curious little boy enjoying a wintry day. You may recall that Martin Perry was a shepherd in the Snowdonia Mountains of Wales. This box figurine is reminiscent of the wind-swept beauty of this mountainous region. In Version 1, Wolfie's face appears inside while his posterior peeks out of the box. The interior of Version Infinity has a sled named Rosebud, a reference to Citizen Kane. Hallmarks include ©, moon, HBC logo, ed.#, and M.

Something's Gotta Give

Item No.: TJSESA97
Artist: PC
Size: 51x50x82
Status: Ltd Time
Carving Date: 97
Release Date: Apr 97
Last Order Date: Dec 97
Issue Size: 16,368

Santa is stuck in the chimney on this box figurine. On the underside of the lid there is a heart with an arrow. The teddy bear wears a tag "JJ", a former girlfriend of Peter's, who received the bear as a gift. The mouse is tucked in under a reindeer near the chimney's corner. The interior on the first 500 pieces contained stockings and earrings, along with the inscription "Not Made in Korea." A fireplace was later added to the interior and the inscription removed. Hallmarks include ©, heart, HBC logo, ed.#, Pc, and MCMXCVII.

Harmony Kingdom Box Details

TIMED EDITIONS
MILLENNIUM

Noah's Quark
Item No.: TJSEMM1
Artist: MR
Size: 102x178x133
Status: Ltd Time
Carving Date: 00
Release Date: Jun 00
Last Order Date: Dec 01
Issue Size: 4478

Blasting into the new millennium at warp speed, "Noah's Quark" boldly goes where no Box Figurine has gone before. This timed edition from the Millennium Series encapsulates what may be in store for the next 1000 years and comments on the past 1000. Within the interior, a hi-tech couple pilots the ship. They represent the 21st century ideal - casual yet ambitious - with hi-tech clothes and hi-tech bodies. Yet right behind them, animal mayhem conquers man and his machines. A robot, basing its judgement on its database, reaches the conclusion that the dog's tail should be bobbed. Tubs the Turtle promptly pulls the robot's plug. In cahoots with Tubs, a hare logs onto the Internet to find a site on dismantling artificial intelligence. Despite efforts to control and manipulate the cosmos, man's best-laid plans can still be undone by nature. Below deck the couple's genetically engineered supplies are stored. Tiny, helpless cattle and gigantic beets and carrots show the grotesque result of genetic manipulation. A disenfranchised lion reigns over potted plants and an artificial jungle. The fish is preserved as an exotic example of a forgotten species from a forgotten environment. A distraught pig looks over the scene. Some things never change, however. A cat still stalks its prey with usual disdain for human activities and Lord Byron still needs to sweep up. Down in the very bowels of the ship is an angel, now relegated below decks, no longer respected or needed now that humankind thinks itself the Creator. The fallen angel has taken up gambling with a wolf in sheep's clothing. But on the outside of the ship is a glimmer of hope. Noah himself sits on a ledge of the spacecraft. He's seen it all before and knows nature's cycles will begin and end - a symbol of human endurance through the ages. Hallmarks include ©, double diamond, HBC logo, ed.#, and M.

Y2HK

Item No.: TJSEY2K
Artist: MR
Size: 127x90x115
Status: Ltd Time
Carving Date: 98
Release Date: Jan 99
Last Order Date: Dec 99
Issue Size: 15,594

On The Bridge: Two burley seamen argue about who is steering the boat, both not realising that the propellers are not actually in the water. Behind them, a bird holds a blank map that the puzzled navigator attempts to decipher. Is the bird's nest atop the funnel to stop pollution? A mink has escaped from a fur farm, and an extinct dodo gazes wistfully at her egg. A poetic vulture (Have a Heart) confers with a wolf in sheep's clothing (Mutton Chops).

On the Bow: The cannon points into the future. The military man in blue and his canine companion keep lookout to prevent warfare.

On the Stern: The voluptuous woman serenely steers the boat using a low-tech tiller. She is our Earth mother, representing fertility and protection. Nonetheless, the pig thinks about jumping ship as he's heard that the burley seamen love BLT's.

On the Mid-Ship: A zebra and lion dine together peacefully. Will it last? Sitting on the steps is "The Garden Prince," who has abdicated as host of The Garden Party to come along for the Millennium ride. Mad Murphy, always involved in intrigue and adventure, joins the crew, while Rocky plays sax for Santa, who belts out a hearty "Ho Ho Ho." The commotion doesn't seem to affect the amorous lovebirds that are nestled beak to beak.

Inside The Cabin: Two angels are gambling with cards, a reference to Albert Einstein's famous quotation, "God does not play dice." While they bet on the outcome of the year 2000, they guard the silver seed, nature's genetic future. Behind them, a man scrubs a pig in the hope that anachronistic dogma will disappear from the world's religions and leave the earth a place of peace.

Inside The Hull: Consumption is the theme of the hull. Lord Byron quietly creates the eco-system in the stern of the ship. It is clear that the large gold fish will not fit through the porthole. On the port side, the seal represents nature biting back. The dinosaur gazes lovingly at its new parent, the scientist. The bug near the dinosaur eggshell is, of course, the Millennium Bug. Below the bug, an ape receives instructions from top deck. He is happy and helpful, unlike the larger ape opposite him (man's dual nature). Tubs the Turtle makes a hasty exit.

Inside The Latrine: Don't open the door to the latrine. You might shock Dolly, the first genetically cloned animal who is enjoying a quiet moment with *The Financial Times*.

Hallmarks include ©, star, HBC logo, ed.#, and M.

TIMED EDITIONS
Romance Annual

Love & Peace

Item No.: TJSER00
Artist: SD
Size: 39x107x122
Status: Ltd Time
Carving Date: 00
Release Date: Jun 00
Last Order Date: Jun 21, 01
Issue Size: 7006

A pair of gentle doves, symbols of purity and spiritual love, gaze into each other's eyes and coo softly. Other symbols of love surround them. The birdbath is shaped like a heart, and tiny pink hearts float in the water. Along the side of the basin grows a wild red rose bush. The pansies reference Shakespeare's Ophelia, who drowned for love of Hamlet: "Pansies, that's for thoughts." Within Version 1, the doves' clutch of eggs is snug in their nest. The eggs are transformed into hearts within Version Infinity. Hallmarks include ©, double diamond, HBC logo, ed.#, and S.

Love Nest

No.: TJSER98
Artist: DL
Size: 66x66x85
Status: Ltd Time
Carving Date: 98
Release Date: Nov 98
Last Order Date: Jun 21, 99
Issue Size: 11,975

The second Romance Annual features two lovebirds entwined, beak to beak, upon a nest woven with ribbons and flowers. Special messages for lovers are carved throughout this box figurine. Hallmarks include ©, star, HBC logo, ed.#, and DL.

Pillow Talk
Item No.: TJSER97
Artist: DL
Size: 123x70x83
Status: Ltd Time
Carving Date: 97
Release Date: Nov 97
Last Order Date: Jun 21, 98
Issue Size: 13,488

David says that the inspiration for this first Romance Annual was the enduring nature of love, as swans pair for life. The plumage on each swan lifts up to reveal two hidden compartments, one containing a rose in memory of Princess Diana, and the other containing a pillow that may be removed to reveal a red heart. David's acorn is between the leaves on the base. The first 3,660 have swans with red beaks and blue pillows, the next 404 have yellow beaks and blue pillows, and the rest of the edition has yellow beaks and light green pillows. Hallmarks include ©, heart, HBC logo, ed.#, and DL.

Rhapsody In Blue
Item No.: TJSER02
Artist: PC
Size: 50x61x76
Status: Timed
Carving Date: 01
Release Date: Oct 01
Last Order Date: Jun 21, 03
Issue Size: Not Available

Ballroom dancing is surely one of the most unusual hobbies an octopus could possibly have, but this amorous pair are giving it a go. The octopus reading the "Tango Made Easy" manual has "SAM" written in the pattern on his head, a reference to Peter Calvesbert's first-born son Samuel. The other, more romantic partner grips a rose in its beak. On the Version One interior is one of the octopus's sacks of "best ink," which is used for defence. Inside the Infinity Version is an eight-legged cat. The artist's signature mouse peers out from inside one of the sixteen coiled tentacles on the box. Hallmarks include ©, smiley face, HBC logo, ed.#, and PC.

Sea of Love
Item No.: TJSER01
Artist: MB
Size: 86x51x108
Status: Ltd Time
Carving Date: 01
Release Date: May 01
Last Order Date: Jun 21, 02
Issue Size: 4109

A pair of colourful puffins preen each other tenderly on this timed edition Romance Annual. They stand on a log, which is inscribed at both ends with words of love: "Forever Together" and "If you'll be mine, two hearts entwine." Grafitti covers the log. "Terry and Marie forever" refers to Master Carver Monique Baldwin's mother and father and "R & J be mine" refers to Ray and James, Monique's grandparents. 18.6.75 is Monique's birthday and No. 3 is her lucky number. "RB?" represents her brother, who seems to have a different girlfriend every week, and "Marry me 2005" is for a friend who vows to be married by that year. "AP & FP" inscribed in a heart refers to Alfie and Flo Perry, the resident pooches at Wimberley Mills, who love each other in a brother/sister sort of way. The interior of the Version One conceals the keys to two hearts. Version Infinity shows two rings on a pillow on the inside. Hallmarks include ©, smiley face, HBC logo, ed.#, and eye.

Tender is the Night
Item No.: TJSER99
Artist: MP
Size: 91x76x123
Status: Ltd Time
Carving Date: 99
Release Date: Sep 99
Last Order Date: Jun 21, 00
Issue Size: 9561

The third Romance Annual attests to the cerebral nature of love. A wise owl carries in his beak a red rose for his mate who gazes at him wistfully. Both of their faces have a blush of pink, symbolizing their passion. The interior of Version 1 portrays an enlightened owl in Zen meditation. The Infinity Version has a bouquet of roses. Hallmarks include ©, moon, HBC logo, ed.#, and M.

LIMITED EDITIONS
ANIMALS

Beer Nuts

Item No.: TJLECAN2
Artist: MB
Size: 57x82x114
Status: Ltd Ed
Carving Date: 01
Release Date: Apr 01
Last Ship Date: Mar 02
Issue Size: 2001

The Canadian adventures of Mad Murphy and Moose continue! National symbols of Canada abound on this Box Figurine. Two beavers, Canada's national animal, appear on the piece, one chewing on Moose's skis, the other hitching a free ride on his back. Moose's blanket is emblazoned with a maple leaf and the hat on his head looks suspiciously like standard issue for the RCMP (Royal Canadian Murphy/Moose Police). The area is littered with beer bottles and cans. A few are even stuck in Moose's antlers and a keg is under his belly. Moose has strapped a second keg around his neck, just in case he gets lost or stranded as he evades the RMCP. For ammunition the desperadoes have stockpiled snowballs for those sudden battles with Sgt. Jacques Strappe. The ten snowballs represent Canada's ten provinces. Inside the box is Mad Murphy, who has again foiled the RCMP's attempts to find and capture him. Carvings include "Rich Little," a famous Canadian impersonator; "DB McKenzie" for two well-known brothers; "Sir John EH" for Sir John A. McDonald, Canada's first Prime Minister, and a play on the Canadian expression "eh"; and "BA ❤ BA" stands for "Bryan Amyot loves Brenda Amyot"(his wife). The 2001st piece in the edition is a special color variation. Hallmarks include ©, smiley face, HBC logo, and eye.

Confined Claws

Item No.: TJCICA3
Artist: MB
Size: 76x61x57
Status: Ltd Ed
Carving Date: 00
Release Date: Apr 01
Last Ship Date: Not Available
Issue Size: 1750

A litter of seven kittens climb on a Chesterfield armchair. Look hard to find the hungry little kitty searching for food. The interior features four tiny mice. This limited edition of signed and numbered pieces was available only through Collect it! magazine. Hallmarks include ©, double diamond, HBC logo, and eye.

Creature Comforts

Item No.: TJHICA
Artist: MP
Size: 64x64x76
Status: Ltd Ed
Carving Date: 99
Release Date: Jul 99
Last Ship Date: Aug 99
Issue Size: 1000

Two dogs sit serenely upon an overstuffed chair, while a sly cat attempts to steal away with their plate of morsels. The interior features one of the cats from "Disorderly Eating" overindulging himself. Available to stockists in the U.K. only, this piece is signed and numbered. Hallmarks include ©, moon, HBC logo, and M.

Danger's Darlings

Item No.: TJHIDO2
Artist: MR & SD
Size: 72x64x72
Status: Ltd Ed
Carving Date: 00
Release Date: May 00
Last Ship Date: Jul 00
Issue Size: 1500

This limited edition box figurine was made available in the UK only. Hallmarks include ©, double diamond, HBC logo, and S.

Disorderly Eating

Item No.: TJCICA
Artist: MP
Size: 76x70x76
Status: Ltd Ed
Carving Date: 99
Release Date: Jul 99
Last Ship Date: Jul 99
Issue Size: 1000

Two cats overindulge themselves as they slouch in an overstuffed chair. The interior features a mouse nibbling on Swiss cheese. This signed and numbered piece was a *Collect it!* exclusive, featured in the August 1999 issue of this British collectible magazine. It was sold directly to *Collect it!* readers. "Creature Comforts" is its companion piece. Hallmarks include ©, moon, HBC logo, and M.

Fishy Business

Item No.: TJCICA2
Artist: MR & AR
Size: 72x68x90
Status: Ltd Ed
Carving Date: 00
Release Date: May 00
Last Ship Date: Jul 00
Issue Size: 1500

This pair of frisky felines was available only through Collect it! magazine.

Hallmarks include ©, moon, HBC logo, and M.

Killing Time

Item No.: TJLEWH
Artist: DL
Size: 144x94x94
Status: Ltd Ed
Carving Date: 96
Release Date: Apr 97
Last Ship Date: Feb 98
Issue Size: 3600

This box figurine features orca whales. Inside there is a seashell which screws off to reveal a pearl, inscribed with the words, "Property of King Neptune." Also inside is a rodent in scuba gear. The colour of the sand varies from black, reminiscent of the mud flats of Weston-Super-Mare near Chalford (first 350), to pale yellow (next 687), then back to black. Each piece is hand-numbered and bears the artist's monogram. Hallmarks include ©, diamond, clock with month 11, and DL.

Pieces Of Eight

Item No.: TJLEPA
Artist: DL
Size: 85x73x109
Status: Ltd Ed
Carving Date: 97
Release Date: Jan 98
Last Ship Date: May 98
Issue Size: 5000

This box figurine portrays colourful parrots. The interior features a screw-off pirate's hat, and the pirate's bounty, coins. The acorn is tucked underneath a parrot's tail. Three colour variations were created: brown, red, and blue. There were approximately 2,500 each of the red and blue versions and very few brown. Some artist proofs were released as well. Each piece is hand-numbered and bears the artist's monogram. Hallmarks include ©, heart, HBC logo, ed.#, and DL.

Pregnant Paws

Item No.: TJHID03
Artist: MB
Size: 83x63x71
Status: Ltd Ed
Carving Date: 00
Release Date: Apr 01
Last Ship Date: Not Available
Issue Size: 1750

Seven puppies, rescued from an animal shelter, sit in comfortable security on a Chesterfield armchair. This piece is signed and numbered. Hallmarks include ©, double diamond, HBC logo, and eye.

Rover's Wreck

Item No.: TJHIDWO
Artist: AB
Size: 56x60x56
Status: Ltd Ed
Carving Date: 00
Release Date: Oct 00
Last Ship Date: Jan 01
Issue Size: 1750

Rover's Wreck is Sheba's partner in the treasure hunt. Rover was not as lucky as Sheba, who found a sack of emeralds. Hallmarks include ©, double diamond, HBC logo, and gecko.

Sharazade

Item No.: TJDLLECA
Artist: DL
Size: 83x41x53
Status: Ltd Ed
Carving Date: 02
Release Date: May 02
Last Ship Date: Not Available
Issue Size: 3600

Sharazade nestles down inside one of Wizard Fezziwig's magic slippers. She joined him shortly before his ascendancy to the position of Court Magician, although, it is true, his powers have seen better days. In short, he has become somewhat absent-minded. This morning has been a long and frustrating one, as Fezziwig came down the worn stone steps of the workshop to light the furnace and give the cauldron a wake-up stir, and then went on to curse as he wandered the icy flagstones searching for his other magical slipper. "Have you seen it Sharazade? No, of course not..." And so on, muttering to himself. Sharazade purrs gently to herself, sitting in plain view near the alchemy table. On the interior, an old lamp is marked with a tag indicating that it works as good as new. Hallmarks include ©, smiley face, HBC logo, and DL.

Sheba's Ship

Item No.: TJTICCA
Artist: AB
Size: 56x58x60
Status: Ltd Ed
Carving Date: 00
Release Date: Oct 00
Last Ship Date: Jan 01
Issue Size: 1750

Decked out in a vintage diving suit, Sheba the cat is hauled from the seabed on a casket full of treasure but seems to have little interest in anything other than the fish in hand! 'Nuestra Senora de Atocha' carved on the chest is a reference to the largest and richest treasure to be found in history. Hallmarks include ©, double diamond, HBC logo, and gecko.

True North

Item No.: TJLECAN
Artist: AR
Size: 57x57x76
Status: Ltd Ed
Carving Date: 99
Release Date: Jan 00
Last Ship Date: Aug 00
Issue Size: 2000

This limited edition pays tribute to furry and famous Canadians. In addition to the varied array of wildlife depicted on the box figurine's exterior, a selection of well-known Canadians are referenced as well. Did you know that musicians Neil Young, Leonard Cohen, and Joni Mitchell; comedians Dan Ackroyd, Jim Carrey, Phil Hartman, and Leslie Neilson; TV personalities Pamela Anderson, Alex Trebek, and William Shatner; and directors/authors James Cameron, William Gibson, and Marshall McLuhan were all born in Canada? Other details include the inscription A + G on the tree trunk, referring to master carver Ann Richmond and her significant other/business partner Gary. A happy-go-lucky Murphy hides in the interior. Hallmarks inlcude ©, moon, HBC logo, and M.

Unbearables

Item No.: TJLEBE
Artist: PC
Size: 176x129x150
Status: Ltd Ed
Carving Date: 94
Release Date: Jan 95
Last Ship Date: Feb 99
Issue Size: 2500

Unbearables, first in the series of signed and numbered multi-compartment limited edition box figurines, depicts a picnic overrun by eight very hungry and curious bears. The group of six humans and their three dogs have learned a valuable lesson regarding Nature's powerful forces. A shattered television has fallen victim to one of the hairy characters. The mouse is hiding beneath a bear's bottom, next to the dog on top of the picnic table. Carved into the tabletop is a message about Anne Archer, one of Peter's favourite actresses. The wine bottles bear the names "Noel" and "Lisa". Also carved into the table is "Broadway GG", which is a widely used golf club. "Hogs" is carved into an overturned chair, referring to Peter's affection for Harley Davidson motorcycles. The first 772 boxes had empty interiors. The remaining pieces had a mini "Unbearables" inside. Each piece is hand-numbered, signed by the artist and accompanied by a certificate of authenticity. Interior hallmarks include © and HBC logo.

Zamboni

Item No.: TJLECAN3
Artist: MB
Size: 69x51x64
Status: Ltd Ed
Carving Date: 02
Release Date: Apr 02
Last Ship Date: Jul 02
Issue Size: 1000

"Zamboni" is a sad little elephant, perhaps because he wants to drive the zamboni, the ice-cleaning machine at the hockey arena. On the interior of the box, a mouse kicks back and relaxes with his feet propped up on a peanut. Hallmarks include ©, moon, HBC logo, and eye.

LIMITED EDITIONS
BIBLICAL SERIES

Babbling Heights

Item No.: TJLETO
Artist: MR
Size: 127x154x178
Status: Ltd Ed
Carving Date: 01
Release Date: Feb 02
Last Ship Date: Aug 02
Issue Size: 750

This spectacular limited edition box figurine is the fourth in Harmony Kingdom's Biblical Series. Depicted is the construction of the Tower of Babel. According to Genesis, men intended to build the tower to reach as high as heaven. Such an enterprising project was possible because everyone spoke the same language. But God foils the plan, "confounds their speech" by creating different languages and scatters the people. The three figures in the foreground may have just been struck by the drastic change: one can't believe his ears, another covers his mouth in amazement and a third screams into his cell phone in a futile attempt to be understood. In another modern touch, three monkeys perched on the tower see no, hear no and speak no evil. The interior of the first level of the tower reveals a spiral ramp leading up past the sun and the moon. Inside the second level, a man on a ladder comes face to face with an angel guarding the entrance to heaven. Perhaps it is this close encounter with divinity that has sparked imaginations for centuries? Hallmarks include ©, smiley face, HBC logo, and an R carved under the smiley.

Harmony Kingdom Box Details

Noah's Lark
Item No.: TJLENO
Artist: PC
Size: 170x106x143
Status: Ltd Ed
Carving Date: 95
Release Date: Sep 95
Last Ship Date: Oct 98
Issue Size: 5000

Noah's Lark is second in the series of signed and numbered multi-compartment limited edition box figurines. This four compartment box is home to 103 creatures, including Noah, who reclines on the roof of his arc. Two mice hide near Noah, one in his beard, and the other underneath him. Nearby Noah is a lone frog in search of its mate who has, unfortunately, become a tasty morsel for the snake. The beaver snacks upon the ark. On the door of the cabin is a sign bearing the message "DALY WINS" referring to the winner of the Scottish Open in 1995. The lifeboat says "GRIFFIN" referring to Griffin Mill, the former home of HK. "A.L.F." (The Animal Liberation Front) is carved into the hull beneath the cow. Inscribed in the wake at the bow of the ship is "TA PAUL." "Ta" is the English equivalent of a quick thank-you, and Paul first suggested the idea of creating a Noah's Ark box. In the wake is a boat inscribed with "GREEN" on one half and "EACE" on the other, an ironic, nautical accident. Also floating in the water is a set of "JAWS," a rabbit, a penguin, and a mermaid, who holds the title plaque for this box. Inside the box is Noah's family, passing the time with a game of Monopoly™. Peter's signature changed in August 1997, from "PW Calvesbert" to "P. Calvesbert." Each piece is hand-numbered, signed by the artist and accompanied by a certificate of authenticity. Hallmarks include HBC logo.

Original Kin
Item No.: TJLEGA
Artist: PC
Size: 130x128x137
Status: Ltd Ed
Carving Date: 97
Release Date: Jun 97
Last Ship Date: July 98
Issue Size: 2500

Original Kin is third in the series of signed and numbered multi-compartment limited edition box figurines depicting the origin(s) of man: the biblical account, evolution, and the extraterrestrial theory. Adam and Eve bear resemblance to Peter and Andrea. The garden contains four palm and three deciduous trees. One is in full leaf, another has a tree spirit face, and the third a sign to the River Gihon. The River Pison is also depicted. Eve is being urged by the serpent to pick from the forbidden Tree of Conscience. Several fruits have already been eaten. Adam is carrying a book of animal names to assist him in his 9-5 job of naming the inhabitants of the garden. Adam bears the scar of the rib removal. Even the Garden of Eden does not escape the tin can pollution. And a dartboard, last seen on board Noah's Lark, appears again. Peter's pet cockatiel,

Spike, is sitting on Adam's shoulder and his dog, Murphy, is bursting through the undergrowth. The handbag looks suspiciously like snakeskin, or so the serpent surmises. Inside, Adam and Eve have packed a suitcase ready for banishment from the garden. In addition to clothes they will need, it contains their UK passports, and Dr. Who's famous coloured scarf. The box figurine is also home to three dinosaurs, and eight aliens with their space ship. The mouse is hiding under the serpent. Each piece is hand-numbered, signed by the artist and accompanied by a certificate of authenticity. Hallmarks include ©, heart, HBC logo, and PC.

Sin City
Item No.: TJLESI
Artist: PC
Size: 195x204x116
Status: Ltd Ed
Carving Date: 98
Release Date: Jun 98
Last Ship Date: May 02
Issue Size: 5000

Sin City is fourth in the series of signed and numbered multi-compartment limited edition box figurines, featuring the seven deadly sins housed within an overcrowded zoo. Peter says that this piece was an excuse for him to include as many animals in a box as he could (143, not including the seven interior compartments or the humans). Inside each of the compartments is a sin being committed by the zookeeper, who bears strong resemblance to Peter. The loose feathers are a reminder of a collard dove that had a fight with Peter's cat, Algy. The "Algy EGL" poster refers to Algy breaking his leg two weeks later. A dog falls through the roof, a reference to Murphy who fell through the false ceiling at Martin's factory. An elephant has three earrings, although with the size of his ears, he has room for many more. A duck billed platypus tries to absorb the aphrodisiac properties of the rhino horn. Peter's new Ford Ka is mentioned twice. Martin's dog, Alf, has his name hidden on a tortoise's back. One of the bears is sick after eating chips, while another has kicked the beak off a flamingo. A meerkat suffers from food poisoning. Noel Wiggins looks out of a gate with one of his Harmony Ball ties. The cancelled Edison poster is a reference that Sin City was not ready in time for this exposition. Each piece is hand-numbered, signed by the artist and accompanied by a certificate of authenticity. Hallmarks include ©, star, HBC logo, ed.#, and Pc.

Harmony Kingdom Box Details — Page 163

LIMITED EDITIONS
BLACK BOX

Bum Wrap
Item No.: TJBB02
Artist: PC
Size: 59x76x68
Status: Ltd Ed
Carving Date: 02
Release Date: Mar 02
Last Ship Date: Sep 02
Issue Size: 5000

The 2002 Black Box echoes the vulture theme of the first Black Box, introduced in 1998. Three vultures feast on a hapless zebra, the perennial wildlife documentary victim. Watching vultures feed, it seems nothing would shock them. Would it be a terrible faux pas to appear suddenly from where the sun don't shine? Judging from the scowling faces, the book of "Vulture Etiquette" evidently says yes. A pretzel by the wayside remains untouched - having heard of President Bush's mishap the birds have decided to leave this dangerous morsel alone. The interior shows a hamburger, feather, knife and fork. "20022002" highlights the palindromic nature of this year. Around the inside of the lid are myriad references to fast food. The mouse is located behind a vulture's leg. Hallmarks include ©, peace sign, HBC logo, and Pc.

Have A Heart
Item No.: TJBBVU
Artist: PC
Size: 48x51x75
Status: Ltd Ed
Carving Date: 96
Release Date: Jan 98
Last Ship Date: Jun 98
Issue Size: 3600

This "good-looking" vulture is sitting on a sawn-off elephant's foot, resting his card on a hyena's headless body, and composing a love poem: "Roses are red, violets are blue, I ate the head, but the heart is for you." The heart in question is gift wrapped and marked "To A" (Andrea). Inside the piece is another heart with the inscription "HKM." Peter cannot remember the significance of these initials. Originally intended as a special 1997 Valentine's piece, this box figurine was considered too tasteless and juvenile to release. Collectors learned of its existence, and by popular demand, it was released as the first HK "Banned Box," in suitable black livery and limited to an edition of 3600. Due to a moulding flaw, many of the vultures are without toenails. "Valentine" and "14 FEB" appear on some early pieces. Hallmarks include ©, diamond, clock face with month 8, HBC logo, and Pc.

Nose Bleed

Item No.: TJBB00
Artist: PC
Size: 76x44x82
Status: Ltd Ed
Carving Date: 99
Release Date: Jan 00
Last Ship Date: Feb 02
Issue Size: 5000

Mother Nature's version of a tank, the formidable rhinoceros knows no predator other than humankind. Poachers have hunted the tough-skinned beasts nearly to extinction for the sake of their horns, which have supposed medicinal properties. In this box figurine, the rhinos exact their revenge by harvesting human noses. The newspaper headline notes, "Manilow and Pinocchio Missing" - could they be prime targets for nose poachers? One of the rhinos has shot Peter in the foot with a gun called "Old Rhinoblasty," a take on "rhinoplasty," or the ubiquitous nose job. "AK74" is inscribed on the butt of the rifle, a favoured weapon of terrorists and poachers. The vulture keeps an eye out for any spare noses for lunch, and a bag of freshly picked noses rests under Peter's foot. Around the base are the names of rhino species with the numbers of each believed to exist. In one interior compartment are four human skulls. In the second, some of the animals from Ed's Safari bus seek refuge. Hallmarks include ©, double diamond, HBC logo, and Pc.

Road Kill

Item No.: TJBB99
Artist: PC
Size: 70x56x71
Status: Ltd Ed
Carving Date: 98
Release Date: Jan 99
Last Ship Date: Apr 99
Issue Size: 5000

This second box figurine in the Black Box series is a tribute to the countless victims of road accidents. A group of animals sit on a cloud in heaven, bearing the tyre marks of their demise. All have been elevated to angel status and have wings, except for the snake and Peter's visiting mouse. A hedgehog peers out beneath a badger who clutches an exhaust pipe, while another badger holds the tail of a squirrel. The rabbit prepares to detonate a bomb that is inside the box; he seeks revenge on the car - the instrument of their deaths. 'For Kelly' on the tail refers to a pet dog that once belonged to Peter's wife. Many famous people who died in traffic accidents are commemorated directly or indirectly: 688 LTV75 - number plate of Mercedes in which Princess Diana killed; 130 'Little Bastard' J.D. - James Dean's car; AYNE MANSFIELD - missing initial J as actress reputed to have been decapitated; A. CAMUS - French-Algerian existential writer; QUEEN ASTRID - Belgian monarch; T. REX - rock band of British pop star Marc Bolan; MARY JO KOPECHNE - friend of Ted Kennedy, died in Chappaquidik Bridge accident; THELMA & LOUISE - film characters; GRACE KELLY - actress and princess of Monaco; KENNY - South Park TV cartoon character, dies a different way during every episode. Hallmarks include ©, star, HBC logo, and Pc.

Harmony Kingdom Box Details

Road Kill's Revenge

Item No.: TJBB01
Artist: PC
Size: 63x102x83
Status: Ltd Ed
Carving Date: 01
Release Date: Feb 01
Last Ship Date: Jan 02
Issue Size: 5000

Two years ago Harmony Kingdom's "Road Kill" commemorated the sheer numbers of wildlife slaughtered on the roads of Britain. It is apparent, though, that the woodland creatures of North America are every bit as abysmal at crossing a busy road as their British counterparts. However, while British animals just accept their fate and say "Sorry, I hope I didn't get too much blood on your tyres," American animals are more likely to shout obscenities and even up the score a little. They've "borrowed" a vehicle of their own...the worm has turned. The opossum is acting as lookout and the owl is keeping score with stick figures drawn on the jeep. The white-tailed deer is steering, albeit with his hind feet. A host of others, including a raccoon, fox, porcupine, bear, otter, skunk, rabbit, snake, chipmunk, woodchuck, and weasel are just along for the ride. And yes...that man they have just run over was carrying a white cane and a Braille book. The animals' excuse is that they have poor eyesight, but that doesn't prevent humans from running them over. Will they get away with it? The interior of the larger compartment shows a mole at the controls, a fitting choice for a driver because of its celebrated short sightedness. Under the bonnet (hood) the surprised expression of the latest target is revealed. Anagrams of some large tyre manufacturers, including Bridgestone, Michelin, Goodyear, Dunlop, and Pirelli, adorn the wheels. The signature mouse was on holiday during the carving of this Box Figurine, so his stand-in, a peregrine falcon, can be seen next to the owl. The year "2001" is inscribed under the rabbit's ear and Peter Calvesbert's initials are found on the bear's paw. Some possible baby names (Sam, Milly) are also hidden under the blind man's hat. Hallmarks include ©, smiley face, HBC logo, and Pc.

LIMITED EDITIONS
Clair de Lune

Colette & Cat
Item No.: CLLECT
Artist: JB
Size: 95x132x67
Status: Ltd Ed
Carving Date: 99
Release Date: Jun 00
Last Ship Date: Not Available
Issue Size: 3600

One of Colette's cats, decked out in bathing cap, contemplates getting in the tub with her.

Josephine & Cat
Item No.: CLLECD
Artist: JB
Size: 89x74x90
Status: Ltd Ed
Carving Date: 99
Release Date: Jun 00
Last Ship Date: Not Available
Issue Size: 3600

Pots of rouge and face paint, powders and perfumes, hair combs and lotions - what a lot of fun cat toys!

Justine & Cat
Item No.: CLLECB
Artist: JB
Size: 92x105x77
Status: Ltd Ed
Carving Date: 99
Release Date: Jun 00
Last Ship Date: Not Available
Issue Size: 3600

One of Justine's cats joins her on the bed for a mid-afternoon nap.

Kiki & Cat
Item No.: CLLECS
Artist: JB
Size: 199x60x76
Status: Ltd Ed
Carving Date: 99
Release Date: Jun 00
Last Ship Date: Not Available
Issue Size: 3600

Kiki curls up with a favorite feline companion.

Mme. Colette
Item No.: CLLENT
Artist: JB
Size: 95x132x67
Status: Ltd Ed
Carving Date: 99
Release Date: Jun 00
Last Ship Date: Not Available
Issue Size: 2500

Through her job as ghostwriter of a former princess's memoirs, Colette met and made friends with the Left Bank literati. She herself has become the thinly disguised heroine of at least six novels and scores of memoirs. Colette serves Formosa oolong tea, Pernod, and small crustless cucumber sandwiches at her Friday night salons.

Mme. Josephine
Item No.: CLLEND
Artist: JB
Size: 89x74x90
Status: Ltd Ed
Carving Date: 99
Release Date: Jun 00
Last Ship Date: Not Available
Issue Size: 2500

Famous and fawned over, Josephine's every move is reported in the press and her style imitated throughout the Continent. Dressed gratis in creations by Patou and Poiret, she is so proud of her figure that she often removes her clothes and dances barefoot at parties.

Mme. Justine

Item No.: CLLENB
Artist: JB
Size: 92x105x77
Status: Ltd Ed
Carving Date: 99
Release Date: Jun 00
Last Ship Date: Oct 01
Issue Size: 2500

Everyone revels in Justine's ready wit, roguish humour, and knowledge of everybody and everything. It is said that she never lets truth get in the way of a good story. She is known to prowl the night streets, dressed as a male gangster.

Mme. Kiki

Item No.: CLLENS
Artist: JB
Size: 199x60x76
Status: Ltd Ed
Carving Date: 99
Release Date: Jun 00
Last Ship Date: Not Available
Issue Size: 2500

Kiki ran away to Paris at the age of thirteen and drifted for a time until she found work as an artist's model. She speaks not a word of English, but her warm nature transcends language and she is extremely well liked by everyone.

LIMITED EDITIONS
Harmony Circus

Bozini The Clown
Item No.: HCZLECL
Artist: DL
Size: 38x32x39
Status: Ltd Ed
Carving Date: Feb 96
Release Date: Jun 98
Last Ship Date: Not Available
Issue Size: 10,000

This limited edition clown box figurine was created to say farewell to the Harmony Circus, which retired July 1998. Each piece is hand-numbered and comes with a certificate of authenticity. Hallmarks include diamond, clock face with month 2, HBC logo, and DL.

Harmony Circus Matched Numbered Set
Item No.: HCSET
Artist: DL
Status: Ltd Ed
Release Date: Apr 96
Last Ship Date: May 02
Issue Size: 1000

Matched numbered set of all 19 pieces in the Harmony Circus. All hand-numbered and bearing the artist's monogram.

Madeline Of The High Wire
Item No.: HCZLEMA
Artist: DL
Size: 31x36x46
Status: Ltd Ed
Carving Date: Feb 96
Release Date: Jun 98
Last Ship Date: Not Available
Issue Size: 10,000

This limited edition trapeze artist box figurine was created to say farewell to the Harmony Circus, which retired July 1998. It was named in honour of Madeline Acton, Harmony Kingdom's special events coordinator. Each piece is hand-numbered and comes with a certificate of authenticity. Hallmarks include diamond, clock face with month 2, HBC logo, and DL..

LIMITED EDITIONS
Harmony Garden

American Beauty
Item No.: HGLELR4
Artist: SD
Size: 171x159x121
Status: Ltd Ed
Carving Date: 01
Release Date: May 01
Last Ship Date: Not Available
Issue Size: 3600

This dazzling bouquet of brilliant blossoms conceals some of Lord Byron's most memorable moments from his journey across America. Three vignettes from his log are found in the interior compartments. In the first, Byron is impressed by the glitz and glam of Hollywood, California. He's even purchased superstar sunglasses just for the occasion. Next he treks through the Grand Canyon of Arizona, backpack firmly strapped to his shell. Finally, Byron's reminiscence of the US ends in the state of New York, on the American side of Niagara Falls. Lord Byron reflects upon the water rushing beneath him - what further adventures will he encounter in the stream of time? Hallmarks include ©, smiley face, HBC logo, and S.

Christmas Bouquet
Item No. HG3LEBQC
Artist: MP
Size: 91x97x67
Status: Ltd Ed
Carving Date: 98
Release Date: Jun 99
Last Ship Date: Nov 99
Issue Size: 5000

The lovely holiday bouquet features an interior of Lord Byron wrapping gifts. Each piece is hand-numbered and initialed with MRP. Hallmarks include ©, star, HBC logo, and M.

Double Pink Rose
Item No.: HGLEDPR
Artist: MP
Size: 87x65x53
Status: Ltd Ed
Carving Date: 97
Release Date: Jun 98
Last Ship Date: Oct 98
Issue Size: 5000

Inside this box figurine, Lord Byron is dining at a roadside café. Each piece is hand-numbered and initialed with MRP. Hallmarks include ©, heart, HBC logo, ed.#, and M..

Double Red Rose

Item No.: HGLEDRR
Artist: MP
Size: 87x65x53
Status: Ltd Ed
Carving Date: 97
Release Date: Jan 98
Last Ship Date: Oct 98
Issue Size: 5000

Inside this box figurine, Lord Byron has to make a decision on which direction to travel at the Double Red Rose Crossroads.

Each piece is hand-numbered and initialed with MRP. Hallmarks include ©, heart, HBC logo, ed.#, and M.

Double Sterling Rose

Item No.: HGLEDSR
Artist: MP
Size: 82x60x48
Status: Ltd Ed
Carving Date: 98
Release Date: Jan 99
Last Ship Date: Oct 99
Issue Size: 1500

Throughout 1998, HK issued four limited edition double roses, each with distinctive exterior colouration and interior scenes. As a grand finale to this exceptionally popular series, HK produced "The Double Sterling Rose," limited to an edition of 1500 pieces and initially offered to Queen Empress dealers only. Crafted in solid sterling silver by Robert Glover who does commissions for the British royal family, this piece has been sanctioned by the London Assay Office. The interior portrays Lord Byron and three of his bug friends, hand-in-hand around a bonfire, donning party hats. Lord Byron is enameled in red. Hallmarks include ©, star, HBC logo, M, and RG.

Double Violet Rose

Item No.: HGLEDVR
Artist: MP
Size: 87x65x53
Status: Ltd Ed
Carving Date: 97
Release Date: Jun 98
Last Ship Date: Dec 98
Issue Size: 5000

Inside this box figurine, Lord Byron enjoys an afternoon swim. Each piece is hand-numbered and initialed with MRP. Hallmarks include ©, heart, HBC logo, ed.#, and M.

Double Yellow Rose
Item No.: HGLEDYR
Artist: MP
Size: 87x65x53
Status: Ltd Ed
Carving Date: 97
Release Date: Jun 98
Last Ship Date: Nov 98
Issue Size: 5000

Inside this box figurine, Lord Byron hitchhikes and is picked up by a purple VW bug. Each piece is hand-numbered and initialed with MRP. Hallmarks include ©, heart, HBC logo, ed.#, and M.

Easter Bouquet
Item No.: HG3LEBQE
Artist: SD
Size: 91x97x67
Status: Ltd Ed
Carving Date: 98
Release Date: Mar 99
Last Ship Date: May 99
Issue Size: 5000

This festive bouquet features an interior of Lord Byron colouring Easter eggs. Each piece is hand-numbered and initialed with MRP. Hallmarks include ©, star, HBC logo, and S.

Fall Bouquet
Item No.: HG4LEBQF
Artist: SD
Size: 83x89x89
Status: Ltd Ed
Carving Date: 99
Release Date: Jun 00
Last Ship Date: Nov 01
Issue Size: 3600

A basket of ripe, fresh fruits and flowers sparkle, having just been rinsed under an old-fashioned water spigot. Plump, juicy berries and a collection of gourds and flowers show off the range of autumn's brilliant yellows, oranges, and regal purples. On the interior, Lord Byron visits some friends at their cottage. Under the harvest moon they rake the fallen leaves into a pile, anticipating the joy of jumping in them. Someone has a crush on Byron: his initials are carved inside a heart in the bark of a nearby tree. Hallmarks include ©, moon, HBC logo, M, and S.

Harmony Kingdom Box Details

Halloween Bouquet
Item No.: HG3LEBQH
Artist: MP
Size: 90x84x71
Status: Ltd Ed
Carving Date: 98
Release Date: Jun 99
Last Ship Date: Nov 99
Issue Size: 5000

This autumnal bouquet features an interior Lord Byron busy at work carving a pumpkin. Each piece is hand-numbered and initialed with MRP. Hallmarks include ©, star, HBC logo, and M.

Home Sweet Home
Item No.: HGLELR3
Artist: MB & SD
Size: 400x170x160
Status: Ltd Ed
Carving Date: 99
Release Date: Jan 00
Last Ship Date: Feb 02
Issue Size: 3600

While Lord Byron is off on his spiritual quest in Chapter IV, who tends to his garden? Unbeknownst to our hero, a Lady bug has taken up residence in his original rose garden home. With typical feminine aplomb, she's tidied up, moved things around, and added some fixtures to suit her more comfortable style. See what she's done to Byron's garden in this multi-compartment box figurine. Hallmarks include ©, moon, HBC logo, and M.

Mother's Day Bouquet
Item No.: HG3LEBQM
Artist: SD
Size: 88x91x97
Status: Ltd Ed
Carving Date: 98
Release Date: Mar 99
Last Ship Date: May 99
Issue Size: 5000

This sentimental bouquet features an interior Lord Byron with a box of chocolates addressed to his mother. Each piece is hand-numbered and initialed with MRP. Hallmarks include ©, star, HBC logo, and S.

Rose Basket
Item No.: HGLELR
Artist: MP
Size: 109x83x79
Status: Ltd Ed
Carving Date: 97
Release Date: Jan 97
Last Ship Date: Nov 97
Issue Size: 3600

Inside this box figurine, Lord Byron, in a dream sequence, is golfing on the moon. Each piece is hand-numbered and initialed with MRP. Hallmarks include ©, heart, HBC logo, and M.

Rose Party
Item No.: HGLELR2
Artist: MP
Size: 87x84x94
Status: Ltd Ed
Carving Date: 97
Release Date: Jan 98
Last Ship Date: Aug 98
Issue Size: 5000

Inside this box figurine, Lord Byron's friends host a farewell party for him. Each piece is hand-numbered and initialed with MRP. Hallmarks include ©, heart, HBC logo, ed.#, and M.

Single Orange Rose
Item No.: HGLEOR
Artist: MP
Size: 48x52x53
Status: Ltd Ed
Carving Date: 97
Release Date: Nov 97
Last Ship Date: Mar 98
Issue Size: 3600

Inside this box figurine, Lord Byron is hanging a picture of his favourite female ladybug. Each piece is hand-numbered and initialed with MRP. Hallmarks include ©, heart, HBC logo, and M.

Single Pink Rose
Item No.: HGLEPR
Artist: MP
Size: 48x52x53
Status: Ltd Ed
Carving Date: 97
Release Date: Jun 97
Last Ship Date: Feb 98
Issue Size: 3600

Inside this box figurine, Lord Byron is vacuuming (or "hoovering" as they say in Lord Byron's homeland). Each piece is hand-numbered and initialed with MRP. Hallmarks include ©, heart, HBC logo, and M.

Harmony Kingdom Box Details

Single Red Rose
Item No.: HGLERR
Artist: MP
Size: 48x52x53
Status: Ltd Ed
Carving Date: 97
Release Date: Jan 97
Last Ship Date: Aug 97
Issue Size: 3600

Lord Byron gazes wistfully out the window. Each piece is hand-numbered and initialed with MRP. Hallmarks include ©, heart, HBC logo, and M.

Single Violet Rose
Item No.: HGLEVR
Artist: MP
Size: 48x52x53
Status: Ltd Ed
Carving Date: 97
Release Date: Oct 97
Last Ship Date: Mar 98
Issue Size: 3600

Inside this box figurine, Lord Byron is talking on the telephone. Each piece is hand-numbered and initialed with MRP. Hallmarks include ©, heart, HBC logo, and M.

Single White Rose
Item No.: HGLEWR
Artist: MP
Size: 48x52x53
Status: Ltd Ed
Carving Date: 97
Release Date: Apr 97
Last Ship Date: Oct 97
Issue Size: 3600

Inside this box figurine, Lord Byron is crying. Each piece is hand-numbered and initialed with MRP. Hallmarks include ©, heart, HBC logo, and M.

Single Yellow Rose
Item No.: HGLEYR
Artist: MP
Size: 48x52x53
Status: Ltd Ed
Carving Date: 97
Release Date: May 97
Last Ship Date: Oct 97
Issue Size: 3600

Inside this box figurine, Lord Byron is bathing in his tub. Each piece is hand-numbered and initialed with MRP. Hallmarks include ©, heart, HBC logo, and M.

Harmony Kingdom Box Details

Spring Bouquet

Item No.: HG4LEBQSP
Artist: SD
Size: 83x77x87
Status: Ltd Ed
Carving Date: 99
Release Date: Jan 00
Last Ship Date: Nov 01
Issue Size: 5000

Lord Byron and his friends celebrate the spring with a maypole dance. Hallmarks include ©, moon, HBC logo, and M.

Sterling Rose

Item No.: HGLESR
Artist: MP
Size: 48x51x41
Status: Ltd Ed
Carving Date: 97
Release Date: Jan 98
Last Ship Date: Sep 98
Issue Size: 1000

Throughout 1997, HK issued six limited edition single roses, each with distinctive exterior colouration and interior scenes. As a grand finale to this exceptionally popular series HK produced the "Sterling Rose," limited to an edition of 1000 pieces and distributed exclusively through Queen Empress dealers. Inside, a removable Lord Byron, enameled with red and black, is having a solitary dinner with a candelabrum adorning his table. The base of this solid sterling box figurine reads: "The Sterling Rose, Limited edition of 1000, .925 sterling." Pieces are not hand-numbered but a certificate of authenticity with production number accompanies each.

Summer Bouquet

Item No.: HG4LEBQSU
Artist: SD
Size: 103x99x108
Status: Ltd Ed
Carving Date: 99
Release Date: Jan 00
Last Ship Date: Mar 02
Issue Size: 5000

This beautiful summer bouquet in a rustic pot features an interior scene of Lord Byron ringing up his mum on Mother's Day. Hallmarks include ©, moon, HBC logo, and M.

Winter Bouquet
Item No.: HG4LEBQW
Artist: SD
Size: 89x85x89
Status: Ltd Ed
Carving Date: 99
Release Date: Jun 00
Last Ship Date: May 02
Issue Size: 3600

A terrier pokes his head out of a Santa's bag laden with gifts. The plentiful presents spill over into a basket full of flowers. Inside the compartment, Lord Byron and the Beetle brothers sled down a snowy hill on home made toboggans. Byron calls out to one of the brothers who is heading dangerously for a tree. Or his he showing off his yodelling skill, acquired during his European travels? Hallmarks include ©, moon, HBC logo, M, and S.

LIMITED EDITIONS
Holiday

Adam Binder Cracker Fairies
Item No: CCETICAAB01
Artist: AB
Size: Approx. 30x29x33 ea
Status: Ltd Ed
Carving Date: 01
Release Date: Sep 01
Last Ship Date: Not Available
Issue Size: 1000

This limited edition set of fairies was available in the UK only through thisiscollecting.com. Fairies include: Tinkibella, Stockingfella, Yurigella, Fortunetella, Bellyfilla, Crackersella and Donatella. The fairies came packaged as a set of six red English "crackers." Most sets came with "Stockingfella," but 200 sets came with "Tinkibella."

Holiday Ornament Set
Item No.: TJZSE98
Artist: MP
Size: 25x25x50 ea.
Status: Ltd Ed
Carving Date: 98
Release Date: Oct 98
Last Ship Date: Not Available
Issue Size: 10,000

Our Garden Party host The Garden Prince, Tubs the industrious turtle, romantic adventurer Lord Byron, and Murphy the madcap penguin meet for the first time to bring you a holiday surprise. Donning red caps, they appear together in the holiday ornament set. Hallmarks include star.

Monique Baldwin Cracker Fairies
Item No: CCEHIMB01
Artist: MB
Size: Approx. 26x30x38 ea
Status: Ltd Ed
Carving Date: 01
Release Date: Sep 01
Last Ship Date: Not Available
Issue Size: 1000

This limited edition set of fairies was available in the UK only. Fairies include: Tinkerbelle, Missmella, Heavenanhella, Kissentelle, Crimbonelle, Candispelle and Topsygelle. The fairies came packed as a set of six green English "crackers." Most sets came with "Candispelle" but 200 sets came with "Tinkerbelle."

LIMITED EDITIONS
LONGABERGER

Daisy Basket
Item No.: HGXLG
Artist: SD
Size: 83x83x108
Status: Ltd Ed
Carving Date: 00
Release Date: July 00
Issue Size: 3600

Daisies: they're bursting with the promise of young love, the dewy freshness of a new season, the simplicity of days gone by. "Daisy Basket" is the first collaboration between Harmony Kingdom and The Longaberger® Company.

Morning Glory Basket
Item No.: HGXLG2
Artist: SD
Size: 76x76x102
Status: Ltd Ed
Carving Date: 00
Release Date: Oct 00
Issue Size: 3600

Morning Glories - the majestic and hearty flower that blooms in the early morning hours - have long been a backyard staple in Grandma Bonnie's garden. "Morning Glory Basket" is a unique rendition of the 11th Longaberger May Series Basket.

Peony Basket

Item No.: HGXLG4
Artist: SD
Size: 108x76x76
Status: Ltd Ed
Carving Date: 01
Release Date: Jul 01
Issue Size: 3600

A basketful of aromatic peony blooms can soothe the soul and take one back to a simpler time. This is the fourth Harmony Kingdom box figurine for The Longaberger® Company.

Petunia Basket

Item No.: HGXLG5
Artist: SD
Size: 76x84x95
Status: Ltd Ed
Carving Date: 01
Release Date: Jan 02
Issue Size: 2500

The bright and cheerful colors of the petunia make it one of the most popular flowers. This box figurine is the fifth exclusive in a series for The Longaberger® Company.

Poinsettia Basket

Item No.: HGXLG6
Artist: SD
Size: 86x86x104
Status: Ltd Ed
Carving Date: 01
Release Date: Apr 02
Issue Size: 2500

The Longaberger® Company introduced the Poinsettia Basket during its 1988 Holiday Campaign. This box figurine is the sixth exclusive in a series for The Longaberger® Company.

Snapdragon Basket

Item No.: HGXLG3
Artist: SD
Size: 76x70x127
Status: Ltd Ed
Carving Date: 00
Release Date: May 01
Issue Size: 3600

"Snapdragon Basket" is the third box figurine produced by Harmony Kingdom exclusively for The Longaberger® Company.

LIMITED EDITIONS
MYTHOLOGICALS/TAMIRA'S TREASURES

Cadmius
Item No.: TJMYLEYE
Artist: MH
Size: 79x58x61
Status: Ltd Ed
Carving Date: 02
Release Date: May 02
Last Ship Date: Not Available
Issue Size: 5000

Beckon the yellow dragon, for he is enigmatic and solitary. An accomplished shape-shifter, this perfectionist will show himself only if he believes you deserve to see him. In the East, the yellow dragon is highly revered, ruler of the sunrise, spring and frivolity. The color yellow has been used for royalty and nobility in China, and throughout the East is associated with happiness and grace. The interior shows a bell, one of Cadmius's magical tools. Hallmarks include ©, peace sign, HBC logo, and H.

Cerlulu
Item No.: TJMYLEBL
Artist: MB
Size: 83x51x38
Status: Ltd Ed
Carving Date: 02
Release Date: May 02
Last Ship Date: Not Available
Issue Size: 5000

Behold the blue dragon, for he is an optimist and a harbinger of spring. More humble and carefree than other dragons, the blue dragon is associated with water, compassion, peace and intuition. Since dragons all have a negative side, the blue dragon may also bring rainstorms, whirlpools or insecurity. The color blue denotes a quiet strength and calming authority. The interior features love letters and a necklace with a peace sign pendant. Hallmarks include ©, peace sign, HBC logo, and eye.

Chiaro

Item No.: TJMYLEBK
Artist: MH
Size: 102x61x58
Status: Ltd Ed
Carving Date: 02
Release Date: May 02
Last Ship Date: Not Available
Issue Size: 5000

Bemoan the black dragon, for he is dark and negative. Cloaked in mystery, the black dragon rules the night, the moon and stars. Although often vengeful, he also seeks truth and may offer psychic guidance and helpful magic. Black is a color of mourning in many countries, yet is also worn on formal occasions. The moon and stars on the interior indicate the mystical qualities of the black dragon. Hallmarks include ©, peace sign, HBC logo, and H.

Henna

Item No.: TJMYLEOR
Artist: MB
Size: 51x71x71
Status: Ltd Ed
Carving Date: 02
Release Date: May 02
Last Ship Date: Not Available
Issue Size: 5000

Believe the orange dragon, for she is wise and thoughtful. Shy and wistful, she prefers study over sports, although he is a fast runner. With an excellent memory, the orange dragon embodies all the positive aspects of learning. The color orange indicates warmth, and is associated with the second chakra, which governs creativity and emotion. The book on the interior is inscribed with "Mensa," the association of geniuses, showing Henna's intelligence, and a quill for writing arcane texts. Hallmarks include ©, peace sign, HBC logo, and eye.

Jada

Item No.: TJMYLEGR
Artist: MB
Size: 61x51x66
Status: Ltd Ed
Carving Date: 02
Release Date: May 02
Last Ship Date: Not Available
Issue Size: 5000

Befriend the green dragon, for she is young and mischievous. A forest-dweller and earth-lover, the green dragon is associated with the element of earth, gemstones, endurance and prosperity. Other traits include stubbornness, a fondness of playing small tricks and a tendency to be temperamental. The color green symbolizes freshness, growth and the future. The interior shows a mirror and chalice, two of her magical aspects. Hallmarks include ©, peace sign, HBC logo, and eye.

Harmony Kingdom Box Details

Rufus

Item No.: TJMYLEPI
Artist: MH
Size: 76x61x76
Status: Ltd Ed
Carving Date: 02
Release Date: May 02
Last Ship Date: Not Available
Issue Size: 5000

Beware the red dragon, for he is short-tempered and can be fierce. Extroverted and energetic, he enjoys competition and conquest. The red dragon is associated with the element of fire, the sun, courage and leadership, as well as war, lightning and volcanoes. While many view red as a symbol of danger, some Eastern cultures use red for joyous and festive occasions. A dagger on the interior indicates the warrior nature of red dragons. Hallmarks include ©, peace sign, HBC logo, and H.

Tamira's Treasure

Item No.: TJMYLEDR
Artist: PC
Size: 79x108x181
Status: Ltd Ed
Carving Date: 01
Release Date: Jul 01
Last Ship Date: Not Available
Issue Size: 3600

Dragons mean many different things to different cultures, but in the West dragons traditionally get bad press. When Master Carver Peter Calvesbert imagined his dragon, this friendly face came to mind. Although benevolent, the mythological beast still wields great power, as evidenced by the self-portrait of Peter firmly clamped between wing and tail. The inspiration for the baby dragon came from Peter's first child, Samuel Frederick. This proud parent is a solid bodied figurine, and not a box. Hallmarks include ©, smiley face, HBC logo, and Pc.

LIMITED EDITIONS
ZOOKEEPERS

Family Reunion
Item No.: TJLEMO
Artist: DL
Size: 83x83x105
Status: Ltd Ed
Carving Date: 97
Release Date: Jun 98
Last Ship Date: May 99
Issue Size: 7200

An expressive family of monkeys is the theme for this box figurine. The interior contains the head of Yorrick, Hamlet's one time jester and friend. Unscrew the head to reveal a book inscribed with "Alas Poor Lucy." Colour variations on the berries can be found, ranging from red to orange to yellow. Each piece is hand-numbered, bears the artist's monogram and is accompanied by a certificate of authenticity. Hallmarks include ©, heart, HBC logo, ed.#, and DL.

Gentle Giant
Item No.: TJLEGP
Artist: SD
Size: 76x89x114
Status: Limited
Carving Date: 00
Release Date: Dec 00
Last Ship Date: Dec 01
Issue Size: 5000

Giant pandas have fascinated humans for ages. With his round face, chubby body, and black and white markings, the baby panda looks like one of the cuddliest creatures on earth. Protective mama spends most of her day munching bamboo stems, which she pulls down with a hand-like giant paw that seems to have a thumb. Only about 1000 pandas remain in the wild, with 130 in zoos. Due to their slow growth and breeding rate, panda populations do not recover quickly from hunting and destruction of habitat. Within this limited edition box figurine three oysters, a supposed aphrodisiac, have been added to a stalk of bamboo in the hopes of introducing a little romance into the pandas' lives. Hallmarks include ©, double diamond, HBC logo, and S.

Ivory Tower

Item No.: TJLEOW
Artist: DL
Size: 88x88x113
Status: Ltd Ed
Carving Date: 97
Release Date: Jun 98
Last Ship Date: May 99
Issue Size: 7200

Distinguished owls decorate this box figurine. Along the base is the inscription, "If the oak's before the ash you'll only get a splash" and the score, "Charles 2 NOL 0." Inside is mistletoe with the words "Kiss Kiss." Each piece is hand-numbered, bears the artist's monogram and is accompanied by a certificate of authenticity. Hallmarks include ©, heart, HBC logo, ed.#, and DL.

Play Ball

Item No.: TJLEPO
Artist: DL
Size: 92x92x104
Status: Ltd Ed
Carving Date: 97
Release Date: Jun 98
Last Ship Date: May 99
Issue Size: 7200

Playful polar bears are the subject of this box figurine. The interior contains a spaceship that opens to reveal a three-eyed alien and the inscription "Oates was here." A nose is peaking out from under the scroll with a treasure map for Cathay. Each piece is hand-numbered, bears the artist's monogram and is accompanied by a certificate of authenticity. Hallmarks include ©, heart, HBC logo, ed.#, and DL.

Retired Racers

Item No.: TJLEGR
Artist: DL
Size: 120x69x66
Status: Ltd Ed
Carving Date: 99
Release Date: Jan 00
Last Ship Date: Dec 01
Issue Size: 5000

A manifestation of the art of selective breeding, the greyhound is a sleek and elegant beast. The CL refers both to Catherine Lawrence, the sculptor's baby daughter, and Catherine Leicester, an avid HK collector and dedicated greyhound rescue worker. On the interior relaxes a retired racer receiving a well-deserved rest. Once he competed in the tough and dangerous world of the dog track. Now he feels safe in his newfound home and curls himself into a sleepy ball of fur. Hallmarks include ©, moon, HBC logo, and DL.

ROYAL WATCH COLLECTOR'S CLUB

April's Fool Pewter Pen
Item No.: RW98PEN
Artist: PC
Size: 17x15x142
Status: Ltd Time
Carving Date: 97
Release Date: Apr 98
Last Order Date: Jul 98
Issue Size: 1900

This pewter pen was available as an April Fool's Day offering to active Royal Watch members from April 1, 1998 through July 4, 1998. Aside from the fool himself, the cuckoo is involved in a bit of tomfoolery. It lays its egg in the basket of another bird so someone else has the work of hatching it. Once hatched, the cuckoo pushes the other eggs out of the nest. "PG Rules" refers to Pope Gregory. Hallmarks include ©, star, HBC logo, and M.

Behold The King
Item No.: RW98LI
Artist: DL
Size: 92x70x91
Status: Ltd Time
Carving Date: 97
Release Date: Jan 98
Last Order Date: Mar 99
Issue Size: 8633

This box figurine, featuring a pride of lions, was the 1998 exclusive club redemption piece. The box interior has a miniature crown compartment that opens to reveal a mouse. The mouse is not Peter's signature mouse, as David Lawrence created this piece. Instead, the mouse is part of the fable upon which this figurine was based – the tiny creature pulled the thorn from the mighty lion's paw. Hallmarks include ©, heart, HBC logo, ed.#, and DL.

Beneath the Ever Changing Seas
Issue Size: RW99SS
Artist: DL/MB
Size: 74x52x71
Status: Ltd Time
Carving Date: 98
Release Date: Jan 99
Last Order Date: Dec 99
Issue Size: 26,109

This elegant seashell box figurine features an interior of Lord Byron reading and sunning himself at the seaside. Contained within 1999 membership kits, it was available exclusively to 1999 Royal Watch members. Hallmarks include ©, moon, and HBC logo.

Big Blue

Item No.: RW96WH/RW97WH
Artist: PC
Size: 154x114x119
Status: Ltd Time
Carving Date: 95
Release Date: Jan 96/Jan 97
Last Order Date: Mar 97/Mar 98
Issue Size: 1839/4056

These box figurines, featuring a school of joyous whales, served as both the 1996 charter year club exclusive redemption piece as well as the 1997 redemption piece. The only difference between the two years are the markings on the front of the piece: either "Royal Watch Charter 1996" or "Royal Watch 1997." A small quantity were produced with "Royal Watch Charter 1997" in error. The mouse is hidden in the whales' tales. Hallmarks include apple, clock with month 11, HBC logo, and Pc.

The Big Day

Item No.: RW96
Artist: PC
Size: 58x35x80
Status: Ltd Time
Carving Date: 95
Release Date: Apr 96
Last Order Date: Dec 96
Issue Size: 5125

Carved to celebrate their wedding, this figurine (not a box) is the first in the "Cake Topper" series. Since Peter's wedding coincided with the inauguration of the Royal Watch, this piece was included in the inaugural year's membership kit. Peter's wedding party also received this piece as a gift. Golf clubs are present due to Peter's then new fascination with the sport. Murphy is resting upon Peter's shoeless foot, and Spike is poised on the couple's shoulders. Peter sculpted Andrea with an apron and washing glove as he sarcastically remarks that "women like to wash and cook." "Colwall 30 Sept 95" is the date of their wedding, and the plane tickets with SAA signify their honeymoon to South Africa. Hallmarks include HBC logo.

Birds of a Feather

Item No.: RWMI
Artist: AB
Size: 57x57x89
Status: Ltd Time
Carving Date: 01
Release Date: Jun 01
Last Order Date: Nov 02
Issue Size: 1069

The smart and sexy space cat Minx shows her tender side in this Independent Club exclusive. Minx is extremely fond of her canary, Charlie. Even though she brings him along to detect deadly space gases (much like canaries in coal mines), Minx would be utterly devastated if any harm should befall him. The patches on Minx's space suit show her shared allegiance to the US and the UK. On the interior is a plaque labelled "HOP 2001" to commemorate the House of Peers organization of authorized independent clubs. Hallmarks include ©, smiley face, HBC logo, and gecko.

Bulldog Pin

Item No.: RW02PI
Artist: MB
Size: 46x15x46
Status: Ltd Time
Carving Date: 01
Release Date: Jan 02
Last Order Date: Mar 03
Issue Size: Not Available

This lapel pin is a 2002 gift for joining the Royal Watch Collector's Club.

Byron & Bumbles

Item No.: RW00BB
Artist: MB
Size: 79x70x101
Status: Ltd Time
Carving Date: 99
Release Date: Jan 00
Last Order Date: Mar 01
Issue Size: 6497

Byron fishes with his pal Bumbles in this multi-compartment year 2000 redemption box figurine. Hallmarks include ©, moon, HBC logo, eye and M.

Byron's Lonely Hearts Club
Item No. RW99LB
Artist: MB
Size: 92x76x75
Status: Ltd Time
Carving Date: 98
Release Date: Jan 99
Last Order Date: Mar 00
Issue Size: 8528

This box figurine featuring a bigger-than-life depiction of Lord Byron was one of two 1999 exclusive club redemption pieces. Hallmarks include ©, star, HBC logo, ed.#, and eye.

Cat Pin
Item No.: RW98PI
Artist: PC
Size: 54x47x13
Status: Ltd Time
Carving Date: 97
Release Date: Jan 98
Last Order Date: Dec 98
Issue Size: 26,109

This gift pin, contained within membership kits, was available exclusively to 1998 club members.

Cotton Anniversary
Item No.: RWCTCO
Artist: PC
Size: 60x47x70
Status: Club Special
Carving Date: 98
Release Date: Nov 98

Carved to celebrate their second anniversary, this figurine (not a box) is the third piece in the "Cake Topper" series and is a tongue in cheek depiction of Peter and Andrea after their second year of marriage. As Andrea reads a book entitled "Is Your Husband MAD," Peter sits beside her, covered by a sheet with the words "Hotel Property" written on it. Beside the armchair is another book named "100 Popular Poisons" by Nick O' Teen. Other cotton representations appear on this figurine, including cotton swabs, cotton thread, cottontails, and a cottonmouth snake. This piece is available exclusively to members of The Royal Watch who have been "wedded" to the Royal Watch for three years. Hallmarks include ©, star, HBC logo, ed.#, and Pc.

Harmony Kingdom Box Details

Cow Town
Item No.: RW00MA
Artist: DL
Size: 134x83x63
Status: Ltd Time
Carving Date: 99
Release Date: Jan 00
Last Order Date: Mar 01
Issue Size: 6511

The first prototype of this box had a bifurcated fluke (two finned tail), which made it not a manatee, but a dugong. Fortunately while in Chicago during the 1998 ICE, several HK enthusiasts supplied missing pieces to the jigsaw. Tribute is paid to them in the assorted treasures on the sea bed interior of the box. The jar marked "Pearl Jam" refers to collector Mike Perlman and the key with "JIM" to collector Jim Kessler. "Chessie" is a manatee who has gained fame by swimming up the Chesapeake Bay every summer. "JB Rules" is an accolade to Jimmy Buffet, president of Save the Manatee and popular singer. This 2000 RW redemption was also part of the Zookeepers Series, with an adoption to benefit the Columbus Zoo and Aquarium. Hallmarks include ©, heart, HBC logo, and DL.

Crown Jewel
Item No.: RWFR
Artist: MB
Size: 71x48x76
Status: Ltd Time
Carving Date: 02
Release Date: Jul 02
Last Order Date: Nov 02
Issue Size: Not Available

This is the fourth box figurine made exclusively for Harmony Kingdom's authorized independent club members. This wistful frog has rescued a princess's golden ball and now longs for his kiss. The interior collection of jewels symbolize how valuable collectors are - they are the jewels of the Kingdom. Hallmarks include ©, peace sign, HBC logo, and eye.

Dressed to Kill
Item No.: RWMU
Artist: PC
Size: 61x58x84
Status: Ltd Time
Carving Date: 00
Release Date: Jun 00
Last Order Date: Dec 00
Issue Size: 2315

Mad Murphy strikes again! This time the hooligan penguin poses as an English gentleman. Still trying to kick the cigarette habit (his nicotine patch is still firmly in place) Murphy blows soap bubbles with his pipe. A Harmony Ball tie is draped nonchalantly over his shoulder. In an effort to appear learned he has borrowed a pile of books from the library. The first describes the ills of collecting. "Berk's Peerage" refers to "Burke's Peerage," a not-entirely-accurate British genealogical directory. "Bernie the Beagle" refers to the beloved pet belong to Queen's Courier editor Kim Cinko's family. "The Pop-Up Kama Sutra" defies description. The mouse peeks out from under a tail feather.

On the interior lies a book entitled "Indy Clubs," commemorating the network of HK authorized independent clubs. Hallmarks include ©, double diamond, HBC logo, and Pc.

Fab Five Party Boys
Item No.: RWFAB
Artist: SD
Size: 53x67x54
Status: Ltd Time
Carving Date: 00
Release Date: Jun 00
Last Order Date: Mar 01
Issue Size: 3249

Wolfie takes the wheel as Harmony Kingdom's best-known characters take a joyride in a classic convertible. Despite the flat tyre, the old car still has some appeal. Lord Byron sips a soda and Bumbles munches a candy bar as the scenery whizzes past. Mad Murphy winks knowingly as he sneaks a fag - he's supposed to have quit, but we won't tell if you don't. Tubs the Turtle hangs on in the far back, pushing up through the canvas top. On the interior is a birthday cake iced with a large numeral "5." Charter Year members received a "Fab 5" with a different interior: an unidentified Englishman has fallen victim to the Party Boys' offensive driving. There were 281 Charter Year pieces issued. Hallmarks include ©, double diamond, HBC logo, and S.

Field Day
Item No.: RW00MO
Artist: SD
Size: 43x46x47
Status: Ltd Time
Carving Date: 99
Release Date: Jan 00
Last Order Date: Dec 00
Issue Size: 26,566

This sweet miniature box figurine was one of three Royal Watch gifts for joining in 2000. Hallmarks include ©, moon, HBC logo, M and S.

Friends of the Royal Watch
Item No.: RW98TU
Artist: DL
Size: 36x30x49
Status: Ltd Time
Carving Date: 97
Release Date: Apr 98
Last Order Date: Dec 98
Issue Size: 582

This miniature toucan box figurine was offered to 1998 club members as a gift for signing up three friends (US) or one friend (UK) to The Royal Watch.

Harmony Kingdom Box Details

Haji's Hero
Item No.: RW02EL
Artist: MB
Size: 93x56x83
Status: Ltd Time
Carving Date: 01
Release Date: Jan 02
Last Order Date: Jun 03
Issue Size: Not Available

"Haji's Hero" is a 2002 Royal Watch redemption and also the 2002 Zookeepers Series piece. Adopt an Asian elephant at Dickerson Park Zoo in Springfield, Missouri, and you will receive an adoption packet including a miniature Wee Beastie figurine. Hallmarks include ©, miley face, HBC logo, and eye.

Holding Court II
Item No.: RW01MU
Artist: PC
Size: 114x127x115
Status: Ltd Time
Carving Date: 00
Release Date: Dec 00
Last Order Date: Jun 02
Issue Size: 3852

This year 2001 club redemption is the first snow globe created by Harmony Kingdom. Featured is Mad Murphy with harpoon, surrounded by some menacing fish. The snow globe's name pays homage to "Holding Court," the first piece where Murphy appeared. Hallmarks include ©, double diamond, smiley, HBC logo, and Pc.

Leather Anniversary
Item No.: RWCTLE
Artist: PC
Size: 68x45x83
Status: Club Special
Carving Date: 98
Release Date: Jan 99

This racy depiction of Peter and Andrea's third anniversary is the fourth figurine (not a box) in the "Cake Topper" series. Peter felt that the "biker" theme was tame enough for his mum's mantelpiece. Andrea is featured in a one-piece skin-tight black leather outfit and Peter dresses in his leather-riding garb. There are a couple of hints that Peter is not experienced on two wheels: both tyres are flat and the motorcycle is marked with an "L" (British designation for new drivers – "Learners"). This piece is available exclusively to members of The Royal Watch who have been "wedded" to the Royal Watch for four years. Hallmarks include ©, star, HBC logo, ed.#, and Pc.

Lovers' Leap
Item No.: RW00FR
Artist: SD
Size: 38x43x35
Status: Ltd Time
Carving Date: 00
Release Date: Jan 00
Last Order Date: Dec 00
Issue Size: 26,566

This frog box was one of three miniature figurines given as gifts for joining the Royal Watch in 2000. Hallmarks include ©, moon, HBC logo, M, and S.

Magic Bus
Item No.: RWFAB3
Artist: SD
Size: 51x84x64
Status: Ltd Time
Carving Date: 02
Release Date: Apr 02
Last Order Date: Jun 03
Issue Size: Not Available

The Fab Five have invited some friends for a very English adventure on a double decker bus. The bus's destination, Harmony Gardens, is displayed on the front. The sides are emblazoned with "Royal Watchers" and "The Kingdom." Dog that he is, Wolfie can't resist hanging his head out the open window, even though he's driving. The rest of the gang are all crowded on top. The Garden Prince doesn't seem to appreciate Cricket Charlie's bluesy sax. Lord Byron, sporting a baby bottle, beams at Annabella and their little bug, enjoying the air. Peter's "Mouse That Roared" peeks over Annabella's shoulder, and behind him Bumbles munches on a snack, as usual. Ever the techno-cat, Minx makes a call on her cell phone. The incorrigible Mad Murphy poses as the conductor with his cap and bag. The bus's license plate reads "HK02," an abbreviation for Harmony Kingdom 2002. On the interior, Tubbs the Turtle makes a few mechanical repairs. Charter Year members with seven consecutive years of membership have the opportunity to purchase a special edition, showing Tubbs rolling lucky sevens on a pair of dice. Hallmarks include ©, smiley face, HBC logo, and S.

Merry-Go-Round
Item No.: RW00DO
Artist: SD
Size: 39x35x40
Status: Ltd Time
Carving Date: 99
Release Date: Jan 00
Last Order Date: Dec 00
Issue Size: 26,566

These playful dolphins were one of three miniature box figurines given as the year 2000 gift for joining the Royal Watch Collector's Club. Hallmarks include ©, moon, HBC logo, M, and S.

Minx on the Moon

Item No.: RW01MI
Artist: AB
Size: 57x63x70
Status: Ltd Time
Carving Date: 00
Release Date: Dec 00
Last Order Date: Feb 02
Issue Size: 15,889

Wondering whether she has packed enough for the trip, space fashion conscious Minx patiently waits for Wolfie to return with a trolley for her designer suitcases complete with designer destination labels. Minx has also bought with her Charlie, her pet canary, who doesn't exactly look excited about his virgin voyage. We catch Minx's expression just at the moment when Wolfie tears past her at high speed on an already overloaded trolley. "Typical," she tuts, before picking up her "Rough Guide to Space" and continuing her search for knowledge. Her camera is packed along with a dog training book (to bring Wolfie to heel) and Minx's vice of choice, special dried mice. This box figurine was a club gift for joining the Royal Watch in 2001. Hallmarks include ©, double diamond, HBC logo, and gecko.

Moon Rovers

Item No.: RWFAB2
Artist: SD
Size: 51x83x63
Status: Ltd Time
Carving Date: 01
Release Date: Apr 01
Last Order Date: Jun 02
Issue Size: 1380

It's one giant leap for HK as the Space Gang enjoys a daytrip on the moon. They don't make five-seater moon buggies, but Murphy's not complaining. Neither is anyone else, as he's gone off the patch and has taken to smoking again. Lord Byron seems a little distracted from his driving, having discovered the universe's smallest star. Behind him, Bumbles fears his spacesuit makes him look a bit chubby, but that cream bun is simply irresistible. Despite having been part of the pack for a while now, Wolfie still wears his camoflauge: sheep's clothing pokes out from under his helmet and suit. Minx, checking her makeup in the back seat, knows exactly what kind of dog he is. The interior has a crater, footprints, and an HK flag. Charter Year members were eligible to receive a special variation with a license plate showing "HK6" and "LUNAR1," plus a U.K. or U.S. flag. Hallmarks include ©, double diamond, HBC logo, and S.

The Mouse That Roared
Item No.: RWMO
Artist: PC
Size: 44x57x89
Status: Ltd Time
Carving Date: 96
Release Date: Jul 99
Last Order Date: Dec 99
Issue Size: 3439

This box figurine is a bigger-than-life depiction of Peter's signature mouse. Offered exclusively to members of independent, authorised Harmony Kingdom clubs, the "Jr." medallion around the mouse's neck pays tribute to these "junior" clubs. The mouse cups a miniature elephant in his paws, signifying the might of the independents. Hallmarks include ©, heart, HBC logo, ed.#, and Pc.

Murphy Pin
Item No.: RW99PI
Artist: PC
Size: 38x9x48
Status: Ltd Time
Carving Date: 98
Release Date: Jan 99
Last Order Date: Dec 99
Issue Size: 26,109

This gift pin, contained within membership kits, was available exclusively to 1999 club members. It features one of the most beloved Harmony Kingdom characters – Murphy the scofflaw penguin.

The Mushroom
Item No.: RW98MU
Artist: MP
Size: 83x87x106
Status: Ltd Time
Carving Date: 97
Release Date: Jan 98
Last Order Date: Mar 99
Issue Size: 7908

This box figurine, featuring an elaborate colourful interior library with Lord Byron and bookworms, was the 1998 exclusive club redemption piece. Hallmarks include ©, heart, HBC logo, ed.#, and M.

Mutton Chops
Item No.: RW98MC
Artist: PC
Size: 52x46x58
Status: Ltd Time
Carving Date: 96
Release Date: Jan 98
Last Order Date: Dec 98
Issue Size: 26,028

Based on the Aesop Fable of a wolf in sheep's clothing, this box figurine features two placid sheep and a hungry wolf in sheep's clothing. This gift piece, contained within membership kits, was available exclusively to 1998 club members. The mouse is tucked in the lamb's wool on the wolf's back. Inside are two lamb chops. "TYLS" stands for "Thank You Lynn Stryck," the collector who suggested the idea to Peter. Hallmarks include ©, diamond, HBC logo, ed.#, and Pc.

Night Watch
Item No.: RW01BB
Artist: MB
Size: 102x51x89
Status: Ltd Time
Carving Date: 00
Release Date: Dec 00
Last Order Date: Jun 02
Issue Size: 3697

Byron and Bumbles again team up for the 2001 Royal Watch redemption piece. This time, they are visiting the moon. This box figurine was available to year 2001 Royal Watch members. Hallmarks include ©, double diamond, HBC logo, and eye.

Paper Anniversary
Item No.: RW97PA
Artist: PC
Size: 58x60x79
Status: Ltd Time
Carving Date: 96
Release Date: Jan 97
Last Order Date: Mar 98
Issue Size: 1600

Carved to celebrate their first anniversary, this figurine (not a box) is the second piece in the "Cake Topper" series and is a tongue in cheek depiction of Peter and Andrea after their first year of marriage. Cuddled together on an armchair, they are surrounded by the family pets (Murphy the dog, Spike the cockatiel, Algy the cat, and Peter's mouse). The couple is reading the sports pages in the newspaper, as Peter is a golf fanatic and Andrea has a passion for horses. Peter is wearing his "Yeoman of the Guard" pendant. This figurine was available exclusively to 1997 members of The Royal Watch. Hallmarks include ©, diamond, clock face with month 8, HBC logo, and Pc.

Pell Mell
Item No.: RW99PE
Artist: DL
Size: 88x90x112
Status: Ltd Time
Carving Date: 98
Release Date: Jan 99
Last Order Date: Mar 00
Issue Size: 7470

This box figurine, featuring four majestic pelicans feeding their young, was the 1999 exclusive club redemption piece. Inscribed around the base is the saying, "A wonderful bird is the Pelican" is inscribed around the base, with an anchor carved in the interior. Hallmarks include ©, star, HBC logo, ed.#, and DL.

Psst! Are You a Member?
Item No.: RWHOP00
Artist: SD
Size: 38x6x57
Status: Ltd Time
Carving Date: 00
Release Date: Sep 00
Issue Size: 4000

This pin was given as a gift by HK and HOP to year 2000 members of the Royal Watch and an Independent Authorised Club. Featured are Mad Murphy and the mouse from 1999's independent club piece, "The Mouse That Roared."

Purrfect Fit
Item No.: RW96DL
Artist: DL
Size: 75x59x66
Status: Ltd Time
Carving Date: 95
Release Date: Apr 96
Last Order Date: Dec 96
Issue Size: 5236

This box figurine, featuring a cat in a stylized Victorian boot, was the inaugural club gift contained in 1996 membership kits. One hundred and ninety nine pieces were shipped in the UK to non-members. Hallmarks include ©, RW 96, HBC logo, and DL.

Rule Britannia
Item No.: RW02LI
Artist: PC
Size: 35x55x63
Status: Ltd Time
Carving Date: 01
Release Date: Jan 02
Last Order Date: Mar 03
Issue Size: Not Available

This regal lion is a 2002 club gift for joining. The theme for 2002 is "Rule Britannia." The lion proudly stands with one paw on a sign that reads "Keep Off the Grass." Hallmarks include ©, smiley face, HBC logo, and Pc.

Silk Anniversary
Item No.: RWCTSI
Artist: PC
Size: 51x45x72
Status: Club Special
Carving Date: 99
Release Date: Jan 00

If you have been a member of the Royal Watch Collector's Club for five consecutive years, you are eligible to purchase "Silk Anniversary." Peter's research showed different gifts for the fourth anniversary - silk or books. Combining the two, he sculpted himself and Andrea as a pair of worms - either silkworms or bookworms. The mouse is snuggled between their bellies. One too many holes were carved for the hallmarks, so one was turned into a smiley face. Hallmarks include ©, moon, smiley, HBC logo, and Pc.

Solemate
Item No.: RW99DL
Artist: DL
Size: 58x60x79
Status: Ltd Time
Carving Date: 96
Release Date: Jan 99
Last Order Date: Dec 99
Issue Size: 4005

This box figurine is the companion piece to the inaugural club gift "Purrfect Fit." Offered to 1999 Royal Watch members who pre-ordered their year 2000 and 2001 memberships, the floppy mutt contrasts to the stylized Victorian boot in which it is tucked. The mutt's bone is found inside. Hallmarks include ©, diamond, clock face with month 8, HBC logo, and DL.

Harmony Kingdom Box Details

Softly, Softly
Item No.: RW02OW
Artist: PC
Size: 51x56x117
Status: Ltd Time
Carving Date: 02
Release Date: Mar 02
Last Order Date: Jun 03
Issue Size: Not Available

With their soft feathers, forward-facing eyes and sharp talons, owls are the ultimate nighttime hunters. This beautiful barn owl looks somewhat nonplussed to discover that it has just caught a clockwork mouse. The S.F. initials inscribed on the toy show that it formerly belonged to Samuel Frederick (Calvesbert), the artist's son, before winding up in the bird's claws.

This Royal Watch members-only box figurine also features the return of the discarded tin can, found on many older HK pieces as a reminder of humankind's impact on the environment. Inside are the hapless victims of the day – loads of mice. Hallmarks include ©, peace sign, HBC logo, and Pc.

The Sunflower
Item No.: RW97SU
Artist: MP
Size: 59x70x122
Status: Ltd Time
Carving Date: 97
Release Date: Jan 97
Last Order Date: Mar 98
Issue Size: 5289

This box figurine, featuring Lord Byron seeking advice from a dove, was the 1997 exclusive club redemption piece. The earlier versions have six leaves, and the later models five. Hallmarks include ©, heart, HBC logo, ed.#, and M.

Sweet As A Summer's Kiss
Item No.: RW97DL
Artist: DL
Size: 46x42x49
Status: Ltd Time
Carving Date: Jul 96
Release Date: Jan 97
Last Order Date: Dec 97
Issue Size: 15,885

This box figurine, depicting a sweet summer strawberry and a butterfly, was the club gift contained in 1997 membership kits. Inside are two mice nibbling on the strawberry. David says that this piece was intended to "capture the delicacy and fleeting precious nature of summer." "37" denotes this box figurine as the thirty-seventh piece David carved. Hallmarks include ©, diamond, HBC logo, clock face with month 7 and DL.

Toad Pin
Item No.: RW97PC
Artist: PC
Size: 56x54x15
Status: Ltd Time
Carving Date: 96
Release Date: Jan 97
Last Order Date: Dec 97
Issue Size: 16,310

This gift pin, contained within membership kits, was available exclusively to 1997 club members and is the first pin produced by Harmony Kingdom.

Wolfie In Space
Item No.: RW01WO
Artist: PC
Size: 63x44x70
Status: Ltd Time
Carving Date: 00
Release Date: Dec 00
Last Order Date: Mar 02
Issue Size: 15,889

Wolfie is doing his best to impress Minx at Gatrow Spaceport by jet propelling himself and his luggage trolley around the departure lounge while blowing kisses. But will his tatty spacesuit, with its rips and patches, his cracked helmet, and wellingtons instead of space boots impress the discriminating Minx? Wolfie has obviously exceeded his alcohol and tobacco limit at the duty free shops, but is oblivious to his losses as his purchases are scattered behind him. Inside the box are the largest bottle of aftershave he could find and a book on the celebrated lover "Catanova." Peter's mouse stows away in a shopping bag emblazoned with the slogan of a neighboring planet. Hallmarks include ©, double diamond, HBC logo, and Pc.

Wood Anniversary
Item No.: RWCTWO
Artist: PC
Size: 63x51x76
Status: Club Special
Carving Date: 00
Release Date: Dec 00

As an apology to his wife Andrea, for not being able to transfer her natural beauty to a Box Figurine, Peter has allowed her to have the upper hand in "Wood Anniversary." She saws Peter and his favourite golf club in two. On the floor is a clue as to why: a final demand from Foxwood, a casino Peter visited in America. Murphy plays her usual game trying to outstare a baseball, while puss cowers under the box. A woodpecker observes the action. Peter also sports one of his infamous Harmony Ball ties. As the carving neared completion, Peter and Andrea were elated by the news they were to become parents and so "June 15?" was added to the bottom of the casket as a guess as to when the Calvesbert baby will arrive. The mouse takes shelter under Andrea's arm. Hallmarks include ©, double diamond, HBC logo, and Pc.

THE ELUSIVE FEW

Angel Baroque
Item No.: None
Artist: DL
Size: Not Available
Status: Retired
Carving Date: 95
Release Date: Jun 96
Last Ship Date: Nov 97
Issue Size: 62

Photo Not Available

This box figurine was a precursor to the Angelique series and features two angels, both playing instruments. Two rabbits frame the inscription "In Arcadia Ego" which means "I, too, am in heaven," and a deer and two doves nestle beside the initials DL. Never released in the U.S., and with very limited release in the U.K., this is amongst the rarest HK pieces. Hallmarks include apple, clock face with month 11, HBC logo, and DL.

Panda
Item No.: TJXXPA
Artist: PC
Size: 63x36x49
Status: Retired
Carving Date: 93
Release Date: Dec 93
Last Ship Date: Nov 96
Issue Size: 482

This box figurine is one of the "Elusive Few." Only 100 pieces were released in the U.S. by HBC. The mouse is under the panda's paw. Colouration varies from brown and cream to black and white. This piece does not incorporate inscriptions, inner carving, or hallmarks.

Ram
Item No.: TJXXRA
Artist: MP
Size: 65x40x41
Status: Retired
Carving Date: 90
Release Date: Jan 93
Last Ship Date: Feb 95
Issue size: 423

This box figurine is one of the "Elusive Few." Only 100 pieces were released in the U.S. by HBC. This piece does not incorporate the hidden mouse, inscriptions, inner carving, or hallmarks.

Rooster (Cockerel)
Item No.: XXXTJRO
Artist: PC
Size: 72x40x60
Status: Retired
Carving Date: 93
Release Date: Dec 93
Last Ship Date: Jul 97
Issue size: 539

This box figurine is one of the "Elusive Few." Only 300 pieces were released in the U.S. by HBC. This piece does not incorporate the hidden mouse, inscriptions, inner carving, or hallmarks.

Rooster, Large
Item No.: None
Artist: PC
Size: 112x61x91
Status: Retired
Carving Date: 91
Release Date: Nov 91
Last Ship Date: Apr 94
Issue Size: 821

Photo Not Available

This box figurine is the first elusive and was not released by HBC. "SAC" appears on some pieces; others have a blank placard where "SAC" was removed. As a precursor to the Rooster (Cockerel), this is a larger version. It does not incorporate the hidden mouse, inscriptions, inner carving, or hallmarks.

Shark
Item No.: TJXXSH
Artist: PC
Size: 72x50x55
Status: Retired
Carving Date: 93
Release Date: Dec 93
Last Ship Date: Feb 95
Issue Size: 402

This box figurine is one of the "Elusive Few." Only 100 pieces were released in the U.S. by HBC. The colouration on the eyes may vary, though most are blue or orange. This piece does not incorporate the hidden mouse, inscriptions, inner carving, or hallmarks.

Sheep (Shaggy) Dog
Item No.: XXXTJSD
Artist: PC
Size: 74x32x50
Status: Retired
Carving Date: 93
Release Date: Dec 93
Last Ship Date: Jun 97
Issue Size: 659

This box figurine is one of the "Elusive Few." Only 300 pieces were released in the U.S. by HBC. This piece does not incorporate the hidden mouse, inscriptions, inner carving, or hallmarks.

Shoebill
Item No.: XXXTJSB
Artist: PC
Size: 54x36x65
Status: Retired
Carving Date: 95
Release Date: Sep 95
Last Ship Date: Jun 97
Issue Size: 442

This box figurine is one of the "Elusive Few." Originally released in the U.K., they were removed from circulation in January 1996. In April 1997, HBC offered a limited release of 300 pieces. Hidden in the reeds are "Shoebill" and "P Calvesbert." The signature mouse appeared in the original U.K. pieces, but was missing from most of the re-released boxes. None incorporated inner carvings, or hallmarks, except for the interior HBC logo.

Teapot Angel I
Item No.: None
Artist: DL
Size: 68x79x48
Status: Retired
Carving Date: 95
Release Date: Jun 95
Last Ship Date: Mar 96
Issue Size: 43

This box figurine depicts three angels, one playing a lute, one drinking a cup of tea, and one taking a nap. The lute player has jogged the tea drinker's cup and spilt the tea. Never released in the U.S., and with very limited release in the U.K., this is amongst the most rare of HK pieces. Inside is a letter "N". Hallmarks include ©, HBC logo, 95, I, and DL.

Teapot Angel II
Item No.: None
Artist: DL
Size: 69x64x50
Status: Retired
Carving Date: 95
Release Date: Jun 95
Last Ship Date: Mar 96
Issue Size: 43

This box figurine depicts the aftermath of the spilt tea from Version 1. A broken lute, torn book, and black eye are the result. Hallmarks include ©, HBC logo, 95, II, and DL. Never released in the U.S., and with very limited release in the U.K., this is amongst the most rare of HK pieces.

SPECIAL EDITIONS
BUYING GROUPS

Cosa Nostra
Item No.: TJLEB00S
Artist: AR
Size: 57x57x89
Status: Ltd Ed
Carving Date: 99
Release Date: Jan 00
Last Ship Date: Not Available
Issue Size: 5000

Cats have nine lives, so you needn't worry about our alabaster feline. She will rise from the flames like the mythical phoenix, renewed and more beautiful. This limited edition box figurine has been created for three buying groups - Gifts Creations Concepts, Parade of Gifts, and Parkwest - hence the inclusion of three of Harmony Kingdom's favourite characters within the interior, Byron, Bumbles, and Mad Murphy. Hallmarks include ©, moon, HBC logo, and AR.

Night Light
Item No.: TJLEB00F
Artist: AR
Size: 60x58x70
Status: Ltd Ed
Carving Date: 99
Release Date: Jun 00
Last Ship Date: Dec 01
Issue Size: 3600

Sam the cat lives in a pawnshop, surrounded by an eclectic collection of items. The centre of the display is a lovely antique lamp. Sam's long tail gently wraps around a Chinese vase and polishes away any dust with his feather duster. Several mice help out with the chores. An exotic-looking dog is tied to the lamp. Look carefully at the legs - they seem to have been repaired with the tube of "Uhoo" glue lying nearby. Sam has caught a tiny mouse, which is squashed under the rug beneath his right paw. Hallmarks include ©, double diamond, HBC logo, and AR.

SPECIAL EDITIONS
DISNEY

101 Dalmations
Item No.: WDWR101
Artist: RK
Size: 84x76x71
Status: Ltd to Disney
Carving Date: 01
Release Date: Apr 02

The famous Disney puppies are gathered around watching their favorite television program, unaware that Cruella de Vil lurks nearby. Hallmarks include © Disney.

Alice in Wonderland
Item No.: WDWRAL
Artist: RK
Size: 79x63x82
Status: Ltd to Disney
Carving Date: 01
Release Date: May 01
Issue Size: 1951

The memorable characters from Disney's 1951 classic are featured on this colorful limited edition. Hallmarks include © Disney.

Aristocats
Item No.: WDWRAC
Artist: RK
Size: 64x64x64x
Status: Ltd to Disney
Carving Date: 00
Release Date: Oct 00

This Disney exclusive box figurine shows Thomas O'Malley, Dutchess and the kittens. Hallmarks include © Disney.

Bambi
Item No.: WDWRBA
Artist: PS
Size: 89x71x66
Status: Ltd to Disney
Carving Date: 01
Release Date: Jan 02

Thumper and friends help young Bambi get his legs under him. Hallmarks include © Disney.

Be Our Guest
Item No.: WDWBEAU
Artist: RK
Size: 89x83x102
Status: Ltd to Disney
Carving Date: 00
Release Date: Oct 00

Belle and the Beast share a special dance. Hallmarks include © Disney.

Beauty and the Beast
Item No.: WDWRBB
Artist: RK
Size: 76x66x74
Status: Ltd to Disney
Carving Date: 01
Release Date: Jan 02

Enchanting animated objects that made up the supporting cast of the film here are given star status. Hallmarks include © Disney.

Bibbidi-Bobbidi-Boo
Item No.: WDWCIN
Artist: RK
Size: 152x127x108
Status: Ltd to Disney
Carving Date: 00
Release Date: Aug 00
Issue Size: 400

It's sheer magic when Cinderella meets her prince. Hallmarks include © Disney.

This piece was carved for the Disneyana 2000 Convention.

Cheshire Cat
Item No.: WDWRCC
Artist: PS
Size: 56x46x41
Status: Ltd to Disney
Carving Date: 02
Release Date: Apr 02
Issue Size: 5000

"Alice in Wonderland's" famous Cheshire Cat shows off his infamous grin. Hallmarks include © Disney.

Classic Pooh
Item No.: WDWRPO
Artist: RK
Size: 76x82x76
Status: Ltd to Disney
Carving Date: 01
Release Date: Jul 01
Issue Size: 1926

Pooh and friends wait out a shower in the Hundred Acre Woods. Hallmarks include © Disney.

Disney Multi-Cats
Item No.: WDWRCA
Artist: PS
Size: 95x89x135
Status: Ltd to Disney
Carving Date: 02
Release Date: Apr 02
Issue Size: 1500

Some of Disney's most popular cat characters, both good-hearted and naughty, are shown on this limited edition. Hallmarks include © Disney.

Disney Multi-Dogs
Item No.: WDWRDO
Artist: PS
Size: 157x127x89
Status: Ltd to Disney
Carving Date: 02
Release Date: Apr 02
Issue Size: 1500

Disney's doggie characters gather together for a portrait on this limited edition. Hallmarks include © Disney.

Donald Through the Years
Item No.: WDWRDD
Artist: RK
Size: 64x64x64
Status: Ltd to Disney
Carving Date: 00
Release Date: Oct 00

The history of everybody's favorite duck is encapsulated on this whimsical box figurine. Hallmarks include © Disney.

Fab Five
Item No.: WDWFABFIVE
Artist: RK
Size: 103x95x95
Status: Ltd to Disney
Carving Date: 97
Release Date: Dec 97

"Fab Five" (Disney's item number 15600540) is the second box figurine in the Disney series. Mickey, Minnie, Goofy, Donald and Pluto are crowded into a convertible. Inside is a spare tyre. Hallmarks include ©Disney.

Family Picnic
Item No.: WDWPIC
Artist: RK
Size: 146x127x108
Status: Ltd to Disney
Carving Date: 01
Release Date: Sep 01
Issue Size: 400

This 2001 Disneyana exclusive is limited to 400 numbered pieces. Hallmarks include © Disney.

Feisty Fellow
Item No.: WDWDON
Artist: RK
Size: 102x82x86
Status: Ltd to Disney
Carving Date: 00
Release Date: Jun 00

Moments from Donald's career are featured on this box figurine. Hallmarks include © Disney.

Harmony Kingdom Box Details

Figaro
Item No.: WDWRFI
Artist: PS
Size: 46x38x41
Status: Ltd to Disney
Carving Date: 02
Release Date: Apr 02
Issue Size: 5000

Geppetto's black and white kitten, and Pinocchio's companion, pouts on this Disney exclusive Roly Poly. Hallmarks include © Disney.

Happy Haunts
Item No.: WDWHA
Artist: RK
Size: 92x82x88
Status: Ltd to Disney
Carving Date: 01
Release Date: Jul 01

The first 999 feature spider webs on the exterior, and a creepy crawly spider on the interior. Hallmarks include © Disney.

Jungle Book
Item No.: WDWRJB
Artist: PS
Size: 127x97x119
Status: Ltd to Disney
Carving Date: 02
Release Date: Apr 02
Issue Size: 1500

The characters adapted from Kipling's classic react to King Louie's antics. Hallmarks include © Disney.

Lady and the Tramp
Item No.: WDWRLT
Artist: RK
Size: 64x64x64
Status: Ltd to Disney
Carving Date: 00
Release Date: Oct 00

This box figurine shows characters from Disney's 1955 animated love story. Hallmarks include © Disney.

Harmony Kingdom Box Details

Land Ahoy!
Item No.: WDWBOAT
Artist: RK
Size: 94x114x133
Status: Ltd to Disney
Carving Date: 01
Release Date: Apr 01

A shipload of Disney characters, including Mickey and Minnie Mouse, Pluto and Goofy, set sail on a cruise. Hallmarks include © Disney.

Lion King's Pride Rock
Item No.: WDWLIONKING
Artist: RK
Size: 108x106x101
Status: Ltd to Disney
Carving Date: 98
Release Date: Sep 98

"Lion King's Pride Rock" is the third box figurine in the Disney series. Inside is an etching of a lion cub. Hallmarks include © Disney.

Lucifer
Item No.: WDWRLU
Artist: PS
Size: 51x57x41
Status: Ltd to Disney
Carving Date: 02
Release Date: Apr 02
Issue Size: 5000

The villainous cat from Disney's "Cinderella" earns a solo appearance on this Roly Poly. Hallmarks include © Disney.

Mickey Mouse Club
Item No.: DAMC
Artist: RK
Size: 76x70x75
Status: Ltd to Disney
Carving Date: 02
Release Date: Mar 02
Issue Size: 500

Available only through Disney Auctions, this box figurine shows moments from Mickey's history. Hallmarks include © Disney.

Mickey Through the Years
Item No.: WDWRMM
Artist: RK
Size: 64x64x64
Status: Ltd to Disney
Carving Date: 00
Release Date: Oct 00

This box figurine evokes memories of everybody's favorite mouse. Hallmarks include © Disney.

Mickey's Fire Brigade
Item No.: WDWRFB
Artist: PS
Size: 124x76x71
Status: Ltd to Disney
Carving Date: 02
Release Date: Apr 02
Issue Size: 3000

Mickey, Donald and Goofy rescue Clarabelle Cow, whether she likes it or not. Hallmarks include © Disney.

Nightmare Before Christmas
Item No.: WDWRNM
Artist: RK
Size: 51x51x93
Status: Ltd to Disney
Carving Date: 01
Release Date: Feb 01

This box figurine features Jack Skellington, Sally, the Mayor and Lock, Shock and Barrel. Hallmarks include © Disney.

Off to Neverland!
Item No.: WDWPET
Artist: RK
Size: 82x120x89
Status: Ltd to Disney
Carving Date: 01
Release Date: Sep 01

Join Peter Pan and Wendy for a magical journey. Hallmarks include © Disney.

Part of Your World
Item No.: WDWMER
Artist: RK
Size: 89x83x102
Status: Ltd to Disney
Carving Date: 00
Release Date: Aug 00

Ariel and Eric meet, surrounded by the cast of characters. Hallmarks include © Disney.

Pinocchio's Great Adventure
Item No.: WDWPIN
Artist: RK
Size: 102x46x90
Status: Ltd to Disney
Carving Date: 99
Release Date: Sep 99

"Pinocchio's Great Adventure" is the fifth box figurine in the Disney series. Pinocchio, Geppetto, the Blue Fairy and other characters from this classic tale appear on the box figurine. Inside is Jiminy Cricket. Hallmarks include ©Disney.

Pooh And Friends
Item No.: WDWPOOH
Artist: TM
Size: 77x78x78
Status: Ltd to Disney
Carving Date: 97
Release Date: Aug 97

"Pooh and Friends" is the first box figurine in the Disney series, featuring Winnie the Pooh, Owl, Tigger, Eeyore, Piglet, Kanga, Roo, and Rabbit. Inside is an overflowing honey pot. Hallmarks include ©Disney.

Snow White
Item No.: WDWSNOWWHITE
Artist: RK
Size: 86x85x98
Status: Ltd to Disney
Carving Date: 98
Release Date: Jan 99

"Snow White" is the fourth box figurine in the Disney series. The seven dwarfs encircle Snow White. Inside is a red apple. Hallmarks include ©Disney.

Harmony Kingdom Box Details

Steamboat Willie
Item No.: DASW
Artist: RK
Size: 70x70x82
Status: Ltd to Disney
Carving Date: 01
Release Date: Oct 01
Issue Size: 500

This unique Box Figurine is a Disney Auctions exclusive. It was available only on the Disney Auctions website. Hallmarks include © Disney.

Teacup Twirl
Item No.: WDWAL
Artist: RK
Size: 98x76x102
Status: Ltd to Disney
Carving Date: 01
Release Date: Aug 01

Alice and the White Rabbit go for a wild ride. Hallmarks include © Disney.

To the Laughing Place
Item No.: WDWSP
Artist: RK
Size: 76x95x106
Status: Ltd to Disney
Carving Date: 01
Release Date: Aug 01

The tale of the "Laughing Places' is one of Uncle Remus's stories from Disney's "Song of the South." Hallmarks include © Disney.

Wicked Ways
Item No.: WDWVIL
Artist: RK
Size: 101x76x101
Status: Ltd to Disney
Carving Date: 99
Release Date: Jun 00
Issue Size: 5000

Everyone loves a good villain, and no one makes them better than Disney. Hallmarks include © Disney.

Harmony Kingdom Box Details

SPECIAL EDITIONS
Event Pieces

2001 Memories Dinner Flower Pot
Item No.: ICE01M
Artist: SD
Size: 76x76x44
Status: Ltd to Event
Carving Date: 00
Release Date: Apr 01
Issue Size: 1000

This box figurine was given to attendees of the 2001 Memories Dinner sponsored by Harmony Kingdom at the Rosemont International Collectibles Exposition. Hallmarks include ©, double diamond, HBC logo, and S.

A Day At The Races
Item No.: RW01LEHIMA
Artist: PC
Size: 40x57x83
Status: Ltd to Event
Carving Date: 01
Release Date: Jun 01
Issue Size: 450

The Royal Watch Sixth Birthday Party featured a pantomime horse race. Participants received this exclusive figurine to commemorate the event. Hallmarks include ©, smiley face, HBC logo, and Pc.

Alley Cat's Meow
Item No.: TJMINEVE4
Artist: MB
Size: 64x64x64
Status: Ltd to Event
Carving Date: 99
Release Date: May 00
Issue Size: 3710

This street-wise kitty is the fourth in the Cat's Meow Tour event exclusives. Hallmarks include ©, double diamond, HBC logo, and eye.

Anaheim '01 Minx Pendant
Item No.: XXYAN01Z
Artist: AB
Size: 19x19x51
Status: Ltd to Event
Carving Date: 01
Release Date: Feb 01
Issue Size: 1440

This solid pendant was created for Royal Watch members who attended the 2001 ICE in Anaheim, California and for those who signed up to the club while at the show. "Anaheim 2001" is on Minx's leg.

Harmony Kingdom Box Details

Atlanta '00 Bumbles Pendant
Item No.: XXYAT00Z
Artist: MB
Size: 25x25x38
Status: Ltd to Event
Carving Date: 99
Release Date: Mar 00
Issue Size: 2000

This pendant was given to current Royal Watch members attending the International Collectibles Exposition in Atlanta in May 2000, and to those who registered at the show.

Atlantic City '02 Murphy Pendant
Item No.: XXYAC02Z
Artist: SD
Size: 20x25x38
Status: Ltd to Event
Carving Date: 01
Release Date: Mar 02
Issue Size: 775

This pendant was intended to be given to Royal Watch club members, and those who joined the club, at the Atlantic City International Gift and Collectible Exposition. Although the Atlantic City show was cancelled, the pendants were made available as a donation to Harmony Kingdom Authorized Independent Clubs.

Bela
Item No.: TJEV01D
Artist: AB
Size: 38x41x44
Status: Ltd to Event
Carving Date: 01
Release Date: Sep 01
Issue Size: 5751

The US and Canadian versions include an oak leaf inscribed on the interiors, while in the UK a sprig of ivy appears carved on the insides. There are 575 Hard Bodies world wide. One set was inlaid with gemstones and hand painted by Artistic Director Martin Perry. Hallmarks include ©, smiley face, HBC logo and gecko.

Bumbles on Planet Paradise
Item No.: XXYPP01Z
Artist: MB
Size: 25x19x38
Status: Ltd to Event
Carving Date: 01
Release Date: Feb 01
Issue Size: 250

Bumbles the Bee salutes Harmony Kingdom collectors from his vantage point on Planet Paradise. This pendant was a gift given at the Paradise Found event at Anaheim, 2001.

Byron's Bacchanal
Item No.: TJICE00M
Artist: SD
Size: 76x63x63
Status: Ltd to Event
Carving Date: 99
Release Date: Mar 00
Issue Size: 1000

This colourful collection of fruit opens to reveal Lord Byron dining with three friends at the Atlanta 2000 ICE Memories Dinner, hosted by Harmony Kingdom. This box figurine was given as a gift to all attendees. Hallmarks include ©, heart, HBC logo, and S.

Camelot
Item No.: TJROSE99
Artist: PC/MB
Size: 84x45x62
Status: Ltd to Event
Carving Date: 98
Release Date: Jun 99
Issue Size: 800

This box figurine is a modified version of "Catch A Lot," retired three months prior to Harmony Kingdom's Grand Investiture at which "Camelot" was the special event piece. Medieval twists were added to "Camelot," including Lord Byron fighting off a massive sea monster. This is the first collaboration between Peter Calvesbert and Monique Baldwin. The interior depicts a swarm of boats. The mouse is inside a life preserver. Hallmarks include ©, star, HBC logo, Pc, and eye.

Cat Nap's Meow
Item No.: TJMINEVE3
Artist: SD
Size: 69x66x48
Status: Ltd to Event
Carving Date: 00
Release Date: Mar 00
Issue Size: 3893

This is the third event piece for the Cat's Meow Tour. Hallmarks include ©, double diamond, HBC logo, and S.

Cat's Meow
Item No.: TJMINEVE
Artist: PC
Size: 45x25x58
Status: Ltd to Event
Carving Date: 99
Release Date: Oct 99
Issue Size: 4068

This figurine was available exclusively to those who attended signing events where Noel Wiggins or Nick Dangar were present. Hallmarks include ©, moon, HBC logo, and Pc.

Chucky Pig
Item No.: XXXTJCP
Artist: PC
Size: 53x42x60
Status: Donation
Carving Date: 96
Release Date: Aug 99
Retired Date: Aug 99
Issue Size: 300

This is the first box figurine produced by Harmony Kingdom exclusively for fundraisers. Over $150,000 (USD) was raised from the proceeds. Harmony Kingdom donated two each to Queen Empress dealers hosting a "Queen of the Jungle" event. These dealers auctioned or raffled their pieces for charitable causes of their choosing. Harmony Kingdom also donated one piece to each of the independent, authorised Harmony Kingdom clubs, who donated at least 50% of the proceeds to a selected charity. The box figurine is elegant and stylized, yet it depicts a wood louse (Chucky Pig is the British euphemism for this insect). The interior contains the HBC logo. Hallmarks include ©, diamond, clock face with month 2, HBC logo, and Pc.

Harmony Kingdom Box Details

Clair
Item No.: XXYCLC
Artist: JB
Size: 76x95x89
Status: Ltd to Event
Carving Date: 99
Release Date: Jun 00
Issue Size: 450

This exclusive box figurine, given as a gift to Clair de Lune attendees, depicts Clair, for whom the collection and convention were named. Hallmarks include ©, moon, HBC logo, and M.

Clair de Meow
Item No.: TJMINEVE5
Artist: JB
Size: 51x47x74
Status: Ltd to Event
Carving Date: 00
Release Date: Sep 00
Issue Size: 3642

This is the fifth in the series for the Cat's Meow Tour event pieces. Hallmarks include ©, double diamond, HBC logo, and M.

Crooze Cat
Item No.: XXYTJCC
Artist: PC
Size: 40x63x63
Status: Ltd to Event
Carving Date: 99
Release Date: Sep 99
Issue Size: 739

This figurine was available exclusively to those who attended Primordial Crooze. Each participant was allowed to purchase up to two pieces. Peter began to sculpt this piece aboard the cruise. Hallmarks include ©, moon, HBC logo, and Pc.

Dragon Breath
Item No.: XXYTJZDR
Artist: DL
Size: 30x35x46
Status: Ltd to Event
Carving Date: 96
Release Date: Jun 99
Issue Size: 360

The charming dragon depicted in this miniature box figurine is fighting his fiery breath the best way he can - with a toothbrush. This piece was given as a gift to anyone who placed a reservation for Clair de Lune, Event 2000, by 15th of September 1999. Hallmarks include ©, diamond, HBC logo, and M.

Earl Cadogan's Tea Party
Item No.: TJEV02TP
Artist: MB
Size: 57 x 59 x 76
Status: Ltd to Event
Carving Date: 02
Release Date: Apr 02
Issue Size: 4000

Staffordshire, home of the center of English porcelain production, was also home to Earl Cadogan. He was the first Englishman to own a curiosity piece from China known as a "wine pourer." Since the vessel was packed in tea leaves to keep it from breaking on the long voyage, the British assumed that it was to be used to brew tea. Thus, the European concept of the teapot was born. Today, a Cadogan is a type of lidless teapot. The water is poured in through a hole in the bottom, and then the pot is quickly turned right side up. An interior funnel prevents leaking. This box figurine was exclusively available at the August 2002 HK Tea Party events. Hallmarks include ©, peace sign, HBC logo, and eye.

Edison '98 Angel Pendant
Item No.: XXYED98Z
Artist: DL
Size: 35x26x46
Status: Ltd to Event
Carving Date: 96
Release Date: Apr 98
Issue Size: 1064

This box figurine pendant was given to current Royal Watch members attending the International Collectibles Exposition in Edison, New Jersey in April 1998, and to those who registered at the show.

Edison '98 Lovebird Pin
Item No.: XXYED98P
Artist: PC
Size: 43x48x19
Status: Ltd to Event
Carving Date: 95
Release Date: Apr 98
Issue Size: 428

This pin was given to those who attended the Memories Dinner held at the International Collectibles Exposition in Edison, New Jersey in April 1998.

Fang

Item No.: TJEV01B
Artist: AB
Size: 41x38x51
Status: Ltd to Event
Carving Date: 01
Release Date: Sep 01
Issue Size: 5751

The US and Canadian versions include an oak leaf inscribed on the interiors, while in the UK a sprig of ivy appears carved on the insides. There are 575 Hard Bodies world wide. One set of was inlaid with gemstones and hand painted by Artistic Director Martin Perry. Hallmarks include ©, smiley face, HBC logo, and gecko.

Fat Cat's Meow

Item No.: TJMINEVE2
Artist: MB
Size: 64x64x64
Status: Ltd to Event
Carving Date: 99
Release Date: Jan 00
Issue Size: 4243

The Cat's Meow Tour of 2000 featured a series of event box figurines, all with feline themes. "Fat Cat's Meow" is the second in the series. Hallmarks include ©, double diamond, HBC logo, and eye.

Fred

Item No.: TJICE01M
Artist: AB
Size: 38x38x38
Status: Ltd to Event
Carving Date: 00
Release Date: Feb 01
Issue Size: 3500

"Fred" is part of a dynamic duo of Roly Polys made especially for the International Collectible Expositions in Anaheim and Rosemont, 2001. "Fred" comes with "Homer," his companion cat. Both are engraved "ICE 2001." 350 Hard Body sets and 175 color variation sets are included in the edition. The color variation "Fred" has yellow ears and blue/green eyes. Hallmarks include ©, double diamond, HBC logo, and gecko.

Harmony Kingdom Box Details

Fred

Item No.: TJKIT01M
Artist: AB
Size: 38x38x38
Status: Ltd to Event
Carving Date: 00
Release Date: Mar 01
Issue Size: 1000

"Fred" is part of a set of Roly Polys made especially for the Canadian Collectible Show in Kitchener, 2001. "Fred" is packaged with "Homer," his companion cat. Both are engraved "Kitchener." 100 Hard Body sets are included in the edition. Hallmarks include ©, double diamond, HBC logo, and gecko.

Gobblefest

Item No.: TJEVGO99
Artist: PC
Size: 64x70x76
Status: Ltd to Event
Carving Date: 99
Release Date: Sep 99
Issue Size: 13,501

This box figurine, depicting a festive turkey, was the special event piece for HK's third annual in-store celebrations held November 1999. Each piece was boxed in tamper proof shrink-wrap packaging so the variation surprises weren't known until opened. 10,500 pieces ("The Grey Back" variety) depict an interior of Governor Bradford, founder of Plymouth Colony, negotiating a treaty with Massasoit, chief of the Wampanoag tribe. It is said that the two became fast friends and threw a big party that they called "Thanksgiving." One thousand pieces ("The Yellow Back" variety) are colour variations with the same interior. Five hundred pieces ("The Arrow") are mould variations, with an arrow piercing Governor Bradford's hat. Fifteen hundred pieces ("The Christmas Cracker") for the U.K. and Canada have a unique interior portraying Christmas crackers, parcels, a bottle, and holly. One piece is jewel encrusted and painted by Martin Perry. Hallmarks include ©, moon, HBC logo, and Pc.

Hip Huggers

Item No.: XXYCLH
Artist: SD
Size: 57x31x63
Status: Ltd to Event
Carving Date: 99
Release Date: Feb 00
Issue Size: 450

This box figurine, featuring two acrobatic hippos, was given as a gift to attendees of the June 2000 Clair de Lune Convention in Lake Geneva, Wisconsin. Hallmarks include ©, double diamond, HBC logo, and S.

Homer

Item No.: TJICE01C
Artist: AB
Size: 38x38x38
Status: Ltd to Event
Carving Date: 00
Release Date: Feb 01
Issue Size: 3500

"Homer" is part of a dynamic duo of Roly Polys made especially for the International Collectible Expositions in Anaheim and Rosemont, 2001. "Homer" comes with "Fred," his companion cat. Both are engraved "ICE 2001." 350 Hard Body sets and 175 color variation sets are included in the edition. The color variation "Homer" has yellow ears and blue/green eyes. Hallmarks include ©, double diamond, HBC logo, and gecko.

Homer

Item No.: TJKIT01C
Artist: AB
Size: 38x38x38
Status: Ltd to Event
Carving Date: 00
Release Date: Mar 01
Issue Size: 1000

"Homer" is part of a set of Roly Polys made especially for the Canadian Collectible Show in Kitchener, 2001. "Homer" is packaged with "Fred," his companion mouse. Both are engraved "Kitchener." 100 Hard Body sets are included in the edition. Hallmarks include ©, double diamond, HBC logo, and gecko.

Hope and Glory

Item No.: RW02HIMA
Artist: PC
Size: 51x41x108
Status: Ltd to Event
Carving Date: 02
Release Date: Jun 02
Issue Size: 300

The pantomime horse from the 2001 RW Birthday Party makes a repeat appearance on the exclusive for the 7th Birthday Party. The theme of the secrets honors the World Cup, which was being played at the time of the event. "Becks" on the back of the shirt refers to English football player David Beckham, and the bandage represents his injured foot. The red cross on the hooves are representative of the flag heralded throughout the country during the World Cup matches. The pony's tail is tagged "Peter Seaman," a reference to the hair style worn by England's goalie. "Sven" is England's coach, Sven Eriksson. "Golden Jubilee 1952-2002" refers to the 50th anniversary of Queen Elizabeth II's coronation. The mouse peeks out of the horse's sleeve. Hallmarks include ©, peace sign, HBC logo, and Pc.

House Party

Item No.: TJEVHOL01A,
TJEVHOL01P
Artist: AB & PC
Size: 95x63x89
Status: Ltd to Event
Carving Date: 01
Release Date: May 01
Issue Size: 851 (TJEVHOL01A),
1372 (TJEVHOL02P)

Adam Binder Variation

Peter Calvesbert Variation

The House of Lords, Harmony Kingdom's highest level of dealership, takes its name from a chamber of the British Parliament. Members of the House of Lords are known as Peers. Three animals, a badger, pig and fox, engage in some of the activities of the members of the British House of Lords. They also represent three environmental issues in Britain. The badger reads his agenda: a discussion of the foot and mouth epidemic, followed by lengthy subsidised lunch at one of the many nearby pubs. His environmental statement is against the gassing of badgers. The pig is sleeping off his heavy, boozy luncheon, clutching a hot water bottle to his belly. His concern is foot and mouth. The fox appears to protest hunting. The pheasant under the badger agrees with the fox. The back of the bench is covered in grafitti. "1852 Pugin" refers to the man who rebuilt the House of Lords in 1852. "Iron Lady Rust in Peace" and "I (heart) Thatcher" refer to former Prime Minister Margaret Thatcher. "Wot no peers" references the fact that peers may soon become an endangered species.

Another hunting protest is scrawled above the number for a high-class madam "Miss Whiplash." Peter Calvesbert's signature mouse is tucked under the fox's chin. On the interior are four snapping turtles going "blah blah blah," as this is what the function of the House of Lords seems to be. This piece was carved as a special event piece for the 2001 House of Lords tour. Due to the events of September 11, 2001, the tour was cancelled. Hallmarks include ©, smiley face, HBC logo, gecko, and Pc.

It's A Knockout
Item No.: RW00LEHIPI
Artist: MP
Size: 49x49x73
Status: Ltd to Event
Carving Date: 00
Release Date: Jun 00
Issue Size: 450

This pair of boxing pigs was given as a gift at the Royal Watch Fifth Birthday event, held in England in 2000. Hallmarks include ©, diamond, HBC logo, and M.

Last Cat's Meow
Item No.: TJMINEVE6
Artist: MB
Size: 79x69x63
Status: Ltd to Event
Carving Date: 99
Release Date: Oct 00
Issue Size: 2088

This cat blows farewell kisses, as it is the last in the series of exclusives for the 2000 Cat's Meow Tour. Hallmarks include ©, double diamond, HBC logo, and eye.

Long Beach '97 Rose Pendant
Item No.: XXXHGLB97
Artist: DL
Size: 25x27x36
Status: Ltd to Event
Carving Date: Oct 96
Release Date: Apr 97
Issue Size: 552

This box figurine pendant was given to current Royal Watch members attending the International Collectibles Exposition in Long Beach, California in April 1997, and to those who registered at the show.

Long Beach '99 Lord Byron Pendant

Item No.: XXYLB99Z
Artist: MB
Size: 19x24x33
Status: Ltd to Event
Carving Date: 99
Release Date: Apr 99
Issue Size: 2000

This solid bodied pendant was given to current Royal Watch members attending the International Collectibles Exposition in Long Beach, California in April 1999, and to those who registered at the show. Lord Byron wears a green jacket and red baseball hat, both with designer HK insignia. Hallmarks include moon and HBC logo.

Lord Foxglove

Item No.: TJEV01T
Artist: MB
Size: 76x70x63
Status: Ltd to Event
Carving Date: 00
Release Date: Jun 01
Issue Size: 3000

This distinguished gentleman toad was available at August 2001 "Pond Party" in-store events. The interior features a mouse sunbathing on a lily pad. Hallmarks include ©, double diamond, HBC logo, and eye.

Lord of the Aisles

Item No.: TJICE02
Artist: AB
Size: 65x68x89
Status: Ltd to Event
Carving Date: 01
Release Date: Dec 01
Issue Size: 2000

For those who have attended shows in the past, you know Harmony Kingdom's proud "Lord of the Aisles" tradition. Independent Authorized Clubs, collectors, retailers and other HK enthusiasts march through the aisles of the trade show, accompanied by pipe and snare and the waving flags of the clubs. This event is captured in 2002's IGCE show exclusive, called "Lord of the Aisles." This Box Figurine by Adam Binder is his second IGCE exclusive, and Harmony Kingdom's fifth. Some of HK's favourite animals, cats and dogs, enact the "Lord of the Aisles" march in true 1776 fashion, complete with fife and drum. A colour variation on 200 boxes is especially patriotic, with red, white and blue coats. On the interior, a young rabbit enjoys the show. "Lord of the Aisles" was available only at the 2002 International Gift and Collectibles Expositions in Rosemont. Hallmarks include ©, smiley face, HBC logo, and gecko.

Lucky Streak

Item No.: TJICE02D
Artist: PC
Size: 41x50x67
Status: Ltd to Event
Carving Date: 01
Release Date: Jan 02
Issue Size: 250

This little dragon was available to attendees of Breakfast With An Artist at the 2002 International Gift and Collectibles Expositions in Atlantic City and Rosemont. A color variation was produced, one for Atlantic City and one for Rosemont (125 of each). Poker chips on the Atlantic City version are marked with "A," and the Rosemont variation has poker chips marked with "R." Hallmarks include ©, smiley face, HBC logo, and PC.

Newark '98 Angel Pendant

Item No.: None
Artist: DL
Size: 35x26x46
Status: Ltd to Event
Carving Date: 96
Release Date: Aug 98
Issue Size: 295

This box figurine pendant was given to current Royal Watch members attending the Newark Show in Nottingham England in August 1998, and to those who registered at the show.

Nick

Item No.: TJEVSA00
Artist: AB
Size: 38x44x44
Status: Ltd to Event
Carving Date: 00
Release Date: Oct 00
Issue Size: 10,626

Nick, along with his companion, Rudy, was the event exclusive figurine for 2000's Winterfest in-store events. Special variations include:

US Version: American flag on back of Nick's jacket. 7000 boxes with standard paint, 700 boxes with vivid paint, 700 Hard Bodies.

UK Version: British flag on back of Nick's jacket. 1500 boxes with standard paint, 100 boxes with vivid paint, 50 Hard Bodies.

Canadian Version: Canadian flag on back of Nick's jacket. 500 boxes with standard paint, 50 boxes with vivid paint, 25 Hard Bodies.

Hallmarks include ©, double diamond, HBC logo, and gecko.

Oktobearfest

Item No.: TJEVBE97
Artist: PC
Size: 55x56x55
Status: Ltd to Event
Carving Date: 96
Release Date: Oct 97
Issue Size: 13,500

This box figurine was for HK's first annual in-store event and available at select retailers during the autumn months of 1997. The tree stump around which the bears play is inscribed with the Calvesbert family tree. "JC," "MAR," and "1816" represent John Calvesbert, who married Mary Ann Rudland on Christmas Day, 1816. Inside is a South African 10 cent coin from Peter's honeymoon. Hallmarks include ©, diamond, HBC logo, ed.#, and Pc.

Pearl

Item No.: XXYCLP
Artist: PC
Size: 51x63x63
Status: Ltd to Event
Carving Date: 99
Release Date: Jan 00
Issue Size: 450

This box figurine, depicting a bejeweled Pearl (Clair's cat), was given as a gift to attendees of the June 2000 Clair de Lune Convention in Lake Geneva, Wisconsin. Hallmarks include ©, moon, HBC logo, and Pc.

Planet Paradise

Item No.: XXYHGRH
Artist: MB, AB, PC
Size: 57x57x69
Status: Ltd to Event
Carving Date: 00
Release Date: Jan 01
Issue Size: 250

Three artists, Peter Calvesbert, Monique Baldwin and Adam Binder, collaborated on this special piece made for the Paradise Found event, held during the 2001 Anaheim ICE. On the interior, Minx watches, aghast, as a meteor falls on Wolfie. Hallmarks include ©, double diamond, HBC logo, and eye.

Portrait of an Artist as a Young Bloke

Item No.: EVPP00
Artist: PC
Size: 89x89x197
Status: Donation
Carving Date: 89
Release Date: Aug 00
Issue Size: 220

This solid-body figurine is an amusing self-portrait of Peter Calvesbert. It was one of Peter's very first carvings, dating back to 1989. Select stores who hosted an HK Beach Party in August 2000 were given this piece to auction or raffle for the charity of their choice. Hallmarks include ©, HBC logo, and Pc.

Primordial Sloop

Item No.: XXYTJXXLTUPC
Artist: PC
Size: 140x140x166
Status: Ltd to Event
Carving Date: 98
Release Date: Apr 99
Issue Size: 800

This box figurine, a transformation of "Primordial Soup," was made for the first annual HK Convention - Primordial Crooze - a five day floating fiesta. Given as a gift to each attendee, the piece depicts a boat and its passengers forging through a sea of turtles. Tubs captains the ship. "Long Beach" denotes the start of the trip aboard Royal Caribbean's Viking Serenade, which sailed to Baja Mexico. This piece is covered with hundreds of turtles, one holding a ribbon reading, "Linford" for the British athlete Linford Christy, and another a pendant with "ZH" for Zoe Heller, a famous British Journalist. "NOEL," for Noel Wiggins, is carved into a turtle shell. Hallmarks include star, HBC logo, and P.C. on lid.

Pumpkinfest

Item No.: TJEVPU98
Artist: DL
Size: 55x56x55
Status: Ltd to Event
Carving Date: 96
Release Date: Oct 98
Issue Size: 10,433

This box figurine was for HK's second annual in-store event and available at select retailers from October 30 through November 1 1998. A boy angel, dressed in a devil's costume for Halloween, is sitting cross-legged atop a Jack-O-Lantern. A miniature "Oktobearfest" is inside, though a small quantity is missing the interior "Oktobearfest". Edition 1 has no hallmarks. Hallmarks on Edition 2 onward include ©, diamond, HBC logo, ed.#, and DL.

Queen of the Jungle

Item No.: TJEVQJ99
Artist: DL
Size: 86x76x89
Status: Ltd to Event
Carving Date: 98
Release Date: Aug 99
Last Ship Date: Aug 99
Issue Size: 3750

This gorilla box figurine is the first Queen Empress event exclusive piece. It was offered at "Queen of the Jungle" events held worldwide the last weekend of August 1999. The queen gorilla, wearing silver tiara, nestles her baby while the king gorilla cautiously gazes forward protecting his family. He is perched atop a safari hat. Where has its wearer gone? The compass points northwest, which may offer a clue but his belongings, including knapsack and shorts, are found within the box figurine. Hallmarks include ©, star, HBC logo, ed.#, and DL.

Queenie & Prince Charming

Item No.: EVQP00
Artist: AR
Size: 76x76x89
Status: Ltd to Event
Carving Date:99
Release Date: Aug 00
Issue Size: 2500

Queenie is a multi-compartment box figurine and is one of the exclusives for the Queen Empress and Princess Dealer events for 2000. While on the beach, she picked up a pretty purple shell, only to realise with some horror later that the shell's occupant would like to steal her towel. Behind her back, another Nature vs. Man scenario plays out as a seagull eyes up the tasty goodies in her picnic basket. In the compartment under her décolletage is a crown, symbolising Harmony Kingdom's Queen Empress and Princess Dealers. The interior of the picnic basket contains a sash and rosette. Queenie's companion, Prince Charming, is a much thinner man in a beach chair. Despite the anchor tattoo on his upper arm, he seems to be quite the landlubber. His pale English skin tends to burn easily, so he applies a tube of "Fake Tan" instead. The sand around his striped beach chair is littered with his debris: a beer can, remains of a sardine sandwich, and magazines called "Ellie" and "Mr. Universe." A crab makes off with his watch - hopefully it's waterproof. On the interior, a crown emblazoned with a "P" pays homage to Harmony Kingdom's Princess Dealers. Hallmarks include ©, moon, HBC logo, and AR.

Rosemont '96 Frog Pendant
Item No.: TJZFRR
Artist: PC
Size: 29x28x48
Status: Ltd to Event
Carving Date: 95
Release Date: Jun 96
Issue Size: 403

This box figurine pendant was given to current Royal Watch members attending the International Collectibles Exposition in Rosemont, Illinois, in June 1996, and to those who registered at the show.

Rosemont '97 Puffin Pin
Item No.: XXYRO97P
Artist: PC
Size: 57x51x10
Status: Ltd to Event
Carving Date: 97
Release Date: Jun 97
Issue Size: 177

This pin was given to those who joined HK on their first annual "Three Hour Tour" aboard a yacht on Lake Michigan during the International Collectibles Exposition in Rosemont, Illinois, in June 1997. The same pin, but with "Harmony Kingdom" replacing "Rosemont" was given to charter members of the Royal Watch U.K. and Australia (qty 104) and to collectors attending the HK reception at the Collect '99 Wembley Fair (qty 91).

Rosemont '97 Rose Pendant
Item No.: XXXHGRO97
Artist: DL
Size: 27x28x35
Status: Ltd to Event
Carving Date: 96
Release Date: Jun 97
Issue Size: 847

This box figurine pendant was given to current Royal Watch members attending the International Collectibles Exposition in Rosemont, Illinois, in June, 1997, and to those who registered at the show. This piece was identical to that given to collectors at the Long Beach show held two months prior, but "Rosemont" is inscribed onto this piece and Lord Byron was added inside.

Rosemont '98 Angel Pendant
Item No.: XXYRO98Z
Artist: DL
Size: 35x26x46
Status: Ltd to Event
Carving Date: 96
Release Date: Jun 98
Issue Size: 1912

This box figurine pendant was given to current Royal Watch members attending the International Collectibles Exposition in Rosemont, Illinois, in June 1998 and to those who registered at the show.

Rosemont '99 Lord Byron Pendant
Style: XXYRO99Z
Artist: MB
Size: 19x24x33
Status: Ltd to Event
Carving Date: 99
Release Date: Jun 99
Issue Size: 1956

This solid bodied pendant was given to current Royal Watch members attending the International Collectibles Exposition in Rosemont, Illinois, in June 1999, and to those who registered at the show. Lord Byron wears a green jacket and red baseball hat, both with designer HK insignia. Hallmarks include moon and HBC logo.

Rosemont '00 Bumbles Pendant
Item No.: XXYRO00Z
Artist: MB
Size: 25x25x44
Status: Ltd to Event
Carving Date: 99
Release Date: Mar 00
Issue Size: 2000

This pendant was given to current Royal Watch members attending the International Collectibles Exposition in Rosemont, IL in June 2000, and to those who registered at the show.

Rosemont '01 Minx Pendant

Item No.: XXYRO01Z
Artist: AB
Size: 19x19x51
Status: Ltd to Event
Carving Date: 01
Release Date: Feb 01
Issue Size: 1600

This solid-bodied pendant was created especially for Royal Watch members who attended the June 2001 ICE in Rosemont, Illinois and for those who signed up to the club while at the show. "Rosemont 2001" is carved on Minx's leg.

Rosemont '02 Murphy Pendant

Item No.: XXYRO02Z
Artist: SD
Size: 20x25x38
Status: Ltd to Event
Carving Date: 01
Release Date: Mar 02
Issue Size: 925

This solid-bodied pendant was created especially for Royal Watch members who attended the 2002 International Gift and Collectible Exposition and for those who signed up to the club while at the show.

Rudy

Item No.: TJEVRU00
Artist: AB
Size: 38x44x44
Status: Lt to Event
Carving Date: 00
Release Date: Oct 00
Issue Size: 10626

Rudy, along with his companion, Nick, was the event exclusive figurine for 2000's Winterfest in-store events. Special variations include:

US Version: 7000 boxes with standard paint, 700 boxes with vivid paint, 700 Hard Bodies.

UK Version: 1500 boxes with standard paint, 100 boxes with vivid paint, 50 Hard Bodies.

Canadian Version: 500 boxes with standard paint, 50 boxes with vivid paint, 25 Hard Bodies.

Hallmarks include ©, double diamond, HBC logo, and gecko.

Secaucus '96 Frog Pendant

Item No.: TJZFRS
Artist: PC
Size: 29x28x48
Status: Ltd to Event
Carving Date: 95
Release Date: Apr 96
Issue Size: 210

This box figurine pendant was given to current Royal Watch members attending the International Collectibles Exposition in Secaucus, New Jersey, in April 1996 and to those who registered at the show.

Signing Line

Item No.: TJICE00
Artist: PC
Size: 54x79x76
Status: Ltd to Event
Carving Date: 99
Release Date: Apr 00
Issue Size: 5000

For an unprecedented third consecutive year, Harmony Kingdom has been selected to create the International Collectibles Exposition exclusive. In keeping with ICE box figurines of years past, "Signing Line" humorously depicts enthusiasts in their quest to perfect their collections. Featured here are a cat and dog collector in queue for Mad Murphy to sign their ICE pieces from 1998 and 1999. Each animal is covered with promotional pins that are passed out during the ICE by exhibiting companies. The canine collector sports a tee shirt emblazoned with "HK Tour 2000 - Atlanta, Rosemont, Hawaii" - Hawaii being Peter's preferred location for the next ICE. At the his feet are the batteries which have fallen out of his camera; practical matters often fall by the wayside in the signing line frenzy. Does the watch mark on his left wrist indicate that he's a watchdog, or does it signify the hours sometimes spent waiting to meet the artist and have favourite pieces signed? The inscription between his legs refers to Kat Spagnola, HBC's former webmistress. On one of the bags is a Union Jack encouraging people to "buy British"- unless it moos, a reference to "mad cow" disease. One of the cat's badges is marked "TD" in homage to HK collector Tom Di Nardi. Another badge has PJ with a tongue in cheek line through it - no PJ's in the exhibition hall please! This is the second reference to Pioneer Joe (a.k.a. Joe McLaughlin, HK webmaster and HOP officer) on an ICE piece. More badges include a smiley face, and "N + L" for HK co-founders Noel Wiggins and Lisa Yashon. Murphy wears a nicotine patch in an attempt to keep his New Year's resolution to quit smoking. On the back of the base is a cryptic arrangement of letters. Peter says that these have to do with the colourful Harmony Ball ties that he's so fond of wearing at ICE events. While all the clues to the code are on the box, he won't give the answer away just yet. 4500 of the 5000 piece edition feature an interior of grape, cherry, and banana symbols on slot machines. 500 collectors will hit the jackpot if the find the interior with three cherries. Hallmarks include ©, double diamond, HBC logo and PC.

Harmony Kingdom Box Details

Slow Dance (Solid Body)
Item No.: XXYCLT
Artist: PC
Size: 46x51x70
Status: Ltd to Event
Carving Date: 00
Release Date: Aug 00
Issue Size: 715

A mere two hours before the carving demonstration at Clair de Lune Convention 2000, Harmony Kingdom's second multi-day convention held in Lake Geneva, Wisconsin, Peter still had no idea what he would carve. As he wandered around the marina, inspiration struck when he sighted his first snapping turtle. This solid figurine was made available to Clair de Lune convention attendees only. Hallmarks include ©, double diamond, HBC logo, and Pc.

Sneak Preview
Item No.: TJICE98
Artist: PC
Size: 79x73x69
Status: Ltd to Event
Carving Date: 98
Release Date: Apr 98
Issue Size: 5000

McRand International commissioned HK to create an event piece for the 1998 International Collectible Expositions held in Edison, New Jersey in April and Rosemont, Illinois, in June. 2500 pieces were available at each show. Due to unprecedented sales at Edison (all pieces sold out by Saturday afternoon), McRand implemented special procedures to ensure that collectors could purchase only one piece so that more could enjoy them. Five felines are featured on this box, and Mad Murphy makes an appearance with a mouse playing checkers. The game originally began as chess but was difficult to produce. Some boxes still have hints of the chess pieces on the board. Inside are two mice eyeing a mousetrap with cheese. Hallmarks include ©, star and heart, HBC logo, and Pc.

Space Ball Pendant
Item No.: HKUK01SB
Artist: MB
Size: 25x35x44
Status: Ltd to Event
Carving Date: 01
Release Date: Apr 01
Issue Size: 150

This solid-bodied pendant was created especially for attendees of the Royal Watch Sixth Birthday Party event, the Space Ball.

Stoneleigh '98 Angel Pendant

Item No.: None
Artist: DL
Size: 35x26x46
Status: Ltd to Event
Carving Date: 96
Release Date: Aug 98
Issue Size: 270

Photo Not Available

This box figurine pendant was given to current Royal Watch members attending the Collect it! Show in Stoneleigh England in December 1998, and to those who registered at the show.

Swap 'n Sell

Item No.: TJICE99
Artist: PC
Size: 86x83x78
Status: Ltd to Event
Carving Date: 98
Release Date: Apr 99
Issue Size: 5000

Krause Publications commissioned HK to create an event piece for the second consecutive year for the 1999 International Collectible Expositions in Long Beach, California, in April and Rosemont, Illinois, in June. 2500 pieces were available at each show. The piece features three dogs crowded around a swap 'n sell table admiring 1998's ICE piece "Sneak Preview." Mad Murphy counts his coins under the table. "Charge P.J. Double" is a tribute to HK collector Joe McLaughlin. Two hundred pieces portray Peter Calvesbert splayed inside with Groucho Marx glasses "appropriately" positioned. The remaining pieces have a fig leaf replacing the glasses. Hallmarks include ©, HBC logo, ed.#, and Pc.

Talk of the Town

Item No.: TJEVHOL02
Artist: PC
Size: 46x46x91
Status: Ltd to Event
Carving Date: 02
Release Date: Mar 02
Issue Size: 4000

Peter Calvesbert designed this African grey parrot especially for the 2002 House of Lords signing tour. Colour variations show the quill painted various shades and hues. The interior shows a group of eggs with Peter's head hatching from one of them. The inscription "Save the Spix" refers to the Spix macaw, now believed to be extinct in the wild although a few still survive in the collections of rich individuals. The signature mouse peeks out from under the quill. Hallmarks include ©, peace sign, HBC logo, and Pc.

Tin Cat's Cruise
Item No.: TJROSE98
Artist: PC
Size: 56x57x62
Status: Ltd to Event
Carving Date: 98
Release Date: Jun 98
Issue Size: 575

This box figurine, a variation on "Tin Cat" with Mad Murphy and Lord Byron, was made for those who joined HK on their second annual 3-hour tour aboard a yacht on Lake Michigan during the International Collectible Expositions in Rosemont, Illinois, in June 1998. Peter signed each. Hallmarks include ©, star, HBC logo, and Pc.

Tubs Pin
Item No.: XXYTPPC
Artist: PC
Size: 38x6x51
Status: Ltd to Event
Carving Date: 98
Release Date: Apr 99
Issue Size: 566

Tubs the Turtle stands at the pier, waiting to board The Viking Serenade for Primordial Crooze. This pin was given as a gift to all attendees of HK's first annual convention in April '99.

UK '99 Lord Byron Pendant
Item No.: None
Artist: MB
Size: 19x24x33
Status: Ltd to Event
Carving Date: 98
Release Date: Mar 99
Issue Size: 309

This solid bodied pendant was given to current Royal Watch members attending collectible expositions throughout the U.K., and to those who registered at the shows. Lord Byron wears a green jacket and red baseball hat, both with designer HK insignia. Hallmarks include moon and HBC logo.

Wembley 2000 Pendant
Item No.: HKUK00
Artist: MB
Size: 25x35x44
Status: Ltd to Event
Carving Date: 01
Release Date: Sep 01
Issue Size: 320

This pendant was issued at the Collect 2000 Fair at Wembley on September 9 - 10, 2000. A tag carved into the piece reads "HK Y2K." On 290 of the pendants the tag is stained light yellow. On only 30 of the pendants the tag is light purple.

SPECIAL EDITIONS
GCC

Boarding School
Item No.: TJSEG98F2
Artist: PC
Size: 69x49x50
Status: Retired
Carving Date: 96
Release Date: Sep 98
Last Ship Date: Mar 99
Issue Size: 7350

This box figurine, featuring 2 dolphins, 2 baleen whales, 1 hammerhead shark and one great white shark, is the first GCC exclusive created by HK. Inside Mad Murphy has found a treasure chest full of money and is indoctrinating an innocent fish into the ways of greed and materialism. The mouse is behind the tail above the base. Hallmarks include diamond, clock face with month 3, HBC logo, and Pc.

Jump Shot
Item No.: TJLEG99F
Artist: MP
Size: 38x44x76
Status: Ltd Ed
Carving Date: 99
Release Date: Apr 99
Last Ship Date: Nov 99
Issue Size: 3600

The pair of frogs grapple for a basketball in this second "Dueling Duet" box figurine. Each piece is numbered and stamped with the artist's initials. Hallmarks include ©, moon, HBC logo, and M.

Queen's Counsel
Item No.: TJSEG98F
Artist: PC
Size: 51x51x63
Status: Retired
Carving Date: 96
Release Date: Oct 98
Last Ship Date: Dec 98
Issue Size: 9140

This box figurine, featuring bald eagles, is the second GCC exclusive created by HK. Hallmarks include ©, diamond, mirror image clock face with month 1, HBC logo, and Pc.

Thin Ice
Item No.: TJLEG99S
Artist: MP
Size: 48x54x76
Status: Ltd Ed
Carving Date: 96
Release Date: Apr 99
Last Ship Date: May 99
Issue Size: 6000

The pair of "graceful" hippos are seen ice-skating in the first "Dueling Duet" box figurine. Each piece is numbered and stamped with the artist's initials. Hallmarks include ©, diamond, HBC logo, and M.

SPECIAL EDITIONS
GUMP'S CATALOG

Gump's Caw of the Wild
Item No.: XXYTJBBG
Artist: PC
Size: 68x59x87
Status: Retired
Carving Date: 99
Release Date: Jan 00
Last Ship Date: Nov 00
Issue Size: 220

This version of "Caw Of The Wild" was created for Gump's Mail Order Catalogue. Aside from slight colouration changes on the exterior, the interior portrays a miniature nest of eggs.

SPECIAL EDITIONS
Parade of Gifts

Parade of Gifts
Item No.: HGLEC99S
Artist: MP
Size: 83x84x63
Status: Ltd Ed
Carving Date: 98
Release Date: Jan 99
Last Ship Date: Feb 02
Issue Size: 5000

This colourful rose bouquet features an interior Lord Byron marching in a parade with his bug friends, each bearing gifts. This is the first Parade of Gifts buying group exclusive. Each is signed and stamped with Martin Perry's initials. Hallmarks include ©, star, HBC logo, and S.

Pet Parade
Item No.: TJLEC99F
Artist: DL
Size: Cat 29x25x52
Dog 26x35x48
Status: Matched Numbered Ltd Ed
Carving Date: 98
Release Date: Jun 99
Last Ship Date: Feb 02
Issue Size: 5000

These two miniature boxes, one portraying a cat and the other a dog, are packaged together in a set. Each is numbered and stamped with the artist's initials. Hallmarks include ©, moon, HBC logo and DL.

SPECIAL EDITIONS
Parkwest/NALED

Bewear the Hare
Item No.: TJLEP99S
Artist: DL
Size: 67x41x53
Status: Ltd Ed
Carving Date: 96
Release Date: Apr 99
Last Ship Date: Jun 99
Issue Size: 4200

This is the fifth piece in the "Bountiful Basket" series. A mischievous kitten impersonates a bunny with socks on his ears, sitting in a basket of fruit and vegetables. "49" denotes the 49th piece carved by David Lawrence. Each piece is hand-numbered and stamped with the artist's initials. Hallmarks include ©, diamond, HBC logo, and DL.

Harmony Kingdom Box Details

Cat's Cradle

Item No.: TJCA6
Artist: DL
Size: 63x61x63
Status: Ltd Ed
Carving Date: 96
Release Date: Mar 97
Last Ship Date: Nov 97
Issue Size: 1000

This box figurine, featuring a mother cat with baby kittens in a basket, is the first Parkwest/Naled exclusive created by HK and the first piece in the "Bountiful Basket" series. The acorn is near the ball of yarn. Two clothed mice rest on a pillow in the interior. "41" denotes the 41st piece carved by David Lawrence. Each piece is hand-numbered and bears the artist's monogram. Hallmarks include ©, diamond, HBC logo, ed.#, and DL.

Cat's Cradle Too

Item No.: TJCA6B
Artist: DL
Size: 65x62x62
Status: Ltd Ed
Carving Date: 96
Release Date: Aug 97
Last Ship Date: Dec 97
Issue Size: 1000

This box figurine, featuring cats in a basket, is the second piece in the "Bountiful Basket" series. The acorn is near a kitten's hind end. A mouse is buried amidst a pile of laundry in the interior. Each piece is hand-numbered and bears the artist's monogram. Hallmarks include ©, diamond, HBC logo, ed.#, and DL.

Golden Oldie

Item No.: TJLEP01F
Artist: MB
Size: 79x69x63
Status: Ltd Ed
Carving Date: 01
Release Date: Sep 01
Last Ship Date: Apr 02
Issue Size: 1000

The Golden Retriever is one of the most popular dogs, renowned for being friendly, reliable and trustworthy. Energetic and active, the retriever was originally bred as a hunting dog. "Golden Oldie" depicts the lovable character of the golden retriever with its deep, soulful eyes and playful manner. On the interior, a mouse snuggles safely in a slipper; that is, he's safe until the dog decides the slipper is a new toy! Hallmarks include ©, double diamond, HBC logo, and eye.

Harmony Bull
Item No.: TJLEP99F
Artist: PC
Size: 76x51x44
Status: Ltd Ed
Carving Date: 96
Release Date: Jun 99
Last Ship Date: Apr 02
Issue Size: 5600

This box figurine, featuring two cows and two bulls, is the sixth Parkwest/Naled exclusive created by HK. Each piece is hand-numbered and signed by the artist. Hallmarks include ©, an interior HBC logo, and Pc.

Kitty's Kipper
Item No.: TJSEP98F
Artist: DL
Size: 60x60x45
Status: Ltd Ed
Carving Date: 96
Release Date: Sep 98
Last Ship Date: Dec 98
Issue Size: 5600

This box figurine, featuring a basket full of fish and crab with an interested cat, is the fourth piece in the "Bountiful Basket" series. Each piece is hand-numbered and bears the artist's monogram. Hallmarks include ©, diamond, clock face with month 8, HBC logo, and DL.

Naughty & Nice
Item No.: TJLEP02S
Artist: MB
Size: 63x71x51
Status: Ltd Ed
Carving Date: 01
Release Date: Apr 02
Last Ship Date: Not Available
Issue Size: 1200

This orange tiger cat embodies all the various characteristics of cats, ranging from naughty to nice. The interior shows a mouse floating on his back despite the "No Swimming" sign. Hallmarks include ©, double diamond, HBC logo, and eye.

Harmony Kingdom Box Details

Peace Offering
Item No.: TJSEP98S
Artist: DL
Size: 52x54x63
Status: Ltd Ed
Carving Date: 96
Release Date: Apr 98
Last Ship Date: Sep 98
Issue Size: 4200

This box figurine, featuring a basket full of fruit with songbirds, is the third piece in the "Bountiful Basket" series. Each piece is hand-numbered and bears the artist's monogram. Hallmarks include ©, diamond, clock face with month 7, HBC logo, and DL.

Take A Bow
Item No.: TJLEP01S
Artist: MB
Size: 76x89x63
Status: Ltd Ed
Carving Date: 00
Release Date: Dec 00
Last Ship Date: Feb 02
Issue Size: 2000

The pug dog is an intriguing breed of ancient Oriental lineage. The Chinese especially valued those pugs that had three deep wrinkles on the forehead, forming part of the symbol for "Prince." Distinctive and friendly, with deep, soulful eyes, pugs have been popular with monarchs from England's William and Mary to France's Marie Antoinette. Within this limited edition box figurine, a happy cat rubs his tummy after a delicious fish supper. Still, the mouse next to her looks a bit anxious as he thinks he may be next on the menu. Hallmarks include ©, double diamond, HBC logo, and eye.

SPECIAL EDITIONS
QVC

QVC Pin
Item No.: XXYQVC
Artist: MB
Size: 38x6x51
Status: Ltd to Event
Carving Date: 99
Release Date: Aug 99
Issue Size: 7014

This pin features Lord Byron watching television. Created as a QVC exclusive, each HK box figurine featured on the QVC Collectibles Showcase broadcast on 7th of August 1999 included a pin. Hallmarks include moon and HBC logo.

SPECIAL EDITIONS
WILD BIRDS UNLIMITED

Jewels of the Wild
Item No.: TJLEW99S
Artist: DL
Size: 92x88x118
Status: Ltd Ed
Carving Date: 98
Release Date: Jun 99
Last Ship Date: Aug 99
Issue Size: 5000

This three-compartment box figurine is the first exclusive produced for Wild Birds Unlimited stores. It features four orange hummingbirds hovering above a cluster of yellow flowers, with a nest of baby birds tucked amidst the foliage. Within two compartments are babies with beaks wide open. The third contains an upturned honey jar. Voted by Wild Birds Unlimited as the 1999 Vendor Mart Best New Exclusive, each piece is numbered and stamped with the artist's monogram. Hallmarks include ©, star, HBC logo, and DL.

SIDELINES
Pendants

Sterling Silver Baroness Trotter
Item No.: TJZLESSPI
Artist: MP
Size: 13x15x28
Status: Ltd Ed
Carving Date: 99
Release Date: Sep 99
Last Ship Date: Not Available
Issue Size: 5000

This pendant, crafted from solid sterling silver and modelled after the Garden Party pendant by the same name, unscrews to reveal a miniature compartment. Each piece is numbered and sanctioned by the London Assay Office. Robert Glover, whose commissions include the British Royal Family, crafted each.

Sterling Silver Garden Prince
Item No.: TJZLESSFR
Artist: MP
Size: 15x15x28
Status: Ltd Ed
Carving Date: 99
Release Date: Sep 99
Last Ship Date: Not Available
Issue Size: 5000

This pendant, crafted from solid sterling silver and modelled after the Garden Party pendant by the same name, unscrews to reveal a miniature compartment. Each piece is numbered and sanctioned by the London Assay Office. Robert Glover, whose commissions include the British Royal Family, crafted each.

Sterling Silver Lord Byron
Item No.: TJZLESSLB
Artist: MP
Size: 10x15x29
Status: Ltd Ed
Carving Date: 99
Release Date: Sep 99
Last Ship Date: Not Available
Issue Size: 5000

This pendant, crafted from solid sterling silver, unscrews to reveal a miniature compartment. Each piece is numbered and sanctioned by the London Assay Office. Robert Glover, whose commissions include the British Royal Family, crafted each.

SIDELINES
Pens

Scratching Post Pewter Pen
Item No.: HKPEN1
Artist: PC
Size: 13x15x145
Status: Ltd Ed
Carving Date: 97
Release Date: Oct 97
Last Ship Date: Not Available
Issue Size: 10,000

This is the first pewter pen created by Harmony Kingdom. Each is numbered on the nib. Hallmarks include ©, heart, HBC logo, and PC.

Tabby Totem Pewter Pen
Item No.: HKPEN2
Artist: PC
Size: 10x10x143
Status: Ltd Ed
Carving Date: 97
Release Date: Oct 97
Last Ship Date: Not Available
Issue Size: 10,000

This is the second pewter pen created by Harmony Kingdom. Each is numbered on the nib. Hallmarks include ©, heart, HBC logo, and PC.

SIDELINES
Prints

Harmony Circus Serigraph
Item No.: HCLESER
Artist: DL
Size: 445x560
Status: Ltd Ed
Creation Date: 98
Release Date: Jun 98
Last Ship Date: Not Available
Issue Size: 1000

This is the first serigraph by Harmony Kingdom and was created to say farewell to the Harmony Circus, which retired July 1998. Each serigraph is signed by the artist, hand-numbered, and accompanied by a certificate of authenticity.

Harmony Kingdom Box Details Page 245

SIDELINES
Teapots

Crackin' Brew
Item No.: HKTPLECB
Artist: PC & Paul Cardew
Size: 250x190x158
Status: Ltd Ed
Carving Date: 98
Release Date: Apr 99
Last Ship Date: May 99
Issue Size: 3850

Designed by Peter Calvesbert and Paul Cardew, this teapot was the first collaboration between Harmony Kingdom and Cardew Designs. Made in Cardew Design Studios in Devonshire, England, the teapot features favourite Harmony Kingdom animals bursting through the teapot with the box figurine names as graffiti. Inside under the rim of the teapot is "Peter and Paul – two prophets in a pot." Each teapot is hand-numbered and accompanied by a certificate of authenticity.

Yt42hk
Item No.: HKTPLET42
Artist: PC & Paul Cardew
Size: 152x241x203
Status: Ltd Ed
Carving Date: 99
Release Date: Sep 99
Last Ship Date: Not Available
Issue Size: 4850

Designed by Peter Calvesbert and Paul Cardew, this teapot was the second collaboration between Harmony Kingdom and Cardew Designs. Made in Cardew Design Studios in Devonshire, England, the teapot features Lord Byron and Bumbles the bee riding atop the teapot ship into the next millennium. Each teapot is hand-numbered and accompanied by a certificate of authenticity.

Harmony Kingdom Box Details

SIDELINES
Video

Harmony Kingdom Video

Item No.: HKVID
Artist: N/A
Size: N/A
Status: Open
Creation Date: 99
Release Date: May 00

This film short will carry you to the beautiful Cotswolds region of England, cradle of Harmony Kingdom. Meet Artistic Director Martin Perry, Master Carvers Peter Calvesbert and Monique Baldwin, and others whose talents and visions combine to create Harmony Kingdom's unique world of whimsy.

SIDELINES
Wee Beasties

Elephant Wee Beastie

Item No.: XXYRW02EL
Artist: MB
Size: 24x43x33
Status: Zookeeper Donation
Carving Date: 02
Release Date: Mar 02
Last Order Date: Jun 03
Issue Size: Not Available

To adopt an elephant at Dickerson Park Zoo in Springfield, Missouri, first purchase "Haji's Hero." "Haji's Hero" is a Royal Watch Club redemption piece, and you must be a member of the Royal Watch Club to order "Haji's Hero." A Zookeepers Series brochure inside the box includes an adoption form. Send in the form, along with the requested donation to Dickerson Park Zoo. The address is on the brochure. You will then receive a packet of information about the Asian elephant and a miniature Harmony Kingdom piece, the Wee Beastie Elephant.

Helen the Owl
Item No.: XXYTJLEOW
Artist: DL
Size: 25x19x32
Status: Zookeeper Donation
Carving Date: 98
Release Date: Jan 98
Last Order Date: Dec 99
Issue Size: 450

Helen the owl is a resident of the Lincoln Park Zoo in Chicago, Illinois. Collectors were given the opportunity to adopt Helen to improve her habitat, and in exchange receive this miniature owl figurine (a downsized version of "Ivory Tower") along with adoption papers, information on Helen and the habitat where she lives.

Manatee Wee Beastie
Item No.: XXYRW00MA
Artist: SD
Size: 19x25x25
Status: Zookeeper Donation
Carving Date: 99
Release Date: Jan 00
Last Order Date: Jun 01
Issue Size: 1018

The peaceful manatee is the embodiment of "do no harm," yet many are severely injured by boat propellers invading their habitat. The luckier manatees have their wounds tended and then are released back into the wild. The Columbus Zoo in Columbus, Ohio, is the first zoo approved by the U.S. Fish and Wildlife Service as a partner institution in its Manatee Recovery Program, and one manatee, Comet, has already been released back into the wild. Adopting a manatee through the 2000 Zookeepers program helped to defray the cost of caring for the gentle giants, and this Wee Beastie manatee was among the rewards.

Marty the Polar Bear
Item No.: XXYTJLEPO
Artist: DL
Size: 25x19x32
Status: Zookeeper Donation
Carving Date: 98
Release Date: Jan 98
Last Order Date: Dec 99
Issue Size: 450

Marty the polar bear is a resident of the Lincoln Park Zoo in Chicago, Illinois. Collectors were given the opportunity to adopt Marty to improve his habitat, and in exchange receive this miniature polar bear figurine (a downsized version of "Play Ball") along with adoption papers, information on Marty and his habitat.

Pacer the Greyhound

Item No.: XXYTJLEGR
Artist: SD
Size: 26x44x33
Status: Zookeeper Donation
Carving Date: 99
Release Date: Jan 00
Last Order Date: Dec 00
Issue Size: 2000

The graceful greyhound often meets with cruel treatment and suffers through a dangerous racing career. Retired Racers, an organisation in Acton, CA, is devoted to rescuing these noble dogs from the perils of the track and providing good homes for them. Those who participated in the Zookeepers adoption program received "Pacer" the miniature greyhound Wee Beastie, as well as information about their adopted greyhound. A group of 400 gray-painted "Pacers" were released at the 2001 International Collectible Exposition in Anaheim.

Panda Wee Beastie

Item No.: XXYTJLEGP
Artist: SD
Size: 38x44x51
Status: Zookeeper Donation
Carving Date: 00
Release Date: Dec 00
Last Order Date: Dec 01
Issue Size: 600

The Friends of the National Zoo's Giant Panda Conservation Fund is dedicated to supporting the efforts of the Smithsonian's National Zoological Park to save giant pandas through education and scientific research both in the United States and in the animal's natural habitat in China. This year, two young giant pandas, Mei Xiang and Tian Tian, are coming to the Zoo from China. These charming animals will serve as ambassadors for their wild cousins while Zoo scientists learn from them what must be known to save them. By participating in the Zookeepers program, the National Zoo will send you a Panda Wee Beastie.

Pip the Pelican
Item No.: XXYRW99PE
Artist: DL
Status: Zookeeper Donation
Carving Date: 98
Release Date: Jan 99
Last Order Date: Jun 00
Issue Size: 640

Pip the pelican is a resident of Pelican Island in Florida, the U.S.'s oldest wildlife preserve. Collectors were given the opportunity to adopt Pip to improve his habitat, and in exchange receive this miniature pelican figurine (a downsized version of "Pell Mell") along with adoption papers, information on Pip and hid habitat.

Zephyr the Monkey
Item No.: XXYTJLEMO
Artist: DL
Size: 25x19x32
Status: Zookeeper Donation
Carving Date: 98
Release Date: Jan 98
Last Order Date: Dec 99
Issue Size: 450

Zephyr the monkey is a resident of the Lincoln Park Zoo in Chicago, Illinois. Collectors were given the opportunity to adopt Zephyr to improve his habitat, and in exchange receive this miniature monkey figurine (a downsized version of "Family Reunion") along with adoption papers, information on Zephyr and the habitat where he lives.

PICTURESQUE

PICTURESQUE

"Epic Tales In Tile"

Noah's Hideaway
Item No.: PXNBOX
Status: Open
Carving Date: 98
Release Date: Mar 99

This box, by Ann Richmond, displays a tile figurine. Any of the twenty tiles in "Noah's Park" may be used as its lid. Look for the premiere and open editions with distinct interiors.

Byron's Hideaway
Item No.: PXGBOX
Status: Open
Carving Date: 98
Release Date: Jun 99

This box, by Ann Richmond, displays a tile figurine. Any of the twenty tiles in "Byron's Secret Garden" may be used as its lid. Look for the premiere and open editions with distinct interiors.

Storm Brewing
Item No.: PXPC1
Status: Open
Carving Date: 99
Release Date: Jun 99

This 6"x 6" framed tile figurine by Peter Calvesbert portrays a menagerie of animals bursting forth from Noah's ark. The premiere edition portrays Peter peaking out of a tent in the foreground.

Purrfect Tidings
Item No.: PXXMASCA
Status: Open
Carving Date: 99
Release Date: Sep 99

This 6"x 6" framed tile figurine by Ann Richmond portrays peaceful kittens around a Christmas tree opening their gifts.

Ruffians' Feast
Item No.: PXXMASHO
Status: Open
Carving Date: 99
Release Date: Sep 99

This 6"x 6" framed tile figurine by Ann Richmond portrays boisterous dogs enjoying a Christmas feast.

Noah's Park

Item No.: PXNA1-PXNE4
Status: Open
Carving Date: 98
Release Date: Mar 99

This is the first series in the Picturesque Collection. Comprised of twenty 4"x 4" tile figurines, it portrays Noah and his companions after the flood. "The Lost Ark" is the centerpiece, carved by Peter Calvesbert. All other tiles by Ann Richmond.

- Sky Master
- Sun Catcher 
- The Lost Ark 
- Whirligig Rainbow 
- Thunder Dome 
- Whale Watch 
- Krakatoa Lounge 
- Mark of the Beast 
- Cliff Hangers 
- Dolphin Downs 
- Beaky's Beach 
- Bungees in the Mist 
- Heart of Darkness 
- Flume Lagoon 
- Glacier Falls 
- Point Siren Song 
- Pelican Bay 
- Tilt-A-Whirl 
- Flamingo East 
- Nessie's Nook 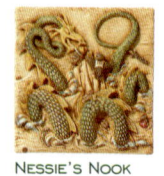

Page 252

Harmony Kingdom

Byron's Secret Garden

Item No.: PXGA1-PXGE4
Status: Open
Carving Date: 98
Release Date: Jun 99

This is the second series in the Picturesque Collection. Comprised of twenty 4"x 4" tile figurines, it portrays Lord Byron's enchanted garden. Each tile by Ann Richmond.

Sun Worshipper	Bell Tower	Martin's Minstrels	Slow Downs		Two Blind Mice
Mum's Reading Room	Swing Time	Fountain Blue	Gourmet Gazebo		Webmaster's Woe
Garter of Eden	Bumble's Bridge	Zen Garden	Love's Labours		A Frog's Life
Byron's Bower	The Long Sleep	Honey Brew	Cata's Pillow		Mayfly Madame

Harmony Kingdom

Page 253

Wimberley Tales
Item No.: PXWA1-PXWD5
Status: Open
Carving Date: 99
Release Date: Sep 99

This is the third series in the Picturesque Collection. Comprised of twenty 4"x 4" tile figurines, it portrays the fictional town of Wimberley, named after Wimberley Mills. Each tile by Mark Ricketts. Pre-production colouration pictured. Colour on production tiles more vivid.

The Builder	The Clouds	The Chimney	The Artist
The Scientist	The Sun	The Rooftop	The Lawyer
The Chef	The Sea	The Lovers	The Birthday
The Doctor	The Fireman	The Teacher	The Baker
The Dentist	The Harlot	The Masquerade	the Butcher

Page 254

Harmony Kingdom

PICTURESQUE
LIMITED EDITIONS

Best In Show
Item No.: PXLEMA2
Status: Ltd Ed
Carving Date: 00
Release Date: Dec 00
Issue Size: 2000

This 9"x 6.75" framed tile figurine by Ann Richmond portrays a fracas at the Pony Club.

The Howling Tree Inn
Item No.: PXXMASLEHO
Status: Ltd Ed
Carving Date: 00
Release Date: Jun 00
Issue Size: 3000

This 6"x 6" framed tile figurine by Ann Richmond portrays the local hounds enjoying some Christmas cheer.

Mrs. Lillipurr's Lodgings
Item No.: PXXMASLECA
Status: Ltd Ed
Carving Date: 00
Release Date: Jun 00
Issue Size: 4200

This 6"x 6" framed tile figurine by Ann Richmond portrays the local cats carolling in the village square.

Showboat
Item No.: PXLEMA
Status: Ltd Ed
Carving Date: 00
Release Date: Dec 00
Issue Size: 2000

This 9" x 6.75" framed tile figurine by Ann Richmond portrays a snobbish rider and her mount about to end up in the water jump area.

APPENDIX/INDEX
Alphabetically listed by box name

Artist
AB = Adam Binder
AR = Ann Richmond
DL = David Lawrence
JB = Julie Bharucha
MB = Monique Baldwin
MH = Mel Heald
MP = Martin Perry
MR = Mark Ricketts
PC = Peter Calvesbert
PS = Patrick Romandy-Simmons
RK = Robert King
SD = Sherman Drackett
TM = Theresa Miller

Place of Origin (P)
C = China
E = England
E/C = England & China
U = United States

Issue Price (IP)
See Page 37 for Key
N/C = No Charge
N/A = Not Available

Status (ST)
D = Donation
L = Limited
O = Open
R = Retired
S = Special
T = Timed
V = Event
F = Fixed

Name	Item No.	Artist	P	IP	ST	PG
101 Dalmatians	WDWR101	RK	C	P30	O	205
2001 Memories Dinner Flower Pot	ICE02M	SD	C	N/C	V	214

A
Name	Item No.	Artist	P	IP	ST	PG
A Day at the Races	RW01LEHIMA	PC	E	N/C	V	214
Adam Binder Cracker Fairies	CCETICAB01	AB	E	P44	L	176
Albatross	HG4AL	MB	C	P06	O	121
Alfred	TJRPFR2	AB	E	P26	O	102
Algenon	TJCA8	PC	E	P06	R	38
Alice In Wonderland	WDWRAL	RK	C	P08	L	205
All Angles Covered	TJME	PC	E	P04	R	38
All Ears	TJRA	PC	E	P04	R	39
All Tied Up	TJSN	PC	E	P04	R	39
Alley Cat's Meow	TJMINEVE4	MB	E	P06	V	214
Alpine Flower	HG3AL	MB	C	P06	O	121
American Beauty	HGLELR4	SD	C	P18	L	171
Anaheim '01 Minx Pendant	XXYANO1Z	AB	C	N/C	V	214
Angel Baroque	N/A	DL	E	P06	R	201
Antarctic Antics	TJXLPE	PC	E	P15	R	95
Antipasto	TJAE	PC	E	P06	R	39
Antony & Cleopatra	TJ2NCA	AB	E	P29	R	115
April's Fool Pewter Pen	RW98PEN	PC	C	P06	T	186
Aria Amorosa	TJES	PC	E	P06	R	40
Aristocats	WDWRAC	RK	C	P06	O	205
Artful Dodger	TJH08	PC	E	P06	O	40
At Arm's Length	TJOC	PC	E	P04	R	41
At The Hop	TJRA2	PC	E	P04	R	41
Atlanta '00 Bumbles Pendant	XXYATOOZ	MB	C	N/C	V	215
Atlantic City '02 Murphy Pendant	XXYACO2Z	SD	C	N/C	V	215
Awaiting A Kiss	TJLFR	PC	E	P08	O	86

B
Name	Item No.	Artist	P	IP	ST	PG
Babbling Heights	TJLETO	MR	E	P40	L	161
Baby Boomer	TJKA	PC	E	P06	R	41
Baby On Board	TJAR	PC	E	P04	R	42
Back Scratch	TJCA2	PC	E	P04	R	42
Bad to the Bone	TJH07	PC	E	P06	O	42
Ball Brothers	HCBA	DL	E	P04	R	137
Bambi	WDWRBA	PS	C	P35	O	206
Bamboozled	TJPA	PC	E	P06	O	43

Name	Item No.	Artist	P	IP	ST	PG
Barney & Betty	TJ2NPI	AB	E	P29	R	115
Baroness Trotter	TJZPI	PC	E	PO1	R	97
Be Our Guest	WDWBEAU	RK	C	P11	O	206
Beak To Beak	TJLB	PC	E	PO4	R	43
Beau Brummell	TJHO5	PC	E	PO6	O	44
Beau Geste	ANSEO1	AB	E	PO6	T	143
Beauregard & Baby's Bed	CLCB	JB	C	PO6	O	134
Beauty & the Beast	WDWRBB	RK	C	P35	O	206
Beer Nuts	TJLECAN2	MB	E		L	156
Begonia	HGBE	MP	C	PO6	R	121
Behold The King	RW98LI	DL	E	P15	T	186
Bela	TJEVO1D	AB	E	P27	V	215
Beneath The Ever Changing Seas	RW99SS	DL/MB	C	N/C	T	186
Benny	TJRPHE	AB	E	P26	R	102
Beppo And Barney The Clowns	HCCL	DL	E	PO4	R	137
Best In Show	PXLEMA2	AR	C	PO8	L	254
Bewear The Hare	TJLEP99S	DL	E	PO6	L	239
Bibbidi-Bobbidi-Boo	WDWCIN	RK	C	P39	L	206
Big Blue	RW96/97WH	PC	E	P11	T	187
Birds of a Feather	RWMI	AB	E	PO6	T	188
Blue Heaven	TJDO2	PC	E	PO6	O	44
Blue Moon	TJSESNO1	SD	C	PO4	T	143
Boarding School	TJSEG98F2	PC	E	PO6	R	237
Bog Hopper	TJIFR	AB	E	P28	O	117
Bon Bon	ANSEOOB	DL	C	PO4	T	144
Bon Chance	ANBO	DL	E	PO4	R	119
Bon Enfant	TJ96AN	DL	E	PO4	T	144
Bones	TJRPHSK	AB	E	P26	R	102
Bonnie & Clyde	TJ2NFR	AB	E	P29	F	115
Boris	TJRPHMU	AB	E	P26	F	102
Botero	TJRPTU	AB	E	P26	R	103
Bozini The Clown	HCZLECL	DL	E	PO3	L	170
Braganza	TJDLCA4	DL	E	PO6	O	44
Brando	TJRPHO	AB	E	P26	R	103
Brean Sands	TJCB2	PC	E	PO4	O	45
Bulldog Pin	RWO2PI	MB	E	N/C	T	188
Bum Wrap	TJBBO2	PC	E	P11	L	164
Bumbles on Planet Paradise	XXYPPO1Z	MB	E	N/C	V	216
Bush Baby	TJNBU	PC	E	PO6	R	112
Byron & Bumbles	RWOOBB	MB	C	P11	T	188
Byron's Bacchanal	TJICEOOM	SD	C	N/C	V	216
Byron's Hideaway	PXGBOX	AR	C	PO8	O	251
Byron's Lonely Hearts Club	RW99LB	MB	C	PO9	T	189
Byron's Secret Garden Set	PXGSET	AR	C	P22	O	253

C

Name	Item No.	Artist	P	IP	ST	PG
Cactus	HGCA	MP	C	PO6	R	122
Cadmius	TJMYLEYE	MH	E	PO6	L	181
Camelot	TJROSE99	PC/MB	E	N/C	V	216
Candy	TJRPBE	AB	E	P26	F	103
Cannery Row	TJCA12	PC	E	PO6	O	45
Carnation	HG5Ca	SD	C	P28	O	122
Cass	TJRPCA3	AB	E	P26	O	103
Cat Nap's Meow	TJMINEVE3	SD	E	PO6	V	217
Cat Pin	RW98PI	PC	E	N/C	T	189
Cat's Cradle	TJCA6	DL	E	PO5	L	240
Cat's Cradle Too	TJCA6B	DL	E	PO5	L	240
Cat's Meow	TJMINEVE	PC	E	PO2	V	217

Name	Item No.	Artist	P	IP	ST	PG
Catch A Lot	TJWH4	PC	E	P06	R	46
Catch As Catch Can	TJCA10	PC	E	P28	O	100
Caw Of The Wild	TJBB	PC	E	P06	O	46
Celeste	ANCE97	DL	E	P06	T	145
Cerlulu	TJMYLEBL	MB	E	P05	L	181
Chaney	TJRPHGE	AB	E	P26	F	104
Changing Of The Guard	TJCH	PC	E	P04	R	47
Chatelaine	TJAN	DL	E	P04	T	145
Chiaro	TJMYLEBK	MH	E	P06	L	182
Cherry Blossom	HG4CB	MB	C	P06	O	122
Cheshire Cat	WDWRCC	PS	C	P26	L	207
Christmas Bouquet	HG3LEBQC	MP	C	P11	L	171
Chrysanthemum	HGCH	MP	E/C	P05	R	122
Chucky Pig	XXYTJCP	PC	E	N/C	D	217
Circus Ring	HCCR	DL	E	P15	R	137
Clair	XXYCLC	JB	C	N/C	V	218
Clair de Meow	TJMINEVE5	JB	E	P06	V	218
Classic Pooh	WDWRPO	RK	C	P08	L	207
Clever Constantine	HCCO	DL	E	P04	R	138
Close Shave	TJHE3	PC	E	P04	R	47
Colette & Cat	CLLECT	JB	C	P09	L	167
Confined Claws	TJCICA3	MB	E	N/A	L	156
Cookie's Jar	TJCA11	PC	E	P06	O	47
Cosa Nostra	TJLEBOOS	AR	C	P07	L	204
Costello	TJRPCR	AB	E	P26	R	104
Cotton Anniversary	RWCTCO	PC	E	P02	S	189
Count Belfry	TJZBA	DL	E	P01	R	97
Courtiers At Rest	TJZTU	PC	E	P01	R	97
Cow Town	RWOOMA	DL	C	P11	T	190
Crack A Smile	TJIAL	AB	E	P28	O	117
Crackin' Brew	HKTPLECB	PC	E	P19	L	246
Cranberry	HGCR	MP	E/C	P05	R	123
Creature Comforts	TJHICA	MP	E	P10	L	157
Croc Pot	TJAL2	PC	E	P06	R	48
Crooze Cat	XXYTJCC	PC	E	P06	V	218
Crown Jewel	RWFR	PC	E	P06	T	190
Curly	TJRPPI	AB	E	P26	R	104
Cyril	TJRPSE	AB	E	P26	O	104

D

Name	Item No.	Artist	P	IP	ST	PG
Daisy	HGDA	MP	E/C	P05	R	123
Daisy II	HG5DA	SD	C	P28	O	123
Daisy Basket	HGXLG	SD	C	P32	L	179
Damnable Plot	TJBV	PC	E	P04	R	48
Danger's Darlings	TJHIDO2	MR/SD	E	P08	L	157
Day Dreamer	TJPO	PC	E	P04	R	49
Dead Ringer	TJHO3	PC	E	P06	O	49
Den Mothers	TJWO	PC	E	P04	R	50
Disney Multi-Cats	WDWRCA	PS	C	P14	L	207
Disney Multi-Dogs	WDWRDO	PS	C	P14	L	207
Disorderly Eating	TJCICA	MP	E	P10	L	157
Divine	TJRPFR	AB	E	P26	O	105
Dizzie	TJRPMO	AB	E	P26	R	105
Dog Days	TJHO	PC	E	P04	R	50
Dom	TJRPMA	AB	E	P26	R	105
Donald Through the Years	WDWRDO	RK	C	P06	O	208
Double Pink Rose	HGLEDPR	MP	C	P08	L	171
Double Red Rose	HGLEDRR	MP	C	P08	L	172

Name	Item No.	Artist	P	IP	ST	PG
Double Sterling Rose	HGLEDSR	MP	E	P22	L	172
Double Violet Rose	HGLEDVR	MP	C	P08	L	172
Double Yellow Rose	HGLEDYR	MP	C	P08	L	173
Down Under	TJPL	PC	E	P04	R	50
Dragon Breath	XXYTJZDR	DL	E	N/C	V	218
Drake's Fancy	TJLDU4	PC	E	P08	R	86
Dressed to Kill	RWMU	PC	E	P08	T	190
Driver's Seat	TJZE	PC	E	P06	R	51
Duc De Lyon	TJZLI	DL	E	P01	R	97

E

Name	Item No.	Artist	P	IP	ST	PG
Earl Cadogan's Tea Party	TJEVO2TP	MB	E	P06	L	219
Earl Of Oswald	TJZEL	DL	E	P01	R	98
Easter Bouquet	HG3LEBQE	SD	C	P11	L	173
Easy Slider	TJSESNOO	SD	C	P06	T	145
Edison '98 Angel Pendant	XXYED98Z	DL	E	N/C	V	219
Edison '98 Lovebird Pin	XXYED98P	PC	E	N/C	V	219
Ed's Safari	TJSA	PC	E	P04	O	51
Ed's Safari II	TJSA2	PC	E	P06	O	51
Ed's Safari III	TJSA3	PC	E	P06	R	52
Egyptian Rose	HG4ER	MB	C	P06	R	124
Elephant Wee Beastie	XXYRWO2WL	MB	E	N/C	D	247
Elvis	TJRPCA4	AB	E	P26	O	105

F

Name	Item No.	Artist	P	IP	ST	PG
Fab Five	WDWFABFIVE	RK	E	P14	O	208
Fab Five Party Boys	RWFAB	SD	E	P08	T	191
Fall Bouquet	HG4LEBQF	SD	C	P11	L	173
Family Picnic	WDWPIC	RK	C	P39	L	208
Family Reunion	TJLEMO	DL	E	P16	L	184
Family Tree	TJKO	PC	E	P04	R	52
Fang	TJEVO1B	AB	E	P27	V	220
Fat Cat's Meow	TJMINEVE2	MB	E	P04	V	220
Fats	TJRPFI2	AB	E	P26	O	106
Faux Paw	TJLI	PC	E	P06	R	52
Feisty Fellow	WDWDON	RK	C	P11	O	208
Fergie	TJRPRA	AB	E	P26	O	106
Field Day	RWOOMO	SD	C	N/C	T	191
Figaro	WDWRFI	PS	C	P26	L	209
Finky	TJNRO2	PC	E	P02	O	112
Fishy Business	TJCICA2	MR/AR	E	P08	L	158
Fleur-de-lis	ANFL	DL	E	P04	R	119
Flight of Fancy	TJBI2	PC	E	P06	O	53
Forget Me Not	HGFM	MP	C	P06	R	124
Forty Winks	TJHE	PC	E	P04	R	53
Foul Play	TJSK	PC	E	P06	O	54
Francis	TJNEL	PC	E	P02	R	113
Frankie	TJRPHFR	AB	E	P26	F	106
Franklin & Eleanor	TJ2NOW	AB	E	P29	R	115
Fred (ICE)	TJICEO1M	AB	E	P27	V	220
Fred (Kitchener)	TJKITO1M	AB	E	N/A	V	221
Friends In High Places	TJGI	PC	E	P06	O	54
Friends Of The Royal Watch	RW98TU	DL	E	N/C	T	191
Fur Ball	TJCA3	PC	E	P04	O	55
Fuss Pot	TJHO4	PC	E	P06	R	55

Harmony Kingdom — Page 259

Name	Item No.	Artist	P	IP	ST	PG
G						
Garcia	TJRPLI	AB	E	P26	R	106
Garden Prince	TJZFR	PC	E	P01	R	98
Gardenia	HGGA	MP	C	P06	R	124
Gateau	TJDLCA2	DL	E	P06	O	55
Gentil Homme	ANGE	DL	E	P04	R	120
Gentle Giant	TJLEGP	SD	C	P08	L	184
Georgie	TJNDR	PC	E	P02	O	113
Gertrude	TJDLCA3	DL	E	P06	O	56
Gill	HG3GI	MB	C	P06	O	124
Gleason	TJRPGO	AB	E	P26	O	107
Gobblefest	TJEVGO99	PC	E	P07	V	221
Golden Oldie	TJLEPO1F	MB	C	P06	L	240
Grapes	HG4GR	MB	C	P06	O	125
Great Escapo	HCES	DL	E	P04	R	138
Group Therapy	TJAA	PC	E	P04	R	56
Gump's Caw of the Wild	XXYTJBBG	PC	E	P06	R	238
H						
Haji's Hero	RWO2EL	MB	E	P09	T	192
Halloween Bouquet	HG3LEBQH	MP	C	P11	L	174
Hammin' It Up	TJPI	PC	E	P04	R	56
Happy Haunts	WDWHA	RK	C	P14	O	209
Hardy	TJRPBU	AB	E	P26	R	107
Harmony Bull	TJLEP99F	PC	E	P06	L	241
Harmony Circus Matched Set	HCSET	DL	E	P25	L	170
Harmony Circus Serigraph	HCLESER	DL	U	N/A	L	245
Harmony Kingdom Video	HKVID	N/A	U	P42	S	247
Harry	TJNRA	PC	E	P02	R	113
Have A Heart	TJBBVU	PC	E	P08	L	164
Hearts Content	TJIEL	AB	E	P28	O	117
Helen The Owl	XXYTJLEOW	DL	E	N/C	D	248
Henna	TJMYLEOR	MB	E	P06	L	182
Henry	TJRPHI	AB	E	P26	R	107
Henry The Human Cannonball	HCHE	DL	E	P04	R	138
Hibiscus	HG5HI	SD	C	P28	O	125
Hide-And-Seek	TJRH	PC	E	P06	O	57
Hilda	TJRPHWI	AB	E	P26	R	107
Hip Huggers	XXYCLH	SD	E	N/C	V	221
Hitchcock	TJRPHCA	AB	E	P26	R	108
Hog Heaven	TJPI2	PC	E	P04	R	57
Hold That Line	TJXLFO	PC	E	P15	R	95
Holding Court	TJLPE	PC	E	P08	R	86
Holding Court II	RWO1MU	PC	C	P09	T	192
Holiday Ornament Set	TJZSE98	MP	E	P15	L	178
Holy Roller	TJSESA99	PC	C	P06	T	146
Holy Water	TJSESAO2	PC	E	P08	T	146
Home Sweet Home	HGLELR3	MB/SD	C	P20	L	174
Homer (Ice)	TJICEO1C	AB	E	P27	V	222
Homer (Kitchener)	TJKITO1C	AB	E	N/A	V	222
Honeymoon Freesia	HG6FR	SD	E	P05	O	125
Hope and Glory	RWO2HIMA	PC	E	N/C	V	222
Hops	HG3HO	MB	C	P06	O	125
Horn A' Plenty	TJLRH	PC	E	P08	R	85
Horse Play	TJSE	PC	E	P04	R	57
Hot Pepper	HG3HP	MB	C	P06	R	126
House Party	TJEVHOLO1A/P	PC/AB	E	P13	V	223

Page 260   *Harmony Kingdom*

Name	Item No.	Artist	P	IP	ST	PG
Hyacinth	HGHY2	MP	E/C	P05	R	126
Hydrangea	HGHY	MP	E/C	P05	R	126

I

Name	Item No.	Artist	P	IP	ST	PG
Il Bendi	HCBE	DL	E	P04	R	139
In Fine Feather	TJPU	PC	E	P06	R	58
In The Know	TJIHI	AB	E	P28	O	117
Ingenue	ANIN	DL	E	P04	R	120
Inside Joke	TJMO	PC	E	P04	R	58
It's A Fine Day	TJHI	PC	E	P04	R	58
It's A Knockout	RWOOLEHIPI	MP	E	N/C	V	224
Iris	HGIR	MP	C	P06	O	126
Iris II	HG5IR	SD	C	P28	O	127
Ivory Tower	TJLEOW	DL	E	P16	L	185

J

Name	Item No.	Artist	P	IP	ST	PG
Jabba	TJRPHGE	AB	E	P26	F	108
Jada	TJMYLEGR	MB	E	P05	L	182
Jersey Belles	TJCO	PC	E	P04	R	59
Jewels Of The Wild	TJLEW99S	DL	C	P11	L	243
Jingle Bell Rock	TJSESA98	PC	E	P08	T	147
Joie De Vivre	ANJO	DL	E	P04	R	120
Jonah's Hideaway	TJWH	PC	E	P04	R	59
Josephine & Cat	CLLECD	JB	C	P09	L	167
Journey Home	TJLFI	PC	E	P08	R	87
Joyeaux	ANSE99C	DL	C	P06	T	147
Jump Shot	TJLEG99F	MP	C	P06	L	237
Jungle Book	WDWRJB	PS	C	P14	L	209
Justine & Cat	CLLECB	JB	C	P09	L	167

K

Name	Item No.	Artist	P	IP	ST	PG
Keeping Current	TJLDU3	PC	E	P08	R	87
Kennedy	TJRPELD	AB	E	P26	F	108
Khepera's Castle	TJDB	PC	E	P28	R	100
Kiki & Cat	CLLECS	JB	C	P09	L	168
Killing Time	TJLEWH	DL	E	P15	L	158
King of the Hill	TJPG	PC	E	P31	F	59
King of the Road	TJSESAOO	PC	E	P08	T	148
Kit & Caboodle	TJCA14	PC	E	P06	O	60
Kitty's Kipper	TJSEP98F	DL	E	P06	L	241
Knackered Nick	TJSESAO1	PC	E	P08	T	148

L

Name	Item No.	Artist	P	IP	ST	PG
La Gardienne	ANSE98	DL	E	P06	T	149
Ladies In Waiting	TJZCA	PC	E	P01	R	98
Lady & The Tramp	WDWRLT	RK	C	P06	O	209
Lady Luck	TJIDU	AB	E	P28	F	118
Land Ahoy!	WDWBOAT	RK	C	P38	O	210
Last Cat's Meow	TJMINEVE6	MB	E	P06	V	224
Leather Anniversary	RWCTLE	PC	E	P02	S	192
Leatherneck's Lounge	TJIG	PC	E	P06	R	60
Lemon	HG4LE	MB	C	P06	O	127
Let's Do Lunch	TJVU	PC	E	P04	R	60
Liberty And Justice	TJEA	PC	E	P06	R	61
Life's A Picnic	TJBE	PC	E	P04	R	61
Lily	HG5LI	MP	C	P28	O	127
Lion King's Pride Rock	WDWLIONKING	RK	E	P13	O	210

Name	Item No.	Artist	P	IP	ST	PG
Lionel Loveless	HCLI	DL	E	P04	R	139
Liz	TJRPEA	AB	E	P26	O	109
Long Beach '97 Rose Pendant	XXXHGLB97	DL	E	N/C	V	224
Long Beach '99 Byron Pendant	XXYLB997	MB	E	N/C	V	225
Look Before You Leap	TJFR4	PC	E	P06	O	61
Lord Busby	TJZBE	DL	E	P01	R	98
Lord Foxglove	TJEVO1T	MB	E	P06	V	225
Lord of the Aisles	TJICEO2	AB	E	P10	V	225
Lotus	HG4LO	MB	C	P06	O	127
Louis	TJRPEL	AB	E	P26	O	109
Love & Peace	TJSEROO	SD	C	P11	T	153
Love Nest	TJSER98	DL	E	P13	T	153
Love Seat	TJWA	PC	E	P04	R	62
Lovers' Leap	RWOOFR	SD	C	N/C	T	193
Lucifer	WDWRLU	PS	C	P26	L	210
Lucky Streak	TJICEO2D	PC	E	N/C	V	226

M

Name	Item No.	Artist	P	IP	ST	PG
Mad Dogs And Englishmen	TJXLHO	PC	E	P15	R	96
Madeline Of The High Wire	HCZLEMA	DL	E	P03	L	170
Mae	TJRPDO	AB	E	P26	R	109
Magic Bus	RWFAB3	SD	E	P08	T	193
Magician's Top Hat	HCTO	DL	E	P04	R	139
Major Parker	TJZMO	DL	E	P01	R	99
Major's Mousers	TJCA4	PC	E	P06	R	62
Make A Wish	TJIFI	AB	E	P28	O	118
Manatee Wee Beastie	XXYRWOOMA	SD	E	N/C	D	248
Marie & Pierre	TJ2NCA	AB	E	P29	R	116
Marigold	HG3MA	MB	C	P06	O	128
Marmalade & Mao Mao's Mirror	CLCM	JB	C	P06	O	134
Marquis De Blanc	TJZRA	DL	E	P01	R	99
Marsh Marigold	HGMM	MP	E/C	P05	R	128
Marty The Polar Bear	XXYTJLEPO	DL	E	N/C	D	248
Menage A Trois	TJFR3	PC	E	P06	O	62
Merry-Go-Round	RWOODO	SD	C	N/C	T	193
Mickey Mouse Club	DAMC	RK	C	P42	L	210
Mickey Through the Years	WDWRMM	RK	C	P06	O	211
Mickey's Fire Brigade	WDWRFB	PS	C	P11	L	211
Midas Touch	TJFI3	PC	E	P28	O	100
Minx on the Moon	RWO1MI	AB	C	N/C	T	194
Miss Spider In Love	HGMS	MB	C	P11	O	128
Mme. Colette	CLLENT	JB	C	P11	L	168
Mme. Josephine	CLLEND	JB	C	P11	L	168
Mme. Justine	CLLENB	JB	C	P11	L	169
Mme. Kiki	CLLENS	JB	C	P11	L	169
Moggy Bag	TJCA9	PC	E	P28	O	100
Monica	TJRPFI	AB	E	P26	R	109
Monique Baldwin Cracker Fairies	CCEHIMBO1	MB	E	N/A	L	179
Moon Rovers	RWFAB2	SD	E	P08	T	194
Morning Glory	HGMG	MP	E/C	P05	R	129
Morning Glory Basket	HGXLG2	SD	C	P33	L	179
Mostel	TJRPOW	AB	E	P26	L	110
Mother's Day Bouquet	HG3LEBQM	SD	C	P11	L	174
Mother's Day Daffodil	HG6DA	SD	E	P05	O	129
Mr. Sediment's Superior Victuals	HCSE	DL	E	P04	R	140
Mrs. Lillipurr's Lodgings	PXXMASLECA	AR	C	P08	L	255
Mud Bath	TJBO	PC	E	P04	R	63

Name	Item No.	Artist	P	IP	ST	PG
Murphy Pin	RW99PI	PC	C	N/C	T	195
Murphy's Last Stand	TJPB	PC	E	P04	R	63
Mutton Chops	RW98MC	PC	E	N/C	T	196

N

Name	Item No.	Artist	P	IP	ST	PG
Naughty & Nice	TJLEPO2S	MB	E	P06	L	241
Neighborhood Watch	TJRF	PC	E	P04	R	64
Nell	TJNHO	PC	E	P02	O	113
New Baby Sweet Pea	HG6SP	SD	E	P05	O	129
Newark '98 Angel Pendant	N/A	DL	E	N/C	V	226
Nic Nac Paddy Whack	TJHO2	PC	E	P04	R	64
Nick	TJEVSAOO	AB	E	P27	V	226
Nick Of Time	TJSESA	PC	E	P04	T	149
Night Light	TJLEBOOF	AR	C	P07	L	204
Night Shift	TJOP	PC	E	P31	F	64
Night Watch	RWO1BB	MB	C	P09	T	196
Nightmare Before Christmas	WDWRNM	RK	C	P30	O	211
Noah's Hideaway	PXNBOX	AR	C	P08	O	251
Noah's Lark	TJLENO	PC	E	P21	L	162
Noah's Park Set	PXNSET	AR/PC	C	P22	O	252
Noah's Quark	TJSEMM1	MR	C	P18	T	151
Noel	ANSE99T	DL	C	P06	T	149
Nose Bleed	TJBBOO	PC	E	P08	L	165

O

Name	Item No.	Artist	P	IP	ST	PG
Of The Same Stripe	TJTI	PC	E	P04	R	65
Off to Neverland!	WDWPET	RK	C	P14	O	211
Oktobearfest	TJEVBE97	PC	E	P05	V	227
Old Gladstone	TJDLCA	DL	E	P06	O	65
Olde Time Carousel	HCCA	DL	E	P04	R	140
Ollie	TJNOW	PC	E	P02	O	113
On A Roll	TJLDO	PC	E	P08	R	88
One Step Ahead	TJLTU	PC	E	P08	R	88
Open Mike	TJXLBA	PC	E	P15	R	96
Orange	HG3OR	MB	C	P06	O	129
Orange Crush	TJTI2	PC	E	P28	O	101
Original Kin	TJLEGA	PC	E	P20	L	162
Orson	TJRPOC	AB	E	P26	O	110
Ozzie	TJRPHPU	AB	E	P26	R	110

P

Name	Item No.	Artist	P	IP	ST	PG
Pacer the Greyhound	XXYTJLEGR	SD	E	N/C	D	249
Package Tour	TJCM	PC	E	P06	O	66
Panda	TJXXPA	PC	E	P04	R	201
Panda Wee Beastie	XXYTJLEGP	SD	E	N/C	D	249
Paper Anniversary	RW97PA	PC	E	P02	T	196
Parade Of Gifts	HGLEC99S	MP	C	P11	L	239
Paradise Found	TJPPF	PC	E	P04	R	94
Paradise Lost	TJPPL	PC	E	P04	R	94
Part of Your World	WDWMER	RK	C	P11	O	212
Pas de Deux	TJPA2	PC	E	P06	O	66
Pastille	ANSEOOG	DL	C	P04	T	150
Pavareata	HCPA	DL	E	P04	R	140
Pavarotti	TJRPPE	AB	E	P26	O	110
Peace Lily	HGPL	MP	E/C	P05	O	130
Peace Offering	TJSEP98S	DL	E	P06	L	242
Peace Summit	TJWO2	PC	E	P06	O	67

Harmony Kingdom

Name	Item No.	Artist	P	IP	ST	PG
Pearl	XXYCLP	PC	E	N/C	V	227
Pecking Order	TJBM	PC	E	P06	O	67
Peezer, Paws & Po Po's Piano	CLCP	JB	C	P06	O	135
Pell Mell	RW99PE	DL	E	P16	T	197
Pen Pals	TJLPI	PC	E	P08	R	88
Peony	HGPE	MP	C	P06	O	130
Peony Basket	HGXLG4	SD	C	P08	L	180
Pet Parade	TJLEC99F	DL	C	P06	L	239
Petty Teddies	TJTB	PC	E	P06	O	68
Petunia Basket	HGXLG5	SD	C	P33	L	180
Photo Finish	TJMA2	PC	E	P06	R	68
Pieces Of Eight	TJLEPA	DL	E	P16	L	158
Pillow Talk	TJSER97	DL	E	P16	T	154
Pink Paradise	TJFL	PC	E	P04	R	69
Pinocchio's Great Adventure	WDWPIN	RK	C	P13	O	212
Pip The Pelican	XXYRW99PE	DL	E	N/C	D	250
Planet Dustbin	TJPD	PC	E	P06	R	69
Planet Paradise	XXYHGRH	PC/MB/AB	E	N/C	V	227
Play Ball	TJLEPO	DL	E	P16	L	185
Play School	TJFI2	PC	E	P04	R	70
Poinsettia Basket	HGXLG6	SD	C	P34	L	180
Pomegranate	HG3PO	MB	C	P06	O	130
Pondering	TJLDU	PC	E	P08	R	89
Pongo's Palm	TJOR2	PC	E	P06	O	70
Pooh And Friends	WDWPOOH	TM	E	P11	O	212
Poppy	HG4PO	MB	C	P06	R	130
Portrait of an Artist as a Young Bloke	EVPPOO	PC	E	N/C	D	228
Pot Sticker	TJHE4	PC	E	P28	R	101
Potty Time	TJCA15	PC	E	P06	O	70
Powder Room	TJCA13	PC	E	P06	O	71
Pregnant Paws	TJHID03	MB	E		L	159
Pride And Joy	TJLTI	PC	E	P08	R	89
Primordial Sloop	XXYTJXXLTUPC	PC	E	N/C	V	228
Primordial Soup	TJXXLTU	PC	E	P17	R	93
Princely Thoughts	TJFR	PC	E	P04	R	71
Psst! Are you a Member?	RWHOPOO	SD	C	N/C	S	197
Puddle Huddle	TJTO	PC	E	P04	R	71
Pumpkinfest	TJEVPU98	DL	E	P06	V	228
Purrfect Fit	RW96DL	DL	E	N/C	T	197
Purrfect Friends	TJCA	PC	E	P04	R	72
Purrfect Tidings	PXXMASCA	AR	C	P08	O	251

Q

Name	Item No.	Artist	P	IP	ST	PG
Queen Of The Jungle	TJEVQJ99	DL	C	P14	V	229
Queen's Counsel	TJSEG98F	PC	E	P06	R	238
Queenie & Prince Charming	EVQPOO	AR	C	P11	V	229
Quiet Waters	TJLDU2	PC	E	P08	R	89
QVC Pin	XXYQVC	MB	C	N/C	V	243

R

Name	Item No.	Artist	P	IP	ST	PG
Ram	TJXXRA	MP	E	P04	R	201
Ranier & Grace	TJ2NDO	AB	E	P29	R	116
Rather Large Friends	TJRLCA	PC	E	P09	R	92
Rather Large Hop	TJRLRA	PC	E	P09	R	92
Rather Large Huddle	TJRLTO	PC	E	P09	R	92
Rather Large Safari	TJRLSA	PC	E	P09	R	93
Reminiscence	TJEL	PC	E	P04	R	72
Retired Racers	TJLEGR	DL	C	P11	L	185

Name	Item No.	Artist	P	IP	ST	PG
Rhapsody in Blue	TJSER02	PC	E	P07	T	154
Rhododendron	HGRH	MP	E/C	P05	R	131
Road Dogs	HCRO	DL	E	P04	R	141
Road Kill	TJBB99	PC	E	P08	L	165
Road Kill's Revenge	TJBB01	PC	E	P11	L	165
Rocky's Raiders	TJRC	PC	E	P06	R	72
Rooster	XXXTJRO	PC	E	P04	R	202
Rooster, Large	N/A	PC	E	N/A	R	202
Rose	HG5RO	MP	C	P28	R	131
Rose Basket	HGLELR	MP	E	P09	L	175
Rose Bud	HGRB	MB	C	P06	O	131
Rose Party	HGLELR2	MP	C	P15	L	175
Roseanne	TJRPRH	AB	E	P26	R	111
Rosemont '96 Frog Pendant	TJZFRR	PC	E	N/C	V	230
Rosemont '97 Puffin Pin	XXYRO97P	PC	E	N/C	V	230
Rosemont '97 Rose Pendant	XXXHGRO97	DL	E	N/C	V	230
Rosemont '98 Angel Pendant	XXYRO98Z	DL	E	N/C	V	231
Rosemont '99 Lord Byron Pendant	XXYRO99Z	MB	E	N/C	V	231
Rosemont '00 Bumbles Pendant	XXYRO00Z	MB	C	N/C	V	231
Rosemont '01 Minx Pendant	XXYRO01Z	AB	C	N/C	V	232
Rosemont '02 Murphy Pendant	XXYRO02Z	SD	C	N/C	V	232
Rosie	TJRPCA	AB	E	P26	R	111
Rover's Wreck	TJHIDWO	AB	E	P08	L	159
Royal Flotilla	TJZFI	PC	E	P01	R	99
Rudy	TJEVRUOO	AB	E	P27	V	232
Ruffians' Feast	PXXMASHO	AR	C	P08	O	251
Rufus	TJMYLEPI	MH	E	P06	L	183
Rule Britannia	RWO2LI	PC	E	N/C	T	198
Rumble Seat	TJCA5	PC	E	P06	O	73
Rush	TJRPRO	AB	E	P26	R	111

S

Name	Item No.	Artist	P	IP	ST	PG
Saint or Sinner	TJDR	PC	E	P06	O	73
Sammy	TJNRO	PC	E	P02	O	114
Samson & Delilah	TJ2NLL	AB	E	P06	F	116
School's Out	TJFI	PC	E	P04	R	73
Scotland Yard	TJH06	PC	E	P06	O	74
Scratching Post	HKPEN1	PC	C	P06	L	245
Sea of Love	TJSERO1	MB	C	P08	T	155
Secaucus '96 Frog Pendant	TJZFRS	PC	E	N/C	V	233
Sharazade	TJDLLECA	DL	E	P31	L	159
Shark	TJXXSH	PC	E	P04	R	202
Sheba's Ship	TJTICCA	AB	E	P08	L	160
Sheep (Shaggy) Dog	XXXTJSD	PC	E	P04	R	203
Shell Game	TJTU	PC	E	P04	R	74
Shoebill	XXXTJSB	PC	E	P04	R	203
Showboat	PXLEMA	AR	C	P08	L	255
Sid	TJNSN	PC	E	P02	O	114
Side Steppin'	TJCB	MP	E	P04	R	74
Signing Line	TJICEOO	PC	E	P11	V	233
Silk Anniversary	RWCTSI	PC	E	P02	S	198
Simba & Saffron's Settee	CLCS	JB	C	P06	O	135
Sin City	TJLESI	PC	E	P23	L	163
Single Orange Rose	HGLEOR	MP	E	P05	L	175
Single Pink Rose	HGLEPR	MP	E	P05	L	175
Single Red Rose	HGLERR	MP	E	P05	L	176
Single Violet Rose	HGLEVR	MP	E	P05	L	176
Single White Rose	HGLEWR	MP	E	P05	L	176

Name	Item No.	Artist	P	IP	ST	PG
Single Yellow Rose	HGLEYR	MP	E	P05	L	176
Sleepy Hollow	TJLE	PC	E	P04	R	75
Slow Dance	TJTU4	PC	E	P06	O	75
Slow Dance Solid Body	XXYCLT	PC	E	P06	V	234
Snapdragon	HGSN	MP	C	P06	R	131
Snapdragon Basket	HGXLG3	SD	C	P33	L	180
Sneak Preview	TJICE98	PC	E	P09	V	234
Snow Drop	HGSD	MP	E/C	P05	R	132
Snow White	WDWSNOWHITE	RK	E	P14	O	212
Snowdonia Fields	TJSESN99	MP	C	P06	T	150
Softly, Softly	RW02OW	PC	E	P37	T	199
Solemate	RW99DL	DL	E	P04	T	198
Something's Gotta Give	TJSESA97	PC	E	P04	T	150
Space Ball Pendant	HKUKO1SB	MB	E	N/C	V	234
Special Delivery	TJST	DL	C	P06	R	76
Splashdown	TJWH3	PC	E	P06	R	76
Spring Bouquet	HG4LEBQSP	SD	C	P11	L	177
Squee	TJNDO	PC	E	P02	O	114
Standing Guard	TJLWO	PC	E	P08	R	90
Steamboat Willie	DASW	RK	C	P42	L	213
Step Aside	TJLCB	MP	E	P08	R	90
Sterling Baroness Trotter	TJZLESSPI	MP	E	P09	L	244
Sterling Garden Prince	TJZLESSFR	MP	E	P09	L	244
Sterling Lord Byron	TJZLESSLB	MP	E	P09	L	244
Sterling Rose	HGLESR	MP	U	P21	L	177
Stoneleigh '98 Angel Pendant	N/A	DL	E	N/C	V	235
Storm Brewing	PXPC1	PC	C	P08	O	251
Straight From The Hip	TJLHI	PC	E	P08	R	90
Stuffed Shirt	TJCA16	PC	E	P28	O	101
Suave St. John	HCSU	DL	E	P04	R	141
Summer Bouquet	HG4LEBQSU	SD	C	P11	L	177
Sunday Swim	TJDO	PC	E	P04	O	76
Sunflower	HGSU	MP	C	P06	R	132
Sunflower II	HG3SU	MB	C	P06	R	132
Sunflower III	HG5SU	SD	C	P28	O	132
Sunnyside Up	TJLHE	PC	E	P08	R	90
Swamp Song	TJAL	PC	E	P04	R	77
Swap 'n Sell	TJICE99	PC	E	P11	V	235
Sweet As A Summer's Kiss	RW97DL	DL	E	N/C	T	199
Sweet Serenade	TJHU	PC	E	P04	O	77
Sweet Spot	TJLE2	PC	E	P06	O	77

T

Name	Item No.	Artist	P	IP	ST	PG
Tabby Totem	HKPEN2	PC	C	P06	L	245
Take A Bow	TJLEPO1S	MB	C	P06	L	242
Talk of the Town	TJEVHOLO2	PC	E	P36	V	235
Tally Ho!	TJLFH	DL	C	P09	O	91
Tamira's Treasure	TJMYLEDR	PC	E	P17	L	183
Tarka	TJNOT	PC	E	P02	O	114
Tartuffe & Teaser's Tub	CLCT	JB	C	P06	O	135
Tea For Two	TJLWA	PC	E	P08	R	91
Teacher's Pet	TJBI	PC	E	P04	R	78
Teacup Twirl	WDWAL	RK	C	P14	O	213
Teapot Angel I	N/A	DL	E	P02	R	203
Teapot Angel II	N/A	DL	E	P02	R	204
Tender Is The Night	TJSER99	MP	C	P11	T	155
Terra Incognita	TJLMA	DL	E	P11	O	91
The Arch	HCAR	DL	E	P12	R	136

Name	Item No.	Artist	P	IP	ST	PG
THE AUDIENCE	HCAU	DL	E	P17	R	138
THE BIG DAY	RW96	PC	E	N/C	T	187
THE GOOD RACE	TJTU3	PC	E	P28	O	101
THE GREAT ESCAPE	TJBP	PC	E	P06	O	78
THE GREAT ESCAPE II	TJLO	PC	E	P06	O	78
THE HOWLING TREE INN	PXXMASLEHO	AR	C	P08	L	255
THE LAST LAUGH	TJBD	PC	E	P06	O	79
THE MOUSE THAT ROARED	RWMO	PC	E	P06	T	195
THE MUSHROOM	RW98MU	MP	C	P16	T	195
THE RINGMASTER	HCRI	DL	E	P04	R	141
THE SUNFLOWER	RW97SU	MP	E	P10	T	199
THIN ICE	TJLEG99S	MP	C	P06	L	238
TIN CAT	TJSH	PC	E	P04	R	79
TIN CAT'S CRUISE	TJROSE98	PC	E	N/C	V	236
TO THE LAUGHING PLACE	WDWSP	RK	C	P14	O	213
TOAD PIN	RW97PC	PC	E	N/C	T	200
TONGUE AND CHEEK	TJFR2	PC	E	P04	O	80
TONY & GEORGE	TJRPBB	AB	E	P26	F	111
TONY'S TABBIES	TJCA7	PC	E	P06	O	80
TOO MUCH OF A GOOD THING	TJMC	PC	E	P04	R	80
TOP BANANA	TJOR	PC	E	P04	R	81
TOPSY TURVY	TJEL4	PC	E	P06	O	81
TRUE NORTH	TJLECAN	AR	C	P08	L	160
TRUMPETERS' BALL	TJEL2	PC	E	P06	O	81
TRUNK CALL	TJEL3	PC	E	P28	O	101
TRUNK SHOW	TJCR	PC	E	P04	R	82
TUBS PIN	XXYTPPC	PC	E	N/C	V	236
TULIP	HG3TU	MB	C	P06	R	133
TURDUS FELIDAE	TJBR	PC	E	P06	O	82

U

Name	Item No.	Artist	P	IP	ST	PG
U.K. '99 LORD BYRON PENDANT	N/A	MB	E	N/C	V	236
UNBEARABLES	TJLEBE	PC	E	P21	L	160
UNBRIDLED AND GROOMED	TJMA	PC	E	P04	R	82
UNEXPECTED ARRIVAL	TJPE	PC	E	P04	R	83
UNTOUCHABLE	TJHE2	PC	E	P04	R	83
UP TO SCRATCH	TJBA	PC	E	P06	O	83

V

Name	Item No.	Artist	P	IP	ST	PG
VALENTINE ROSE	HG6RO	SD	E	P05	O	133
VICTORIA	TJRPCA2	AB	E	P26	O	112
VIX, VERNE & VELVET'S VANITY	CLCD	JB	C	P06	O	135
VLAD THE IMPALER	HCVL	DL	E	P04	R	142

W

Name	Item No.	Artist	P	IP	ST	PG
WADDLES	TJNDU	PC	E	P02	O	114
WEDDED BLISS	TJITU	AB	E	P28	O	118
WEDDING LILY	HG6LI	SD	E	P08	O	133
WEMBLEY 2000 PENDANT	HKUKOO	MB	E	N/C	V	237
WHALE OF A TIME	TJWH2	PC	E	P04	R	84
WHEN NATURE CALLS	TJPB2	PC	E	P06	R	84
WHO'D A THOUGHT	TJOW	MP	E	P04	R	84
WICKED WAYS	WDWVIL	RK	C	P14	L	213
WIMBERLEY TALES SET	PXWSET	MR	C	P24	O	254
WINSTON	TJRPHO2	AB	E	P26	O	112
WINSTON THE LION TAMER	HCWI	DL	E	P04	R	142
WINTER BOUQUET	HG4LEBQW	SD	C	P11	L	178
WISE GUYS	TJOW2	PC	E	P04	R	85

Name	Item No.	Artist	P	IP	ST	PG
Wishful Thinking	TJTU2	PC	E	P06	R	85
Wolfie In Space	RWO1WO	PC	C	N/C	T	200
Wood ANniversary	RWCTWO	PC	E	P02	S	200

Y

Name	Item No.	Artist	P	IP	ST	PG
Y2HK	TJSEY2K	MR	C	P18	T	152
Yeoman Of The Guard	TJZOW	PC	E	P01	R	99
YT42HK	HKTPLET42	PC	E	P20	L	246

Z

Name	Item No.	Artist	P	IP	ST	PG
Zamboni	TJLECAN3	MB	C	P06	L	161
Zephyr The Monkey	XXYTJLEMO	DL	E	N/C	D	250